Academic Library Impact:
Improving Practice and Essential Areas to Research

Lynn Silipigni Connaway
OCLC Research, Senior Research Scientist and Director of User Research

William Harvey
OCLC Research, Consulting Software Engineer

Vanessa Kitzie
School of Library & Information Science, University of South Carolina, Assistant Professor

Stephanie Mikitish
Rutgers University, User Engagement and Assessment Librarian

ACRL Advancing learning Transforming scholarship
Association of College & Research Libraries
A division of the American Library Association

Academic Library Impact: Improving Practice and Essential Areas to Research

Citation: Association of College and Research Libraries. *Academic Library Impact: Improving Practice and Essential Areas to Research*. Prepared by Lynn Silipigni Connaway, William Harvey, Vanessa Kitzie, and Stephanie Mikitish of OCLC Research. Chicago: Association of College and Research Libraries, 2017.

Association of College & Research Libraries
A division of the American Library Association
Chicago, Illinois 2017

Contents

Foreword

ACRL has long been interested in assessment, accountability, and determining the impact of academic library programs and services. In the early 1980s, ACRL created an Ad Hoc Committee on Performance Measures that issued an RFP and selected Dr. Nancy Van House to develop a manual on assessment.

More recently, in early 2009, the ACRL Board of Directors identified a rapidly growing need to document the contributions academic libraries make to the missions of their institutions and made a commitment to help librarians demonstrate these contributions. This was both in response to the general environment and because ACRL members told us, in membership surveys and focus groups, that demonstrating and communicating the value of academic libraries was and remains a top issue facing the profession. ACRL determined it had a vital role in developing research to support libraries in communicating with campus decision-makers and funders in higher education. In fall 2009, ACRL issued a request for proposal for a comprehensive review of the quantitative and qualitative literature, methodologies, and best practices currently in place for demonstrating the value of academic libraries. We selected Dr. Megan Oakleaf to carry out this work. The subsequent 2010 report, *The Value of Academic Libraries: A Comprehensive Research Review and Report (the "VAL Report")*, represents a seminal work on the subject and has spurred ACRL along with countless libraries to take action to improve their programs and communicate clearly about library contributions to campus communities.

After the report was issued, in April 2011, ACRL adopted a new strategic plan, the Plan for Excellence, with one of three goal areas concentrated on the value of academic libraries. The following month the Board of Directors established and charged a new standing committee to oversee and coordinate ACRL's Value of Academic Libraries Initiative as described in the strategic plan.

The "VAL report" recommended that ACRL:

> create a professional development program to build the profession's capacity to document, demonstrate, and communicate library value in alignment with the mission and goals of their colleges and universities.

To determine how to shape that program we sought advice from a broad range of stakeholders, and convened a summit in 2011 with an IMLS Collaborative Planning Grant (read more in the report *Connect, Collaborate, and Communicate: A Report from the Value of Academic Libraries Summits*).

We took what we learned and, within weeks, we applied for a follow-on IMLS National Leadership Demonstration Grant. In September 2012 ACRL was awarded nearly $250,000 for the project *Assessment in Action: Academic Libraries and Student Success*, which ran for three years and provided an intensive 14-month, team-based format to more than 200 academic institutions. This training continues today as a one-day travelling workshop. Reports on each of the three years of the *Assessment in Action* project, as well as best practices and lessons learned from participants and instructors, will be published by ACRL in late 2017 as *Shaping the Campus Conversation on Student Learning and Experience: Activating the Results of Assessment in Action*. That book will feature an occasional paper which synthesizes the results of the Assessment in Action program, *Creating Sustainable Assessment through Collaboration: A National Program Reveals Effective Practices*, first published by the National Institute of Learning Outcomes Assessment (NILOA) in November 2017.

ACRL's Purpose in Issuing this Report

Leaders of ACRL's VAL committee studied the progress of the association's strategic objectives for their area and identified outstanding gaps where effort should be focused. Knowing that the "VAL report" had stimulated much inquiry into practice and scholarly research, and that the landscape had changed, they recommended that ACRL issue an open and competitive request for proposals to investigate and write a research agenda that provides an update on progress since the 2010 publication of the "VAL report." In April 2016, ACRL issued a call for proposals, asking for an "action-oriented research agenda" that would both examine important questions where more research is needed in areas critical to the higher education sector, and also identify actions academic libraries can take now based on both existing scholarship and practice-based reports. In August 2016, we selected a team from OCLC Research, who has shared many updates on their work through virtual and in-person sessions over the past year. Now we are pleased to be releasing this report, *Academic Library Impact: Improving Practice and Essential Areas to Research*, and the accompanying Literature Analysis Dashboard.

Next Steps for ACRL

This new report is a significant milestone for ACRL's value of academic libraries initiative and for the profession. It clearly identifies priority areas and suggests specific actions for academic librarians and administrators to take in developing programs, collections, and spaces focused on student learning and success. It includes effective practices, calls out exemplary studies, and indicates where more inquiry is needed, with proposed research designs.

ACRL hopes this report will be used as a springboard for action. The Board of Directors has allocated funds for travel scholarships so that librarians can make presentations about the contributions of libraries to their parent institutions at higher education conferences. ACRL has also allocated funds for small research grants so that scholars and practitioners can undertake research in the areas where this report indicates it is most needed. In 2017, ACRL was chosen as a host organization for the American Council of Learned Societies (ACLS) Mellon/ACLS Public Fellows Program, a career-building fellowship initiative designed to expand the reach of doctoral education in the humanities. The Public Fellow placed at ACRL in a two-year staff position will advance research focused on student learning and success and promote findings from this report to resonate across the network of higher education stakeholders. Our fellow is working closely with the VAL Committee to develop the travel scholarship and research grant programs. They will be available through an open, competitive process and we'll be announcing full details in the months ahead.

Academic Library Impact: Improving Practice and Essential Areas to Research summarizes the incredible strides made and best practices developed by the profession in capturing and emphasizing academic libraries' contributions to student learning, success, and experience. ACRL looks forward to an exciting future, including this next generation of research that builds on our extensive assessment knowledge base.

Mary Ellen K. Davis
ACRL Executive Director
mdavis@ala.org

Cheryl Middleton
ACRL President 2017-2018
Associate University Librarian for Research & Scholarly Communication
Oregon State University Libraries & Press
cheryl.middleton@oregonstate.edu

References

Association of College and Research Libraries. *Connect, Collaborate, and Communicate: A Report from the Value of Academic Libraries Summits.* Prepared by Karen Brown and Kara J. Malenfant. Chicago: Association of College and Research Libraries, 2012. Published online at www.acrl.ala.org/value.

Association of College and Research Libraries. *Value of Academic Libraries: A Comprehensive Research Review and Report.* Researched by Megan Oakleaf. Chicago: Association of College and Research Libraries, 2010. Published online at www.acrl.ala.org/value.

Association of College and Research Libraries. *Assessment in Action Bibliography.* Prepared by Chase Ollis and Kara J. Malenfant. Chicago: Association of College and Research Libraries, 2016. Published online at www.acrl.ala.org/value.

Van House, Nancy A., Beth T. Weil, and Charles R. McClure. *Measuring Academic Library Performance: A Practical Approach.* Chicago: American Library Association, 1990.

Introduction: Demonstrate the Library's Value

How well can academic library administrators and staff demonstrate that the academic library is useful to students? Do these administrators and staff have metrics that show how their programs, collections, and spaces impact student learning outcomes and institutional goals? Can they illustrate to provosts* the library's value to support increased spending?

Now more than ever, academic libraries are being asked to demonstrate value to their institutional stakeholders, funders, and governance boards.[1] But because there is a lack of consensus on how to measure library value for student learning and success, these measures often are left to individual campus units to determine.[2] This absence of consensus poses a difficulty for librarians, as they may need to serve several constituencies with very different goals, even at one institution. Across the entire educational landscape, there is even less agreement on how libraries might show substantial contributions to measures such as accreditation, student retention, and academic achievement.[3]

This situation has led the Association of College and Research Libraries (ACRL) to commission an "action-oriented" research agenda. The goal is to investigate how libraries can increase student learning and success while communicating their value to higher education stakeholders. This document consists of the following components:

- a report on all project phases and findings;
- a detailed research agenda based on those findings;
- a visualization component (http://experimental.worldcat.org/valresearch) that filters relevant literature and creates graphics that can communicate library value to stakeholders;
- a bibliography of the literature analyzed;
- and a full bibliography of the works cited and reviewed, which can be found at http://www.oclc.org/content/dam/research/themes/works-cited.pdf.

All components were produced in partnership with OCLC Research and include the analyses of library and information science (LIS) and higher education literature, a focus group interview and brainstorming sessions with academic library administrators at different institution types within the United States, and individual interviews with provosts.

Based on findings from these analyses and feedback from ACRL members, this agenda identifies six priority areas for academic librarians and administrators to use as a guide and facilitator for developing academic services, collections, and spaces focused on student learning and success:

1. **Communicate the library's contributions.**
2. **Match library assessment to institution's mission.**
3. **Include library data in institutional data collection.**
4. **Quantify the library's impact on student success.**
5. **Enhance teaching and learning.**
6. **Collaborate with educational stakeholders.**

*Throughout this report, the term "provost" is used as a catch-all to indicate all senior academic officers. See Appendix C for more details.

Academic librarians, administrators, LIS researchers, and library school students can use research questions developed for each of the six priority areas as a catalyst for the study of college and university student learning and success. These priority areas, suggested actions, and accompanying future-focused research questions are included in the section below and with more detail in the agenda. The agenda also includes effective practices, exemplary studies, and proposed research designs. The suggested actions described in this section are broader than the effective practices in the agenda, which were derived using specific examples from this report.

Communicate the Library's Contributions

As academic libraries strategically evolve to support student learning and success, they must effectively communicate the library's value to those high in their institution's hierarchy. This communication is a vital step when competing for resources within funding and governance structures both in and outside the academic institution.

Communication was the most commonly identified theme in the selected literature and interview data analyzed, and the other five areas support this priority area. If the library matches its assessment to its institution's mission, enhances teaching, quantifies its impact, is included in data collection activities, and collaborates with the principal stakeholders, good communication can happen much more naturally and efficiently.

There is more emphasis on service in the LIS literature and the focus group interviews with library administrators than in the higher education literature and provost interviews.

The increasing importance of communication is a theme in the selected literature, but with more research, come more questions. A significant difficulty in suggesting best practices is the number of factors that can affect with whom to communicate and how. In other words, communication is highly contextual. However, such context must be addressed by librarians, as findings from a recent survey comparing faculty and librarian views of the library suggest that librarians are not effectively communicating their value to entities responsible for funding and governance.[4] There is more emphasis on service in the LIS literature and the focus group interviews with library administrators than in the higher education literature and provost interviews. This lack of focus on service does not mean that provosts perceive library services as redundant and not proactive but indicates that library administrators and staff may not be communicating the breadth of their offerings and their value in the same language used by others in the academic community. While this report uses the word *service* to describe the activities performed by library administrators and staff, they should consider using more direct terminology, such as *programs* or *events*, to describe their activities.

While this report uses the word *service* to describe the activities performed by library administrators and staff, they should consider using more direct terminology, such as *programs* or *events*, to describe their activities.

Suggested Actions

1. Explore ways to effectively communicate both up (to institutional leaders) and out (to other departments and peers).
2. Experiment with both messages and methods.
3. Confer with provosts, who can offer a bird's-eye view of what the library should be doing and how well it is succeeding.[5]
4. Communicate regularly with other stakeholders in the hope of making them feel invested in the library and become library advocates and supporters.

Research Questions Requiring Further Study

1. How can library administrators and staff more effectively communicate their contributions to student outcomes to institutional stakeholders (e.g., administrators)?
2. What types of library services, collections, and spaces matter to institutional stakeholders?
3. To what extent do institutional stakeholders recognize library administrators' and staff's contributions to teaching and learning? What factors affect levels of recognition?
4. How do faculty envision the integration of library services, collections, and spaces for teaching and learning?
5. How can libraries support the information needs of stakeholders related to teaching activities?
6. How are other units effectively communicating with stakeholders?
7. What factors influence librarian communication with academic library users and potential users?
8. How can library administrators and staff leverage social media to increase student engagement?
9. What are the main barriers to communication between library administrators and staff and educational stakeholders (e.g., students, faculty, administrators)?

Match Library Assessment to Institution's Mission

There is a growing trend toward institutional similarity in education as the pressure of rankings causes colleges and universities to emulate their more prestigious counterparts.[6] As institutions gradually come to resemble each other across academic offerings, they also must conversely strive to address the unique needs of specific stakeholders and surrounding communities.[7]

Academic administrators must balance these competing pressures. Striking this balance means that campus units must perform based on both common indicators of quality (such as accreditation) and unique objectives that align with the institutional mission and goals. Stakeholders judge libraries based on how well their services, collections, and spaces align across both these areas.

Although provosts and other academic administrators develop institutional plans, supervise libraries and other institutional units, and allocate funds, few studies published since 2000 have investigated their perceptions of library services, collections, and spaces. In fact, the number of research studies from LIS and higher education journals addressing institutional mission and goals and alignment, which includes accreditation, has decreased from 2010 to 2016. At the same time, practitioners work to align their libraries' services, collections, and spaces with the institutional mission and goals, but findings from interviews with provosts indicate that this alignment must be better communicated. Interviews with academic library administrators and provosts show that accreditation is important to the institution. However, some stakeholders may perceive accreditation as a necessary task accomplished with or without libraries. For this reason, libraries must communicate how they contribute to accreditation and their importance in meeting these standards.

One reason for a discrepancy between library administrators' and provosts' views of the library's importance to achieving institutional goals could be that they have differing views on the library's role within the institution. While interviews with provosts from around the United States show that they are concerned about alignment, a recent study of 722 library directors indicates that they feel less aligned strategically with their supervisors and less valued by their administration than the respondents reported in the 2013 survey.[8] Further, analysis of the LIS literature and information from a focus group interview with academic library administrators indicates that librarians and LIS researchers mention service more frequently than provosts. This finding suggests that librarians and administrators see the library's role in student learning and success outcomes differently.

Suggested Actions

1. Support student success by aligning services, collections, and spaces to support institutional objectives.
2. Include "nontraditional" metrics that show how libraries support goals such as student recruitment and alumni engagement.[9]
3. Go outside of the library to collect data and suggest collaborations with other campus units around common issues.
4. Use terminology similar to that used by others within the academic institution.
5. Work with faculty and staff from teaching and learning support services to build a culture of assessment that effectively demonstrates library alignment with the institutional mission, goals, and priorities.

Research Questions Requiring Further Study

1. In what ways have the support by library administrators and staff of the institution's mission and goals affected student learning and success outcomes?
2. How do libraries fit into the broader array of institutional resources and programs (e.g., writing centers, tutoring)?
3. How do libraries compare to other support units in demonstrating their impact on the institutional mission and goals?
4. How are budget constraints affecting the support by library administrators and staff of the institution's mission and goals related to student learning and success?
5. How do library administrators and staff support accreditation efforts, and are these efforts recognized by the institution?

Include Library Data in Institutional Data Collection

Learning analytics involves "data about learners and their contexts for... understanding and optimising learning and the environments in which it occurs."[10] While research in this area is relatively new, three of the fourteen provosts interviewed for this report described data components that could track student progress at a variety of institutional, programmatic, and course levels. The range of data being tracked by these components offers librarians the opportunity to triangulate their data with those from other departments, improving their visibility to other departments, administrators, and provosts.

Research in this area mirrors that on analytics and privacy and confidentiality in other areas.[11] For instance, one study assesses what analytics related to reading behaviors researchers can collect from individuals reading mass-market e-books versus scholarly journals.[12]

Suggested Actions

1. Know how other academic stakeholders are using learning analytics.
2. Research the safeguards needed to ensure student privacy or confidentiality.
3. Strategically collect data that can be integrated into learning analytics software.
4. Advocate for the inclusion of library data in the volumes of information collected from multiple systems within the academic institution.
5. Integrate library data into campus analytics components.
6. Work with stakeholders to statistically analyze and predict student learning and success based on shared analytics.

Research Questions Requiring Further Study

1. How can library administrators and staff connect their data with student outcomes? To do this effectively, will library administrators and staff need to begin collecting different and additional data?
2. How are other stakeholders in higher education using analytics to affect the areas of teaching and learning and student success, and how can library administrators and staff contribute to these efforts?
3. What types of data do faculty and staff in institutional research units collect that would supplement the data assembled by library administrators and stakeholders to measure the impact of courses, events, and other library services on student learning and success?
4. How can library administrators and staff use triangulated data to demonstrate the impact of library resources and programs on student learning and success?
5. How can library administrators and staff employ mixed methods or multiple methods to demonstrate how student usage of library collections affects retention?
6. How can library administrators and staff balance concerns about maintaining user privacy with the use of individual student data to measure learning and success outcomes?
7. What factors affect librarian decisions regarding the level of confidentiality or privacy of student data?

Quantify the Library's Impact on Student Success

Contributing to student success has become the most significant way that institutions and their constituent units demonstrate value to funding and governance boards. These outcomes often relate to objective indicators of learning, which include assignment completion, semester grades, and graduation rates.

In this agenda's analysis, LIS and higher education literature related to student success peaked in 2013. By 2016, this theme was present in only about half of the documents analyzed. A lack of effective practices and standards regarding student privacy constitutes a significant factor in causing this decline.[13] However, research from the University of Minnesota and the University of Wollongong has employed data collection and analysis methods that facilitate user confidentiality.[14] These methods can be used to re-engage with data-driven research that quantifies student success.

Suggested Actions

1. Identify quantifiable student success indicators at the individual and aggregate levels. These indicators should include enrollment in postsecondary education, grades, persistence to the sophomore year and beyond, length of time to degree, and the student's career after graduation.
2. Partner with other educational stakeholders, including those from other institutions, to identify factors that affect student success before students begin their education at a college or university.
3. Partner with outside stakeholders, such as businesses, to identify factors that influence student success following their undergraduate education.

Research Questions Requiring Further Study

1. How do library resources and programs (e.g., courses, events, etc.) impact indicators of student success?
2. Does access to library collections impact student retention? If so, how?
3. How do library spaces support student enrollment?
4. How does library instruction affect job placement and salary the first year after graduation? Five years after graduation?
5. What effects do libraries have on success outcomes for different types of students?
6. What are the effects of library instruction on success outcomes for diverse student populations (e.g., military students, non-US students, English language learners, nonresidential students, online-only students, etc.)?
7. How are library administrators and staff implementing continuous assessment to facilitate equal access to information for diverse student populations?
8. How can library administrators and staff supplement the data collected by other university departments (e.g., tutoring and writing centers) to document student learning and success?
9. How does library instruction at the secondary or earlier level affect information competencies at the postsecondary level?
10. How have library administrators and staff updated instruction based on the ACRL *Framework for Information Literacy*?[15]
11. What factors affect library contributions to positive student learning outcomes?
12. How can academic, public, and school libraries work together to develop connected informal and formal learning opportunities that lead to measurable student success outcomes (e.g., retention, grades, time to graduation) for community college, four-year college, and university students?

Enhance Teaching and Learning

Librarians frequently have collaborated with course instructors to help improve the course instructors' teaching. At the most basic level, librarians introduce students to the services, collections, and spaces that the library offers. At the highest level, librarians can function as co-instructors.

Learning activities can cover a wider range of activities than simply teaching, however. For instance, librarians often include textbooks and other learning materials in the collections, incorporating teaching faculty in the selection decisions so that the faculty members will use the materials in their courses.[16] This inclusion and selection require librarians to engage and communicate with teaching faculty across various disciplines to coordinate and collaborate on the collection of these resources. Librarians also can align with the institutional mission and goals by developing affordable resources for students of lower socioeconomic backgrounds and electronic resources for distance learning students.

Like other learning outcomes, the use of library materials may not impact specific success measures, but it can enhance more subjective learning goals, such as critical thinking. Due to the less tangible effects of learning resources, higher education stakeholders are determining how best to identify and measure these relationships.[17]

Another, more established outcome related to student learning is engagement. In the last few years, faculty and staff have worked to increase students' engagement both during their time in school and after graduation.[18] Given their experience in providing information literacy instruction, librarians have an opportunity to lead the effort in creating more informed citizens. While LIS research in this area has increased over the last six years, interviews from around the United States indicate that provosts are more likely to associate libraries with student learning outcomes related to services, collections, and spaces than instruction and teaching support. Activities that support these outcomes include training in research skills and how to identify credible information.[19]

Suggested Actions

1. Work with peers and students to identify effective points at which the library can be involved in teaching and learning.
2. Determine the metrics to measure the impact of those changes.
3. Integrate library resources and instruction into academic workflows.
4. Engage with faculty and students to develop everyday support services (such as research and writing workshops) for students. That might involve extending library hours, having services and collections available in nontraditional areas, providing stress-relief services during final exam periods, and so on.
5. Plan to articulate and communicate the ways in which these new activities support teaching and learning outcomes.

Research Questions Requiring Further Study

1. What is the role of library administrators and staff in evaluating teaching and student learning outcomes?
2. What are the most common difficulties faced by library administrators and staff in measuring teaching and learning outcomes?
3. How do library administrators and staff measure the impact of library instruction on student learning outcomes?

4. How can library administrators and staff increase engagement among students?
5. How are library spaces (online or physical) affecting engagement among students?
6. In what ways have library administrators and staff implemented a continuous improvement process to support engaged student learning?
7. How are library administrators and staff implementing new models of outcomes-based measurement to assess the effectiveness of informal (e.g., Greek life, intramural sports) and formal learning opportunities?
8. Where do students go to discover information (e.g., answers to questions, resources for their needs)? If they do not use library websites or online catalogs, what can library administrators and staff do to integrate library discovery systems into academic users' workflows?

Collaborate with Educational Stakeholders

The primary mission of the academic library is to support an institution's research and teaching.[20] This mission obviously necessitates collaboration with other educational stakeholders. Such collaboration includes all librarian efforts to work with those inside and outside their institution to influence student learning and success outcomes.

Findings from this agenda indicate that librarians and others in higher education are collaborating at an increasing rate. Provosts discussed collaboration numerous times in their individual interviews, underscoring the importance of these types of activities across all types of academic institutions. The library administrators in the advisory group also identified several collaborative efforts at both inter- and intra-institutional levels that served to communicate library value.

In Assessment in Action (AiA) projects supported by ACRL and the Institute of Museum and Library Services (IMLS), nearly 200 research teams collaborated with a variety of university units that also support research and teaching. This report also summarizes how these units (e.g., offices of assessment, institutional research, student affairs, information or academic technology, etc.) collaborate to support each other and students, as well as relevant services that bolster student learning and success, such as study abroad.

Suggested Actions

1. Collaborate beyond the academy with other public institutions such as museums, libraries, and archives. A recent study found that public library staff support students in their learning because students will use public libraries if they know the staff or otherwise feel comfortable going there.[21]
2. Study how other librarians have modified services and collections to better support other departments, including joint publications in other fields.[22]
3. Understand that there are different types and levels of collaboration and consider looking at literature from related fields to see what is said about libraries and information-related topics.
4. Work with academic and regional stakeholders, who include administrators, academic services staff, faculty, students, alumni, and other members of local communities, to identify mutual areas of research interest and to initiate collaborative research projects.

Research Questions Requiring Further Study

1. How can library administrators and staff collaborate with staff and faculty members from other academic institutions to increase student learning and success?
2. How can library administrators and staff collaborate with staff and faculty from other academic departments within the same academic institution to increase student learning and success?
3. What can library administrators and staff learn from institutional units that have increased student learning and success? How can library administrators and staff use this information to accomplish these increases and communicate their efforts?
4. What types of collaboration are the most effective in facilitating student learning and success outcomes?
5. How do collaborations between library administrators and staff and other libraries affect contributions to student success outcomes?
6. How can library administrators and staff contribute to areas that demonstrate the most promise for benefiting from library collaboration to increase positive student learning outcomes?

Using This Report

The priority areas, research questions, and other components of this research agenda provide a framework for discussion by key stakeholders. There have been several conference presentations outlining draft stages of the agenda, demonstrating the visualization component, and soliciting comments and suggestions. This agenda culminated in a public release and presentations of the agenda and visualization component.[23]

At the same time, no one project, even one as comprehensive as this, can provide all the information needed to measure the ways in which one library impacts student learning and success. Therefore, academic librarians should use the priority areas and research questions above to guide their efforts. The report, bibliography, and visualization component all need to be customized to suit the individual needs every library has when demonstrating value in student learning and success to its institution.

The audience for this report consists of library administrators and staff, as well as researchers, practitioners, and students in the fields of LIS, higher education, and other allied areas. While this report pertains to academic libraries, library administrators and staff who are undertaking assessment initiatives in auxiliary contexts also can use it to develop services, collections, and spaces and to learn about the practices that have been effective for others. Given that one primary audience for the report is academic library staff, many of whom are practitioner-scholars, we provide guidance on investigating the identified priority areas throughout the report.

The remainder of the report is structured to guide the reader through the steps taken to derive the priority areas and research questions outlined. First, a brief literature review provides an overview of some of ACRL's work on the value of academic libraries and describes how this work informed the development of a codebook. This codebook was then used to identify emerging themes addressed in the three different data sources: 535 selected LIS and higher education documents, focus group interviews with library administrators comprising the advisory group, and semi-structured individual interviews with their provosts. The report outlines how we collected data from these three sources and how we analyzed these data using a codebook, as well as basic and inferential statistics. Next, we discuss findings from each data source, followed by a comparison between the three data sources. We then summarize what we learned by comparing these data sources and identify six priority areas. These priority areas are defined, and we provide an overview of exemplary studies, practices, and research designs for each. In addition, we provide future-focused research questions in each priority area.

Academic librarians, administrators, and LIS researchers, practitioners, and students can use the research questions as a catalyst for the study of college and university student learning and success. After introducing the agenda, the report provides an overview of the development of the visualization component and some examples of how it can be used to address the priority areas and research questions. The report concludes with a discussion of limitations of both the design and creation of the research report, agenda, and visualization component, followed by a conclusion.

Literature Review

This literature review outlines four types of value research conducted by library administrators, library staff, researchers, practitioners, and students. Each type varies by the library resource measured (collection, service, and space), how it is measured (library-centered outcome, student-centered outcome), and the intended audience (librarians, higher education administrators). It appears that over time, there has been a push toward studies intended for higher-level administrators that examine the effect of library resources on institutional-level goals, such as student-centered outcomes. Two of these outcomes, learning and success, are then discussed in detail, including how researchers outside the library study them.

Following this review, we outline key findings from relevant ACRL documents identified by the RFP, which is entitled *Academic Library Impact: Improving Practice and Essential Areas to Research*.[24] These documents were intended to inform the team of themes to look and code for when analyzing relevant literature and interviews. We kept a list of these themes, of which the section *Relevant ACRL Documents* below gives an overview. See *Appendix A: Glossary* for definitions of relevant terms.

Evaluation and Assessment Literature

Evaluation and assessment are two related concepts used to determine the value of academic library collections, spaces, and services. While exact definitions of each vary in LIS and other literature, evaluation tends to be more holistic,[25] occur on a larger scale, focus on more generalized end results, and be written for a wider audience. In other words, an evaluation perspective will take a big picture or helicopter view of a collection, space, or service in a larger (e.g., institutional) context. Assessment provides a more detailed or "on the ground" view of the same. Another way to describe the difference between the two terms is that the purpose of assessment is to facilitate the ongoing improvement of the collection, space, or service that librarians are assessing, and the purpose of evaluation is to measure the library's resources and activities against a predetermined standard of value. To differentiate assessment from evaluation, take information literacy instruction as an example. An assessment would adopt a more focused examination of whether the students learned how to find and evaluate information. An evaluative approach might incorporate a test or survey instrument, such as the Standardized Assessment of Information Literacy Skills (SAILS).

One way to increase the scope of the assessment in this example would be to compare student learning outcomes to those of other sections, either by section average or individual student grades. Based on the performance of their students, librarians could modify their information literacy instruction for the next class. On the other hand, an evaluation of information literacy instruction would primarily be concerned with whether the students met a certain standard after receiving the instruction. A narrower evaluation might only compare assessments of students' information literacy skills, perhaps using SAILS. A broader evaluation might link their results to institutional goals for the attainment of a certain level of information literacy skills or link information literacy to the achievement of more extensive critical thinking skills. Because this report examines the influence of academic libraries on student learning and success, it is more concerned with evaluation, reflected in the report's data collection, data analysis, and priority areas. However, we did include ACRL AiA projects in our content analysis of 535 selected LIS and higher education documents (see *Relevant ACRL Documents* section).[26] Since the terms *evaluation* and *assessment* often are used interchangeably, and assessment can provide contextual details to aid in evaluation studies, the report uses the terms *evaluation* and *assessment* as employed by the authors of the cited work.

The past few decades of LIS literature on academic library value can be differentiated based on the use of evaluation and assessment activities and how departments or units report these activities. We have identified four types of value research conducted by library administrators, library staff, researchers, practitioners, and students. The first type includes library evaluations based on collection size or amount of other library resources. LIS research published before the 1980s tends to fall into this category, but this type of the investigation continues to present day. These evaluations often compare library collection size or composition to national standards, such as the *Standards for College Libraries* or, more recently, the *Standards for Libraries in Higher Education*.[27] They also can include how a library compares to its peers regarding resources, such as space, budgets, or collection size, an approach similar to the statistics compiled by the Association of Research Libraries (ARL).[28] The results of these evaluations usually are intended for other librarians or administrators rather than the staff, faculty, and students of an institution.[29]

The second type of value research includes assessments and evaluations concerning how students, faculty, and staff in colleges and universities use library collections, spaces, and services. Findings from these activities often are framed regarding types of value that concern only libraries. For example, the number of items checked out can be tracked year to year and included in an evaluative report as one indicator of the library's value[30] based on the assumption that if the items are checked out, they support the mission and goals of the institution for teaching, learning, and research. Librarians also can attempt to increase the number of checkouts through better marketing or through buying materials that library users may be more interested in and then assess those efforts via checkout volumes over time.[31] Librarians report these results to other stakeholders, either within or outside the library, and different metrics may appeal to different audiences. The emphasis on collections can be difficult because of shared collections and storage facilities, as well as the availability of online content. For instance, a library administrator or employee might feel that access to a book through interlibrary loan within forty-eight hours is acceptable, while graduate students care more about the number of books that they must request via interlibrary loan because the book they need is not available on campus.

The third type of value research includes assessments and evaluations of how those outside the library perceive and quantify the quality or value of library collections, spaces, and services.[32] The most common types are user satisfaction and return on investment (ROI) studies. User satisfaction studies frequently use the LibQUAL+ survey instrument to collect responses on library quality in three areas: effect of service, information control, and library as place. These areas were found to have statistical validity and reliability over several iterations of the survey, which has been in development since the 1990s and used in thousands of libraries worldwide since 2000.[33] While there has been some criticism over what the LibQUAL+ survey measures and how to interpret the findings, the results of the surveys have been used to aid in library strategic planning, general comparisons of library service perceptions among different groups of users, and benchmarking.[34] Librarians can mix survey results with other data, such as funding and collection size data.[35] ROI studies quantify the economic costs of library collections, spaces, and services and are the most common examples of how the library can be evaluated based on an external standard, in this case the monetary value. These studies lend themselves to comparing libraries with other units in the institution and between institutions. While satisfaction, ROI, and other, similar studies sometimes consider non-library perspectives, studies that examine student-, faculty-, or staff-centered goals and outcomes may be more interesting and useful to those outside of the library.

The fourth type of value research includes assessments and evaluations of how library collections, spaces, and services affect user-centered goals or outcomes.[36] For instance, the number of checkouts for each student may be tracked year to year and then compared to the grade-point average (GPA) of each student.[37] The results would frame the library's value regarding how its collections may have had an impact on the student's GPA rather than the number of checkouts alone. Libraries also engage in benchmarking activities, such as information literacy instruction, linking these activities to student-centered learning and success. In the past few years, an increasing amount of the literature has focused on the significance of the library to students, faculty, and staff.[38] This increase is based on the overall growth in studies and other literature focusing on the themes of collaboration, communication, teaching and learning, student success, and teaching support (see *Data Analysis* section).

Learning and Success

Learning and success are two student-centered outcomes prioritized by the ACRL RFP. Like evaluation and assessment, learning and success are two distinct, yet related terms. The *Oxford English Dictionary* definition of *learn* is "To acquire knowledge of a subject or matter; to receive instruction."[39] One can categorize students' demonstration of learning based on the success of their performance. However, learning and success can be difficult to measure. As the *International Encyclopedia of the Social Sciences* explains:

> The major preoccupation of students [and] learning has been with the experimental manipulation of a variety of variables to determine their lawful relationship to learned changes in behavior. As we shall see, it is easy to list variables that have powerful effects upon performance in the learning situation. What is not so easy is to determine with certainty whether the effect is upon learning or performance.[40]

In other words, it is hard to tell if a university unit, such as the library, has affected the student's learning or the student's ability to perform well in a graded event or other indicator of success, such as eligibility to graduate.

Not only are learning and success difficult to measure, but differentiating the terms also can be problematic. Sometimes one encompasses aspects of the other. For instance, Kuh, Kinzie, Schuh, and Whitt state that student success is "broadly defined to include satisfaction, persistence, and high levels of learning and personal development of the increasingly diverse students enrolling."[41] Another conceptualization puts one in the service of the other. An advisory group member associated student learning with attaining learning goals and objectives and student success with programs to support attainment of those goals (Advisory Group Member LM13). In the AiA program, ACRL has defined projects that "consider any aspect of the library (e.g., collections, space, instruction, reference, etc.) but must ultimately be tied to student learning (e.g., course, program, degree) or success (e.g., retention, completion, persistence)."[42] A fourth conceptualization looks at the qualitative or quantitative measurability of the terms. Under this conceptualization, one may define student success as "quantifiable student attainment indicators, such as enrollment in postsecondary education, grades, persistence to the sophomore year, the length of time to degree, and graduation."[43] We used the fourth definition to connect *student success* to more objective, usually quantifiable outcomes and maintain the distinction between these terms when coding and analyzing the selected documents and interviews. *Teaching and learning* denotes less measurable outcomes.

Measuring Student Learning and Success outside the Library

Student learning and success also prove difficult to measure outside the library. While a literature review and analysis of these topics are outside the scope of this project, a recent study of actions taken by other units or departments in higher education to influence student learning and success outcomes suggests that others are investigating this topic.[44] Although this higher education document did not include the library, the findings indicate that all types of academic libraries (e.g., universities, community colleges) could immediately respond and contribute to the two most effective practices: supporting and collaborating with undergraduate research and creating or redistributing space to facilitate collaborative learning. Findings from the study indicated that actions that are taken to support and work with undergraduate research positively affected critical thinking, attitudes toward literacy, inclination to inquire and lifelong learning, and intercultural effectiveness. Creating or redistributing space to facilitate collaborative learning positively affected critical thinking, the desire for inquiry, lifelong learning, and intercultural effectiveness. In addition to giving more support or collaborating with the institutional departments or units that engage in these practices, library administrators and staff also can work together or learn from those that offer similar resources and services. Examples include the following:

1. *Writing centers or courses.* As indicated by the provost interviews, libraries have the potential to collaborate with other departments or units, such as writing centers, by sharing space (see *Provost Semi-structured Individual Interviews* section). A recent study on the influence of university writing centers on first-year students in a business seminar reported that there is relatively little research into the effectiveness of writing centers at universities.[45] This study used multiple quantitative methods and found that students who visited the writing center scored significantly higher than students who had not. Interestingly, this significant effect applied only to students who received higher grades. An earlier study used mixed methods to evaluate the effectiveness of a writing center course at a university.[46] While a survey of the students who took the course found it to be helpful, there was no significant difference in their grades, which the researchers concluded was an indicator that student evaluations were not appropriate measures of effectiveness. An earlier study using multiple qualitative methods compared the differences between remedial writing courses, a reportedly understudied service despite their widespread availability, at a community college and those offered at a research university.[47] The study findings suggested that various factors, such as the curriculum, pedagogy, and level of resources, such as access to tutors or full-time professors, affected student learning. These studies suggest that writing centers and courses are understudied and that more recent studies are more likely to focus on student success and use multiple or mixed methods. The implication for academic libraries is that writing centers and libraries can mutually benefit from collaborating on student success studies that test the effect of research and writing interventions.
2. *Advising or tutoring consultations.* A library's reference service can be like consulting services, which tutoring, advising, or career services provide. These departments connect students with resources and information. They also can contribute indirectly or directly to students' learning and success. However, the influence of activities, such as tutoring from one department, on learning and success can be difficult to isolate from similar support provided by other units.[48] A recent study of mathematics support at nine higher education institutes in Ireland found that students in a survey believed that mathematics supported their retention and other learning and success outcomes.[49] Qualitative analysis of open-ended survey questions also led to the development of themes related to this type of tutoring. As in many large-scale surveys, the individual respondents were anonymous. However, when looking at data in a single institution, it was common to link resources and activities to individual learning or success. A recent article describes ways to improve advising using technology

and data analytics.[50] The author reports that "the collegiate advising system... is highly inefficient, error-prone, expensive, and a source of ubiquitous student dissatisfaction" but that systems can be improved by utilizing data analytics, specifically by pulling individual student-level data from a variety of sources.[51] This study and the other quantitative studies of departmental or unit influence on student learning and success also suggest that other departments besides the library are comfortable with collecting these sorts of data. The implication for library administrators and staff is that they should learn what data these departments are collecting and identify library data that can help provide a richer picture of the range of academic support services used by students and their effects.

3. *Study abroad.* Study abroad programs were related significantly to intercultural effectiveness[52] and are a high-impact practice for libraries to demonstrate value.[53] Library and non-library administrators, faculty, and staff should work together to provide support for these programs because the students involved comprise a unique type of distance student. Another similarity between research on study abroad and libraries is that community colleges are often underrepresented, as noted in a recent study, which used mixed methods to show that studying abroad positively affects learning and academic success.[54] A difficulty addressed by a study in this topic of research is what to do when the researcher does not have a control group or a group that has not received the resources or services given to the group under study.[55] The researcher used participant age to create two different groups, and because he found that this variable did not have an effect on participants' learning and other outcomes, he concluded that studying abroad did have an effect on student learning, which included better language fluency and an increased interest in world affairs. While one can debate the validity of these results, this study does indicate that others working in the higher education environment are facing challenges like those experienced by library administrators and staff. The implication for library administrators and staff is that while experimental designs may be unfeasible in most contexts, other educational stakeholders face the same issues, and some have implemented creative quasi-experimental designs.

To further investigate the topic of measuring student learning and success outcomes outside the library, questions were added to the provost interview protocol asking how all academic units or departments reporting to them measured and articulated their contributions to student learning and success outcomes (see *Appendix B: Provost Semi-structured Interview Protocol* and *Appendix C: Provosts' Titles and Carnegie Class for Provosts' Universities*).

Relevant ACRL Documents

In addition to the relevant literature areas outlined above, the ACRL RFP specified several of its publications as key documents for review.[56] The project team read these documents before responding to the RFP, which led to the suggested methods as noted in the RFP proposal.[57] A qualitative analysis of themes in the key documents from the RFP led to the formation of two codebooks (see *Appendix D: Codebook* for the codebooks). The definition of a codebook, as well as its purpose, is described in more detail in the *Data Collection* section below. Three of these publications are summarized below to exemplify how these codes emerged.

ACRL's 2010 *VAL Report* provides an overview of how academic librarians articulate value to higher education stakeholders and identifies ten areas of library value. Areas informing the codebooks include student enrollment, retention, and graduation; success; achievement; learning; and support of faculty teaching. Based on these identified areas, the report concludes with a series of recommended next steps. The steps that have the most relevance to this project detail the importance of library administrators and staff not only establishing student outcome measures but also documenting and communicating outcome attainment to higher education stakeholders, as well as engaging in higher education assessment initiatives.[58] While library administrators and staff must determine and establish outcome measures, there appears to be a significant need to link these outcomes to a broader higher education context beyond the library's walls.

Based on these recommendations, ACRL created an action-oriented project, AiA, which built a community of practice around assessment among more than two hundred higher education institutions.[59] Findings from the shared assessment methodologies and tools informing the codebooks show the effectiveness of library assessment when libraries collaborate with other campus units, assessment aligns with institutional goals, and mixed-methods approaches are employed. Codebook values also incorporate findings that emphasize the contribution of library instruction and spaces, as well as collaborative instructional activities, instructional games, and multiple instruction sessions, to student outcome measures.[60]

To capture the broader higher education context of assessment, ACRL regularly completes an environmental scan in odd years[61] and identifies trends in higher education in even years.[62] The 2015 *Environmental Scan* indicates growth of interest among higher education stakeholders in linking the following areas to outcome measures: research data services, discovery services, and the library as a place for student success.[63] These areas are mirrored in "2016 Top Trends in Academic Libraries," particularly the importance of the library in supporting digital scholarship.[64] The report also explains how information literacy assessment has changed to include contributions to student and institutional-level outcomes—the fourth type of value research outlined in the previous section, *Evaluation and Assessment Literature.*[65] As with the prior resources addressed in the literature review, these identified areas informed the development of the initial codebooks, and the *Methods* section discusses these codebooks in further detail.

As mentioned at the beginning of the *Literature Review*, the areas identified in this review informed the following data collection methods: (1) literature review of LIS and higher education literature from 2010 to present that addresses the impact of library resources on student learning and success; (2) the development of an advisory group of academic library administrators at diverse institutions in the United States to participate in focus group interviews and provide feedback on the project; and (3) semi-structured individual interviews with provosts at the same institutions as the advisory group academic library administrators.

Methods

Since a primary audience for this report is practitioner-scholars, we identify the steps, or methods, taken to conduct the research and offer pointers to primers for more detailed discussions of the methods. Defined as "any procedure employed to attain an absolute end," a method is used to characterize a research-related goal or goals.[66] We used both qualitative and quantitative methods, or mixed methods, for data collection and analysis. The use of mixed methods provides a way of viewing and analyzing the data using different analytical lenses, rather than one lens alone, and can provide checks and balances of the data collection and analysis methods as well as the findings.[67] The following section is an overview of the mixed-methods data collection tools used for the three data sources: LIS and higher education literature, a focus group interview, and semi-structured individual interviews. While this overview is not comprehensive, several excellent primers describe qualitative and quantitative research methods.[68] A key component of the data analysis for this project is coding. Coding can be qualitative or quantitative and represents instances where researchers describe a defined unit of data, such as a sentence or paragraph, by assigning it a label, or code. In this report, codes are assigned based on themes identified in the 2010 *VAL Report.*[69]

Data Collection

Selected LIS and Higher Education Literature

We performed a search in both LIS and higher education databases for literature that aligned with the project themes identified in the RFP. Selected LIS databases were Library and Information Science Abstracts (LISA), Library Literature and Information Science Full Text (H. W. Wilson), and Library, Information Science and Technology Abstracts (LISTA). Selected higher education databases were Academic Search Premier, Education Resources Information Center (ERIC), ProQuest Education Journals, and Teacher Reference Center. Papers included in the Association of Research Libraries (ARL) Library Assessment Conference (LAC), AiA projects, and reports published by Ithaka S+R also were included in the analysis. Search delimiters narrowed the results to studies published since 2010, containing themes identified in the 2010 *VAL Report*,[70] and published in the United States, except for studies outside the United States that we deemed relevant.

We reviewed the retrieved documents based on their alignment with the project research outcomes and questions and added and removed documents accordingly. Therefore, the literature review does not represent an exhaustive consideration of all assessment and evaluation research, but rather only literature about student outcomes, libraries, and higher education. We added a total of 535 documents to a bibliography (see *Appendix E: Literature Analyzed Bibliography*) and designated them as either theoretical (31%, *n*=166) or research (69%, *n*=369). Documents coded as theoretical include literature reviews, discussions of a theoretical model or framework, or thought pieces that identify a higher education trend or the way in which a library utilized its resources, which could include its collections, spaces, and services, or a combination of these, to respond to that trend. These theoretical pieces represented what LIS and higher education professionals addressed as emerging and important areas to examine. The documents coded as research involve some data collection and analysis for measuring outcomes or answering practical or empirical questions. These documents identify a higher education trend or the way in which a library utilized its resources, which could include its collections, spaces, and services, or a combination of these, to respond to that trend. The research category includes all AiA projects that have been completed and are accessible from the AiA project page website—a total of 178 studies.[71]

Focus Group Interviews

We created an advisory group to ensure that the findings from this report resonate with professional librarians and administrators in higher education. The members were academic library administrators from fourteen institutions that include community colleges (*n*=2), four-year colleges (*n*=2), and research universities (*n*=10); the members were from secular (*n*=11), nonsecular (*n*=3), public (*n*=9), and private (*n*=5) institutions representing the four geographical regions of the United States (see *Appendix F: Advisory Group Members' Titles and Carnegie Class for Advisory Group Members' Universities* for a full breakdown of Carnegie Classes). Eleven advisory group members addressed the questions we developed (see *Appendix G: Library Administrator Focus Group Interview Protocol* for an interview protocol) via an online focus group interview, which we conducted on Tuesday, October 11, 2016, from 1:00 p.m. to 2:30 p.m. EST. The other three members, who could not attend the focus group, provided written responses to the focus group protocol, which we folded into the analysis.

We conducted the online focus group interview using WebEx conference software, and we recorded audio from the meeting and had it transcribed by an external service. This conference software enabled both audio and visual, meaning that we could see nonverbal behaviors, such as facial expressions. The purpose of a focus group interview is "to explore in depth the feelings and beliefs people hold and to learn how these feelings shape overt behavior,"[72] by beginning with a broad discussion and gradually winnowing down to the core research focus.[73] Researchers can employ focus group interviews for multiple purposes; those most relevant to this project are to "examine known research questions from the participants' perspective"[74] and obtain "participants' interpretations of results from earlier studies," namely from the literature review portion of the study.[75] To this end, we used findings from initial analysis of the literature review themes to structure focus group questions. Project lead Connaway moderated the focus group interview and ensured that participation was equitable, the participants addressed the desired themes, and the session ended on time. While we had developed a protocol for the focus group interview (see *Appendix G: Library Administrator Focus Group Interview Protocol*), Connaway used the protocol as a guide to engender a free flow of discussion around core themes identified in the ACRL documents and by the literature review.[76]

One way to determine the validity of data collection and analysis methods is to ask participants to interpret the data collected and analyzed. This interpretation can inform writing up of findings by the research team. Researchers call this process *member checking*.[77] For this research, we employed member checking by conducting brainstorming sessions with advisory group members. Specifically, those who attended the American Library Association (ALA) 2017 Midwinter Conference in Atlanta, Georgia, in January participated in one of two brainstorming sessions. These sessions provided an opportunity for the advisory group members to review our initial findings, expand upon the identified priority areas, and suggest additional priority areas that we had not defined. We used the results of the brainstorming sessions to refine the research report and agenda further and to inform interpretations of findings.

Semi-structured Individual Interviews

Like focus group interviews, semi-structured individual interviews constitute another method intended to elicit in-depth information from individuals who are knowledgeable about a particular subject.[78] Three team members conducted semi-structured individual interviews with provosts from each of the advisory group members' institutions. Unlike a focus group interview environment, where the intent is to engender conversation among participants conducive to group input and discussion, the provost interviews were conducted to identify the provosts' ideas and thoughts on the academic library's contribution to the institution and the future of higher education. We chose this data source given the lack of studies in the LIS literature concerning assessment that elicit interview data from provosts and other higher education administrators.[79] However, some recent examples of LIS literature employ provost interviews to inform assessment-related recommendations.[80] The interviews were semi-structured, meaning that the interviewer and the provost shared control of the interview. In this way, the provosts could redirect some of the interview topics as desired, and the interviewer could probe in areas of interest.[81]

Between Friday, November 4, and Friday, November 11, 2016, three team members conducted telephone interviews with fourteen provosts. Two team members each interviewed five provosts each, and one interviewed four. As with the focus group interviews, findings from the literature review informed the development of the provost semi-structured individual interview protocol (see *Appendix B: Provost Semi-structured Interview Protocol* and *Appendix C: Provosts' Titles and Carnegie Class for Provosts' Universities*). On average, interviews were forty-five minutes, with the shortest interview taking twenty minutes and the longest sixty minutes. The interviewers took notes during the interviews, and the interviews were audio recorded digitally and sent to an outside agency for transcription. The recording quality of five interviews was not sufficient for transcription, so notes taken during the interviews were used to code and analyze these interviews.

Data Analysis

Once we collected the three data sources (i.e., relevant literature, advisory group interview transcript, provost semi-structured individual interview transcripts), we needed to develop a system to describe the context of each data source, as well as to compare the data sources. To make this comparison, we used coding to develop a standard way to represent the data. Once we applied codes, we could search for and identify patterns among and between the data sources, referred to as "post hoc analysis." This section reviews both phases of data analysis.

Coding

As stated by Connaway and Radford, "To organize and analyze the data collected for a study, it is necessary to place them in categories."[82] An initial identification of categories occurred before the data collection, when we reviewed relevant ACRL documents to identify important categories, or themes (see *Relevant ACRL Documents*).[83] Based on these documents, we developed a codebook to record the themes; we also included definitions and examples for each theme.[84]

After we had identified and analyzed literature review documents, we divided the original codebook into two separate codebooks. The first codebook includes the theme coding scheme, informed by the categories identified within the ACRL documents specified in the ACRL RFP. The second codebook, which contains the research document characteristics, was applied to the LIS and higher education documents identified as research (see *Selected LIS and Higher Education Literature* section). These codes captured information found only in research documents, including information about the populations studied (type of institution, group studied) and methods used, which one can call the demographic characteristics of the documents. We collected these codes to make the studies more accessible and findable when using the visualization component.

As mentioned above, student *learning* and *success* are two distinct terms. When developing the coding scheme, we decided to code any library collection, space, or service objectively tied to a particular grade or outcome as *success*. In this case, "objectively" means that the variables are measurable and usually quantifiable. If the library collection, space, or service did not have a measured or measurable effect on the student or their success, we coded it as *teaching and learning.*

Table 1 depicts sample entries from the project theme codebook, which was applied to all three data sources, while Table 2 depicts sample entries from the research document characteristics codebook, which we applied only to the literature review research documents. Refer to *Appendix D: Codebook* for full versions of both codebooks and *Appendix H: Further Description of the Coding Process for Data Analysis* for a detailed description of the coding process.

Table 1. Excerpt from theme codebook

Higher education trend	*Trend defined*	*Example of library resources that addressed higher education trend*
Teaching and learning (and beyond)	This outcome represents the less objective concepts of learning, such as critical thinking. These encompass the outcomes not covered by the student success theme, which is "quantifiable student attainment indicators, such as enrollment in postsecondary education, grades, persistence to the sophomore year, the length of time to degree, and graduation."[a] Usually not tied to a particular graded assignment or graduation. For more information, please see the discussion on Learning and Success in this report's *Literature Review* section.	Service: Library instruction Space: Collaborative working space for students Collections: Repository of online tutorials not linked to a specific class
Student success (for multiple student groups)	This outcome represents the more objective, usually quantifiable indicators of learning, or "quantifiable student attainment indicators, such as enrollment in postsecondary education, grades, persistence to the sophomore year, length of time to degree, and graduation."[b] These outcomes are related to a particular assignment or semester, such as grades or GPA. They could also be related to whether the student re-enrolled or graduated. For more information, please see the discussion on Learning and Success in this report's *Literature Review* section.	Collections: Physical collections Collections: Digital collections Space: Study spaces Service: Library instruction Service: Collection discovery

a. George D. Kuh, Jillian Kinzie, Jennifer A. Buckley, Brian K. Bridges, and John C. Hayek, What Matters to Student Success: A Review of the Literature, Commissioned Report for the National Symposium on Postsecondary Student Success: Spearheading a Dialog on Student Success (Washington, DC: National Postsecondary Education Cooperative, 2006), 5, https://nces.ed.gov/npec/pdf/kuh_team_report.pdf.
b. Ibid.

Table 2. Excerpt from research document characteristics codebook

Code name	*Code definition*	*Values*
Analysis method—Qualitative	How the data were analyzed via qualitative methods.	Content analysis; Other
Analysis method—Quantitative	How the data were analyzed via quantitative methods.	ANOVA; Regression; X2; Descriptive statistics; Correlation; Other

Descriptive Statistics and Post Hoc Analysis

All three data sources (i.e., selected literature, advisory group interview, and provost semi-structured individual interviews) were coded, and we divided each data source according to its unit of analysis. The units of analysis describe the "what" or "who" being studied or quantified;[85] and we chose the document, the group interview transcript, and the provost interview transcript as the unit of analysis for the three data sources, respectively. For each selected document, we were concerned with whether a code was applied or not, not how many times we used the code. This decision allowed us to see what themes were being discussed frequently and less frequently across the literature. For provost and focus group interviews, we were concerned with how many times advisory group members and provosts discussed each theme, rather than whether they discussed a theme or not. We made this decision given the small sample number of participants in both the focus group and semi-structured interviews. Based on the selected units of analysis, we were, therefore, able to determine the number of documents that discussed each theme and the number of times focus group and semi-structured interview participants discussed each theme. We also wanted to compare how often each data source discussed the themes. To make this comparison, we took the total number of themes coded for each data source and divided them by the number of times each theme was coded, otherwise known as the proportion of themes assigned to each data source.

Within each data source, we also calculated basic descriptive statistics (i.e., mean, median, mode, and standard deviation). This process broadly summarized and described the data, giving us insight when obtaining the findings. We also used post hoc analysis techniques to search for trends and patterns within the three coded data sources. Such methods allowed for additional findings and discoveries beyond what could be uncovered using descriptive statistics.[86] For more details on the specific post hoc techniques used, please see *Appendix I: Description of Post Hoc Techniques Used in Report*. The *Findings* section below addresses the frequency of codes applied to each data source, then compares similarities and differences between the proportion of codes used.

Findings

This section examines key findings from analysis of the three data sources. These key findings include the following:

- *The selected literature focused on service, collaboration, and teaching and learning.* Mission alignment and strategy was discussed more in theoretical documents than in research documents, which signifies that librarians and researchers are not addressing this key theme in their work. Documents from the higher education literature examined service less than those within the LIS research, suggesting a disproportionate focus on this theme among librarians and LIS researchers. We compared the AiA projects to the non-AiA projects, finding that the former sampled from more varied populations and used mixed methods more frequently than non-AiA projects. AiA projects focused more on collaboration, communication, and instruction than non-AiA ones.
- *Focus group interview participants, who are library administrators, prioritized service, collaboration, and communication.* As in the AiA projects, participants also addressed collaboration and communication. However, participants contextualized the need to link both collaboration and communication to the institutional mission, goals, and strategy of the university, rather than isolate both themes within the library.

- *Provosts valued communication and mission alignment and strategy.* Provosts' evaluating communication aligns with the priorities of the AiA projects and advisory group participants. However, provosts discussed mission alignment and strategy to a greater degree than these other data sources. Specifically, provosts further emphasized the importance of librarians communicating how the library contributes to institutional goals by marketing, customer service, and sharing space with other groups, both on and off campus.

We discuss the empirical basis of these findings in more detail below.

Selected LIS and Higher Education Literature

As stated above in the *Data Collection* section, we coded a total of 535 documents using the theme codebook (see *Appendix D: Codebook* for a list of all theme codes). Figure 1 and figure 2 depict the number of documents with each theme. On average, we applied a code to 37 percent of the documents (*n*=199). Themes that are more than one standard deviation (+/–19%, *n*=102) from the mean indicate some of the themes most and least frequently discussed by the literature. Themes most discussed are service (*n*=377, 70%), collaboration (*n*=321, 60%), and teaching and learning (*n*=308, 58%). Those least discussed are provision of technology (*n*=88, 16%), inclusivity/diversity (*n*=67, 13%), and accreditation (*n*=41, 8%).

Figure 1
A word cloud depicting the number of documents coded within each theme

Figure 2
Number of documents within each theme (n=535)

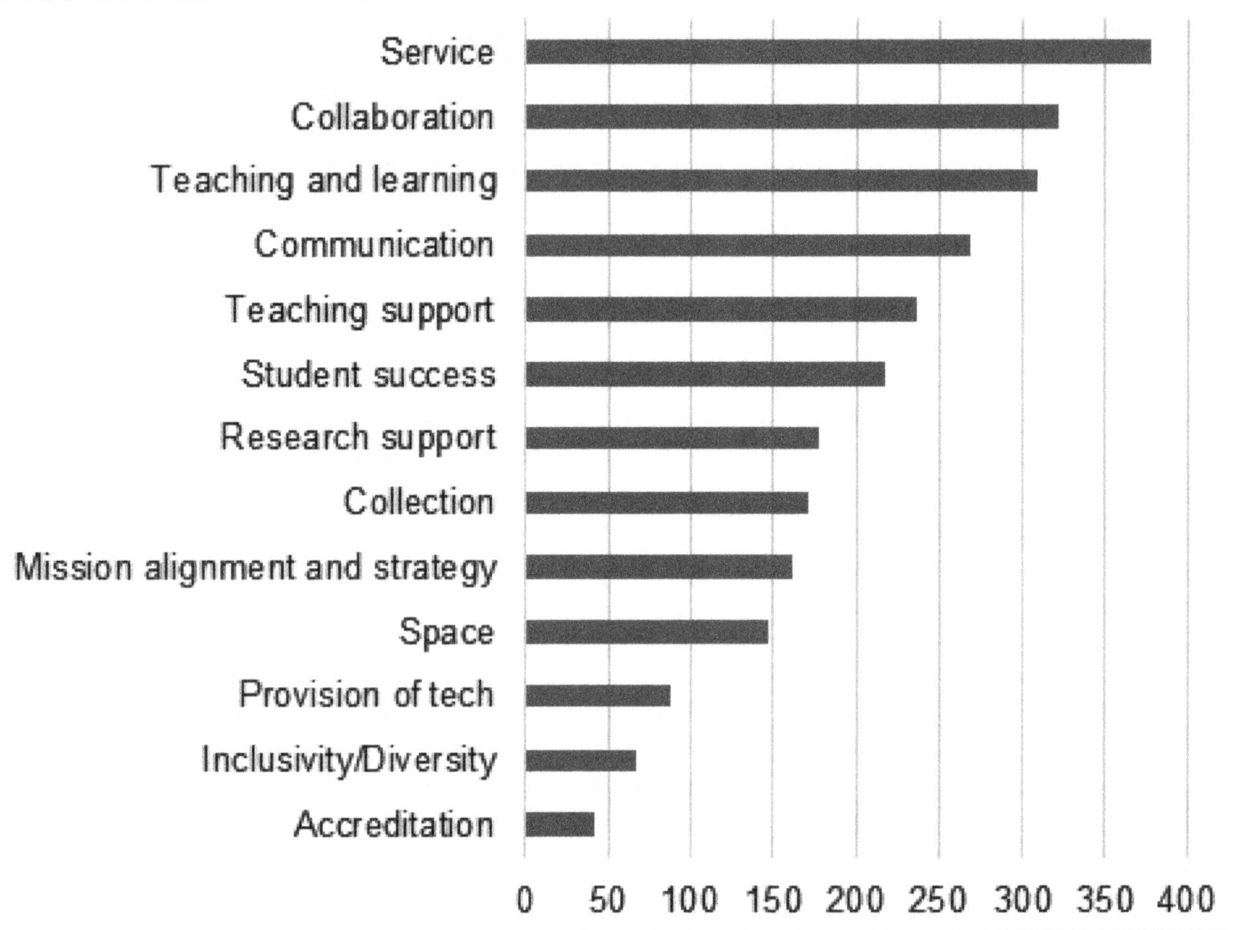

Next, we compared the frequency of codes based on whether a document was coded as theoretical, representing an area or areas identified as important to focus on by library administrators, library staff, researchers, practitioners, and students and supported by prior research (e.g., literature reviews), or practical research, indicating both empirical and action. An overlap between the frequency of codes applied to theoretical and research documents means that library administrators, library staff, researchers, practitioners, and students are addressing significant themes within higher education and LIS, whereas little to no overlap indicates that what they are articulating should be done differs from what they have done, as reflected in the documents reviewed. Since research documents (68%, n=369) outnumber theoretical documents (32%, n=166), we compared their proportions. This comparison is depicted by figure 3.

Figure 3
Differences in proportion of codes between theoretical and research documents

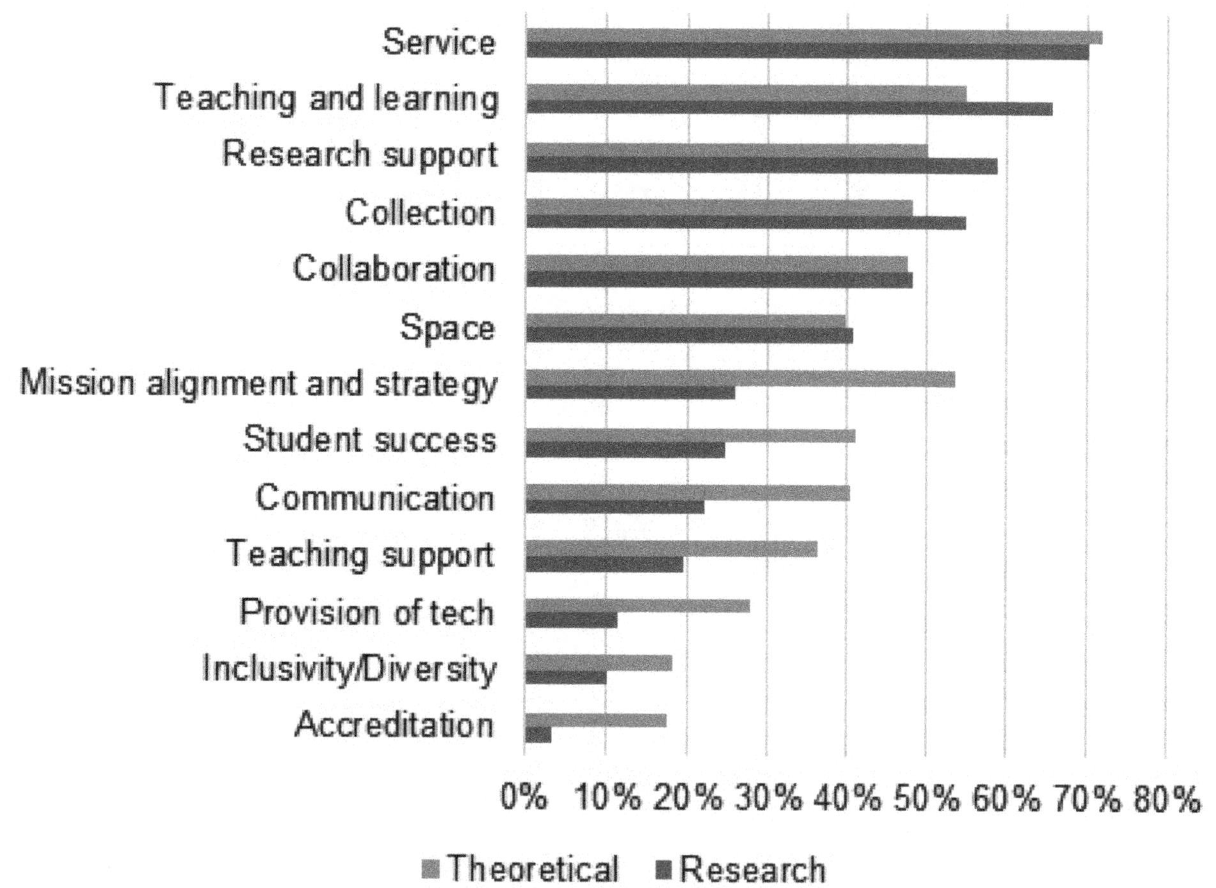

On average, theoretical documents contain 7 percent more codes than research documents. One explanation for this observation is that theoretical documents include literature reviews and predictions of future trends. Therefore, discussing theoretical documents will include more themes as compared to research documents, which empirically investigate one or two themes. Mission alignment and strategy is discussed 28 percent more in theoretical documents than in research documents and is more than one standard deviation of difference from the mean (+/–12%).

We also wanted to determine if the proportion of themes applied changed over time. Table 3 depicts the proportion of themes coded by year. Themes discussed more over time are collaboration, communication, and teaching support. A few themes experienced a decrease in the proportion of codes applied over time. However, the *p*-value determining their significance was higher than 0.05. This *p*-value indicates that while these themes were very likely to trend downward over time, there is less evidence for this observation as compared to those themes that increased over time. Themes that appeared to decrease over time are mission alignment and strategy, research support, and collection.

Table 3. Proportion of themes from codebook applied to documents by year

Themes by year	*2010* % (of 63)	*2011* % (of 20)	*2012* % (of 77)	*2013* % (of 29)	*2014* % (of 109)	*2015* % (of 40)	*2016* % (of 18)
Collaboration	32%	25%	34%	34%	43%	63%	50%
Communication	25%	30%	16%	38%	24%	35%	33%
Accreditation	11%	20%	8%	17%	8%	18%	11%
Mission alignment and strategy	40%	50%	35%	45%	27%	50%	44%
Inclusivity/Diversity	17%	15%	6%	21%	9%	28%	44%
Teaching and learning	59%	50%	42%	41%	53%	60%	61%
Provision of tech	25%	25%	19%	34%	17%	30%	22%
Research support	54%	45%	56%	62%	44%	45%	28%
Student success	24%	30%	23%	66%	27%	73%	67%
Teaching support	30%	30%	26%	52%	26%	38%	61%
Collection	46%	50%	55%	62%	42%	28%	44%
Service	62%	80%	68%	83%	69%	55%	56%
Space	35%	15%	36%	48%	37%	48%	44%

Following this comparison of documents by type (theoretical or research) and year, we compared differences in the proportion of themes discussed in documents from the higher education literature versus the LIS literature. One should note that the search terms used for the database searches included the word *library* and its derivatives. For this reason, this comparison can inform only of differences in the proportion of themes between what the documents say about student learning outcomes as related to libraries within the higher education literature versus the LIS literature, not student learning outcomes in general.

Documents labeled as higher education literature were those retrieved from higher education databases that LIS databases did not index and reports from Ithaka S+R. For this reason, we reviewed 354 of the total 535 documents (66%) when making this comparison, given that we retrieved documents for review that were not indexed by databases (e.g., AiA projects). We designated 5 percent of documents as higher education literature (*n*=18). We also designated 15 percent (*n*=52) as both higher education and LIS literature since both databases indexed them. The remainder of the documents (*n*=284, 80%) were from LIS literature. Figure 4 illustrates the percentage difference between themes coded in the higher education literature, the LIS literature, or both the higher education and LIS literature.

Figure 4
Percentage difference between themes by literature type

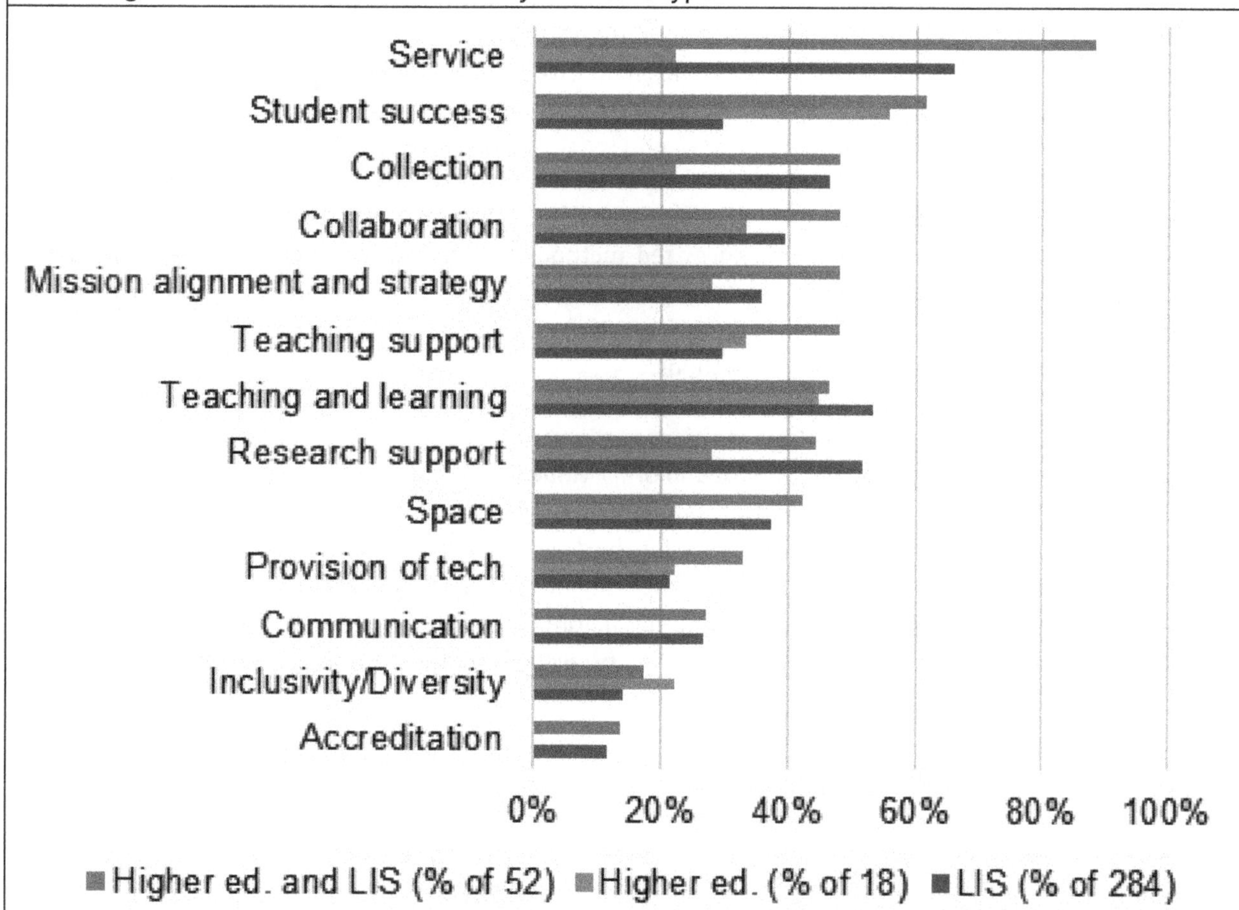

Higher education literature has fewer documents coded for service (22%, *n*=4) as compared to LIS documents (66%, *n*=187) and higher education and LIS literature combined (88%, *n*=46). The LIS documents have fewer codes for student success (30%, *n*=84) as compared to higher education and LIS literature combined (62%, *n*=32).

Analysis of Studies within the Selected Literature Review

Along with the theme codes, we applied the research document characteristics codes to documents coded as research, about 68 percent (*n*=369) of all documents. These latter codes provide more insight into the study details.

Per the selection criteria for the literature review, the studies were conducted in the United States (79%, *n*=290) and distributed evenly throughout the four regions: South (22%, *n*=83), Midwest (22%, *n*=80), West (18%, *n*=65), and Northeast (17%, *n*=62). The majority examined universities (72%, *n*=266), followed by colleges (11%, *n*=39), and community colleges (7%, *n*=27). Fourteen percent (*n*=51) of studies spanned multiple institutions. Most institutions were in the public sector (67%, *n*=227). Populations studied were graduate students (41%, *n*=151), undergraduates (39%, *n*=143), and other groups, such as faculty (27%, *n*=98).

Because we defined *method* for this project as "Any procedure employed to attain a certain end," methods are the specific actions and tools used during data collection and analysis.[87] The most popular data collection methods were quantitative (79%, *n*=292), specifically surveys (41%, *n*=151) and rubrics (28%, *n*=102). Qualitative methods were less used (28%, *n*=102), with interviews constituting the most popular method (18%, *n*=65). The most common data analysis methods also were quantitative (86%, *n*=316), most of which used correlations (52%, *n*=191) and descriptive statistics (37%, *n*=136). Qualitative analysis methods also were used (71%, *n*=262), with content analysis being overwhelmingly employed (69%, *n*=254).

Research approaches constitute the "plans and the procedures for research that span the steps from broad assumptions to detailed methods of data collection, analysis, and interpretation."[88] These approaches fit into three categories: qualitative, quantitative, and mixed methods.[89] The research documents most often used quantitative approaches (92%, *n*=338), followed by qualitative (73%, *n*=271) and mixed methods (67%, *n*=246). Many studies also employed multiple methods (80%, *n*=296). See *Appendix A: Glossary* for definitions stating the difference between mixed and multiple methods.

Given that the data collection and analysis of this report have proceeded iteratively, we added literature for review based on comments by the ACRL board and other valued stakeholders. One significant addition from prior drafts was the addition of 178 AiA projects. We folded findings from analysis of these studies into all previous discussion of selected documents, except for the discussion of theoretical documents (we labeled all AiA projects as research documents) and when comparing documents retrieved from LIS databases to those from higher education ones. In examining the findings before and after this addition, we noted that some key themes and study demographics addressed by the AiA projects were not as prevalent in non-AiA projects.

Differences in AiA Projects versus Non-AiA Projects

A collaborative planning grant funded the AiA program, which involved "senior librarians, chief academic administrators, and institutional researchers."[90] Participation in the program required librarians, administrators, and researchers to collaborate with at least two team members outside of the library. AiA participants were asked by the project requirements to consider any aspect of the library related to assessment, and the requirements also provided examples of inquiry questions.[91] AiA projects all are within the United States except for six in Canada and one in Australia, whereas 11% (*n*=40) of non-AiA projects collected are outside the United States. The team can attribute this finding to the selection criteria of literature reviewed for this project, which emphasized studies within the United States, with a few exceptions from Australia and the United Kingdom. AiA projects are more evenly dispersed throughout the four areas of the United States (Northeast, 25%, *n*=43; West, 20%, *n*=34; Midwest, 28%, *n*=48; South, 26%, *n*=45) as compared to non-AiA projects, which are less representative of the Northeast (9%, *n*=19).

We examined these studies across three areas: institution type, communication and collaboration, and data collection and analysis methods:

- ***Institution type.*** AiA projects concentrate more on community colleges (6%, *n*=22) and colleges (8%, *n*=31) than non-AiA projects (1%, *n*=5; 2%, *n*=8, respectively). AiA projects also focus more on private institutions (18%, *n*=67) than non-AiA projects (8%, *n*=30). Both study types primarily examine universities (non-AiA, 38%, *n*=141; AiA, 34%, *n*=125). Regarding the groups studied, AiA projects focus less on undergraduates. Thirty-three percent (*n*=120) of non-AiA projects examine undergraduates, while 6 percent (*n*=23) of AiA projects do. Instead, AiA projects have a more evenly dispersed focus in the study of graduates, undergraduates, and other populations.
- ***Communication and collaboration.*** In the analysis of theme coding, AiA projects focus more on communication (48%, *n*=178) and collaboration (48%, *n*=178) than non-AiA projects (25%, *n*=91; 39%, *n*=143). On the other hand, AiA projects focus less on space (4%, *n*=13) and research support (1%, *n*=2) than non-AiA projects (36%, *n*=134; 48%, *n*=176). Since participants conducted all AiA projects between 2014 and 2016, AiA projects likely account for the observed increase in focus on communication and collaboration and for the decrease in focus on research support over time within the literature. Although AiA projects concentrate more on collaboration than non-AiA projects, the latter are more collaborative across institutions, with 24 percent (*n*=50) of non-AiA projects conducted at multiple institutions, as compared to only 1 percent (*n*=1) of AiA projects.
- ***Data collection and analysis methods.*** Regarding types of library resources studied, AiA projects focus much more on instruction as a library service (37%, *n*=135) than non-AiA projects (17%, *n*=64). This observation plays out when examining quantitative data collection methods used, with AiA projects more often employing rubrics (22%, *n*=82) to assess instructional effectiveness than non-AiA projects (5%, *n*=20). Regarding methods in general, AiA projects experience a heightened use of quantitative data collection methods (53%, *n*=195) versus non-AiA projects (26%, *n*=97), whereas non-AiA projects employ more qualitative data collection methods (20%, *n*=74) than AiA projects (8%, *n*=28). Both types of studies emphasize quantitative data analysis, but the kind of analysis employed varies. Specifically, 37 percent (*n*=165) of non-AiA projects apply descriptive statistics as a quantitative data analysis method, whereas no AiA projects coded use this analysis method. Instead, 45 percent (*n*=166) of AiA projects employ correlations, whereas 7 percent (*n*=25) of non-AiA projects do. AiA projects also demonstrate a heightened use of mixed methods (45%, *n*=166) as compared to non-AiA projects (22%, *n*=80). See *Appendix A: Glossary* for definitions stating the difference between mixed and multiple methods.

As previously discussed, the themes of collaboration and communication were addressed more frequently in the AiA projects than in the non-AiA projects. These themes also were reviewed by the focus group participants in this project.

Focus Group Interview

Figure 5 depicts the frequency of themes coded within the focus group interview transcript. On average, a theme was coded 21 times (8%) within the transcript. Themes more than one standard deviation away from the mean (+/–6%, *n*=17) are communication (20%, *n*=54), collaboration (17%, *n*=46), and service (16%, *n*=44), all frequently discussed, and accreditation (0%, *n*=0), which was not addressed.

Figure 5
Frequency of themes coded in focus group interview

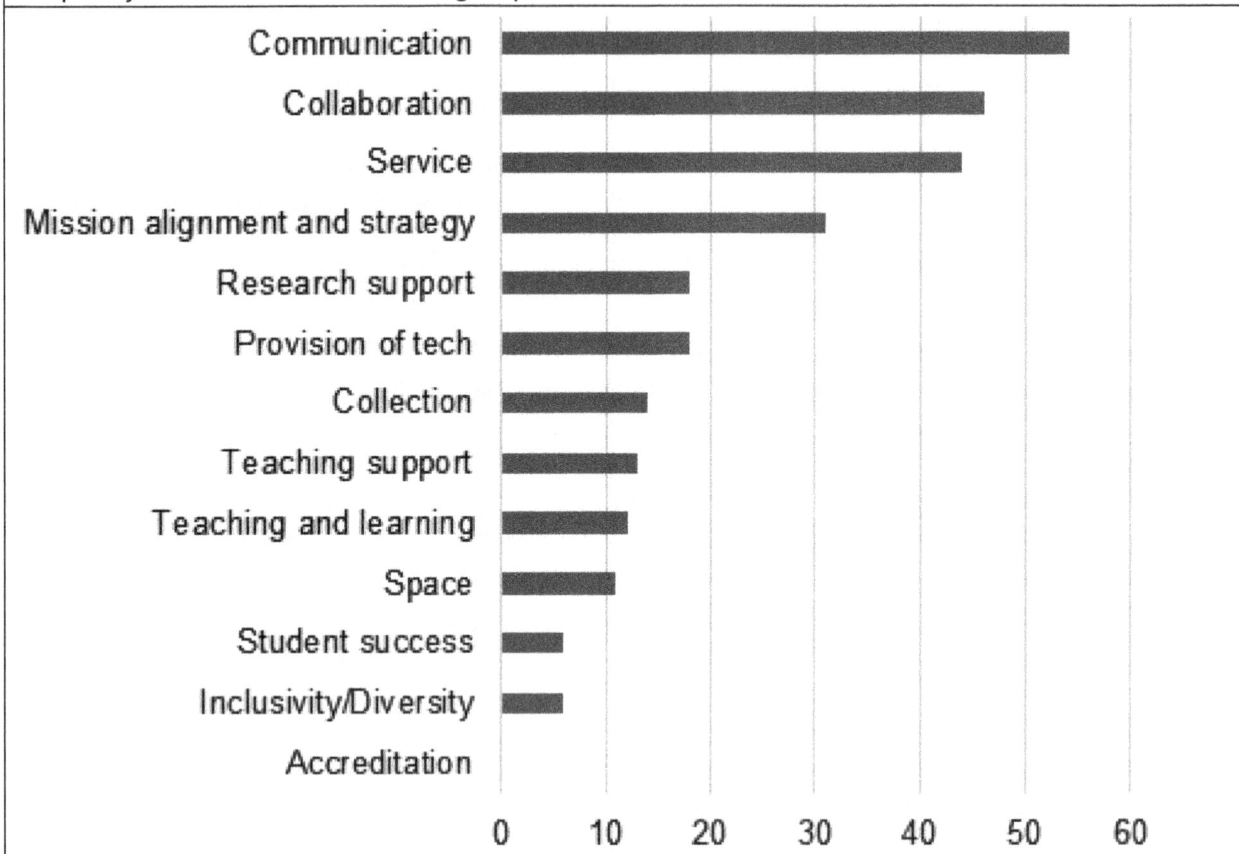

> All of us see our work as directly tied to the mission of the university. And it is what makes academic libraries unique in some ways, but also so successful, that academic libraries, in my opinion, are those that are directly connected to the mission of their unique institution.
>
> —Advisory Group Member LM13

It may be surprising that the focus group interview participants did not discuss student learning (4%, *n*=12) and success (2%, *n*=6), considering how often the literature mentions these themes (learning, 58%, *n*=308; success, 41%, *n*=218). However, as explained by one participant:

> I think probably each of us would have some example of our shared strategic initiatives around enhancing students' success. And promoting innovation and teaching and learning. I think those are probably common across all our institutions. I think what's underlying all of this is that all of us see our work as directly tied to the mission of the university. And it is what makes academic libraries unique in some ways, but also so successful, that academic libraries, in my opinion, are those that are directly connected to the mission of their unique institution. (Advisory Group Member LM13)*

As perceived by this participant, library administrators and staff should continue to position the library's role in enhancing student learning and success as inherent to the mission of the academic institution. This participant felt that being solely concerned with fulfilling library-oriented goals would detract from the effect they would be able to have at the university level. One reason for this observation may be that the participants are administrators in their academic libraries; therefore, their focus is to be strategic and targeted on high-level library goals. It also likely accounts for why themes that implied making connections and establishing relationships outside of the library—collaboration and communication—were among those most frequently discussed (communication, 20%, n=54; collaboration, 17%, n=46).[92]

> One thing I will say is I think it needs to be sort of multi-level communication from the provost to those relationships you have with other units like the centers for teaching and learning, to the academic units, to the individual relationships that librarians and staff have with faculty and students.
>
> —Advisory Group Member LM03

However, making such connections is not as simple as having a conversation with one group or implementing the same strategies to make connections across various ones. Rather, library administrators and staff should continue to engage in outreach beyond the library by recognizing and adapting to the unique "ecosystem" of relationships within the institution (Advisory Group Member LM14). As stated by one participant:

> A lot of what's come out is that we're not islands. Not that we ever were, but I think part of our success in reaching to students and faculty is the way we collaborate with others.... One thing I will say is I think it needs to be sort of multi-level communication from the provost to those relationships you have with other units like the centers for teaching and learning, to the academic units, to the individual relationships that librarians and staff have with faculty and students. You know, all those levels reinforce each other, and any alone doesn't quite work as well. (Advisory Group Member LM03)

As indicated by this participant, establishing multi-level communication requires collaboration. Specifically, library administrators and staff should continue to recognize how the multiple stakeholders within their specific university ecosystem interrelate and leverage their relationships to attain "shared goals," rather than just library-oriented ones (Advisory Group Member LM07). Here are some examples of how focus group interview participants achieved successful collaborations that resulted in communicating value:

* All quotes were lightly edited and abbreviated for clarity.

- Partner with departments to support student research projects by offering instructional courses, publishing research in a student-run journal or institutional repository, and hosting relevant campus events, such as research competitions (Advisory Group Member LM06)[93]
- Invite campus meetings and gatherings to take place in the library building, which increases visibility of the library's space and services among administrators (Advisory Group Member LM08)[94]
- Work with the student government association to advocate to the administration on the library's behalf (Advisory Group Member LM01)[95]
- Partner with faculty members to institute an embedded librarians program, which results in the former advocating on the latter's behalf (Advisory Group Member LM12)[96]
- Establish a marketing communication program that considers the best approaches to engage different user groups, for example, using social media to market to students (Advisory Group Member LM09)[97]
- Build use of special collections materials into course curriculum (Advisory Group Member LM01)[98]
- Examine the learning goals and influential practices articulated by other departments to see where potential synergies are present (Advisory Group Member LM07)[99]
- Collaborate with the career office to articulate library effects on student learning outcomes (Advisory Group Member LM07)[100]

A common thread throughout these examples is that library administrators and staff should continue to denote how the library integrates into the larger university system when focusing on mission alignment and strategy and communicating value. By considering themselves as "university citizens" (Advisory Group Member LM13), library administrators and staff can more easily "capture the senior leadership attention, because what they see is the library as a partner in the academic enterprise, helping other units to achieve these goals that at the highest level have been identified" (Advisory Group Member LM07). It also should be noted that the library engendered collaboration and communication efforts using service-based (16%, *n*=44), rather than collection-based (5%, *n*=14) or space-based (4%, *n*=11) resources. This finding contrasts with provost interviews, which focused on space (9%, *n*=105) almost as much as service (10%, *n*=112). The provosts' increased focus on space as compared to library administrators' is also statistically significant. This finding demonstrates that library administrators and staff may not know how to talk about space and facilities, while provosts and other higher education administrators are interested in seeing a more efficient use of library space and facilities. Therefore, library administrators and staff should craft their terms carefully to align their language with the areas considered vital by provosts. Such alignment will improve communication among library administrators and staff and provosts.

Privacy was mentioned only once but is an important area of exploration. This topic is particularly fraught in the areas of assessment and academic libraries since there is a lack of established effective practices and standards addressing the methods and contexts that may threaten the privacy of students.[101] For this reason, privacy, when broadly defined, can be viewed by library administrators and staff in some instances as less of an ethics issue and more of an impediment, as articulated by one participant:

> I think that to truly be able to look at, and be able to tell those stories, and to come up with those snippets of information that will resonate with other leaders, we have to be willing to do types of data collection that libraries have shied away from in the past. And I think that involves tracking user behavior in a way that we've seen in a couple of the different studies that have looked at retention. But I think that there are ways of extrapolating and growing that out a little bit more so that we are dealing with large datasets.... We could still keep it anonymous when we look at it in aggregate, right? I think that we have to be able to be willing to have conversations on campus about tracking user behavior in ways that libraries just haven't done. (Advisory Group Member LM14)

The methods detailed in this account are in stark contrast to the level of detail that would be available with some of the data components mentioned by three of the provosts in the semi-structured individual interviews. As one provost explained:

> We are creating components that [are on] institutional, programmatic and... course level[s], and having an intervention assigned to each.... Each department will have its own interventions to increase... numbers that are associated with completion. We'll keep track of those through [a] software program that is available to me as well as everybody... at different levels with different permissions. (Provost PP12)

> We have to be willing to do types of data collection that libraries have shied away from in the past. And I think that involves tracking user behavior in a way that we've seen in a couple of the different studies that have looked at retention.
>
> —Advisory Group Member LM14

Although arguments for using individual-level data have been made, and in some cases such usage has been put into practice, certain components can anonymize data or make it available only to specific levels.[102] Library administrators and staff should continue to examine methods and tools, such as software programs, to collect new forms of individual-level data and connect these data to communicating the library's value, while preserving privacy and confidentiality. We have highlighted the University of Wollongong as having done an exemplary study in the *Priority Areas for Future Research and Effective Practices* section below because it has successfully navigated the line between privacy and confidentiality while using individual-level data. Library administrators and staff can use this study as a starting point from which to derive methods and tools that strike this balance. Since we did not ask provosts direct questions about privacy, future research may need to address how those involved in assessment outside the library handle this topic and what practices and norms they have established.

Some of the themes addressed in the focus group interviews also were discussed by provosts. However, provosts also emphasized the integration of these themes with the themes of mission alignment and strategy and space.

Provost Semi-structured Individual Interviews

Figure 6 depicts how frequently the provosts discussed the themes. On average, a theme was coded 88 times (8%) across all provost interview transcripts. Themes that have frequencies more than one standard deviation (+/–1%, n=53) from the mean indicate those considered most and least significant to provosts interviewed. Those considered important to provosts are communication (17%, n=199) and mission alignment and strategy (14%, n=159). Accreditation, on the other hand, was not discussed frequently by provosts (2%, n=18).

Provosts consider communication and mission alignment and strategy to be essential components of academic library value related to student learning and success. Regarding communication, provosts recognize that it is difficult for library administrators and staff to get the attention of potential stakeholders. One reason for this difficulty is the gap in perceptions between stakeholders, such as faculty, and library administrators and staff of what the library does and how it is a valuable member of the academic enterprise.[103] This gap may result in a series of "myths" (Provost PP04) about the library, such as that it provides only collections or that there is no need for libraries since everything can be freely accessed online. As stated by one provost:

> The big myth… is that, that many faculty don't engage with the library, because they feel that, "Well, the library is online." Right? Students can access everything from a distance. (Provost PP04)

To address these gaps, library administrators and staff should continue to become better at communicating the value of their libraries. However, for this communication to be effective, it cannot rely on passive means such as e-mail newsletters. Rather, library administrators and staff must integrate their library's services, collections, and spaces into the lives of its principal stakeholders, such as faculty and students, to achieve this communication. This point is exemplified by the following anecdote from the same provost of a "not helpful" communication strategy:

> A number of years ago, before I started… there was some agreement… to buy huge TV screens… and put them in our library as a means of sharing information for students… [such as] what resources are available to students and, and then it also advertises other things going on on-campus,… award winners and that sort of thing. Well, we have got them by the main entrance of these libraries and I have yet to see a single student interested in those things. These passive forms of communication are not helpful. I would say another e-mail is not helpful. Even a newsletter that is beautiful, by e-mail, [is] probably not helpful. (Provost PP04)

They have to be able to sell to the deans that this is something valuable that the deans want to be a part of, and the deans are going to be impacted by their faculty feeling like that this is a worthy thing because if we use money for one thing, we can't use if for something else. I think customer service… becomes really important in this kind of environment.

—Provost PP07

Instead of such passive communication, library administrators and staff need to become good at "customer service" (Provost PP07). It instills buy-in from other campus stakeholders, who can become the library's "champions," "boosters," and "prophets" (Provost PP02). As noted by one provost:

> I think the key for units like the library, since they are dependent upon the deans, whether for special things or just in that general sort of central cost pool assessment, they have to be able to sell to the deans that this is something valuable that the deans want to be a part of, and the deans are going to be impacted by their faculty feeling like that this is a worthy thing because if we use money for one thing, we can't use if for something else. I think customer service… becomes really important in this kind of environment. (Provost PP07)

To fulfill this role, provosts suggest that library administrators and staff should continue to collaborate with faculty and students, for example, by introducing a liaison program. As conveyed by one provost, it is very important for library administrators and staff to "establish themselves as a critical link or a critical piece" early on by having "intentional interventions" (e.g., in orientations, by going to classes or convincing instructors to bring classes to the libraries, online or on campus; Provost PP05). The goal of library administrators and staff should be to push the library beyond its role as "a service body" and instead integrate the library into the lives of its potential users (Provost PP13). As one provost stated:

> I think that for so long [libraries] have had sort of a role of support rather than integration into work, and I think with the new leadership and the new vision that it is much more of a partnership rather than just sort of a support as needed, so it's much more proactive in its orientation rather than reactive. And I think that culture change is somewhat, it takes time. I think that not everyone recognizes because the way many of our faculty and students have done research now, it is less about going to a physical space but accessing information in their offices.... And so trying to imagine a new way in which it is not just a service model, but it is actually an integration and partnership model, I think that that is one of the challenges of... changing the paradigm. (Provost PP03)

And so trying to imagine a new way in which it is not just a service model, but it is actually an integration and partnership model, I think that that is one of the challenges of... changing the paradigm.

—Provost PP03

This account reiterates a key finding from the *Selected LIS and Higher Education Literature* and *Focus Group Interview* sections above. Library administrators and staff use *service* as an umbrella term to capture more distinct practices, such as teaching or customer service. However, provosts envision service as less explicit and therefore less "proactive" (Provost PP03). Instead, provosts want to see the specific ways that library administrators and staff have collaborated with the principal stakeholders in their institutions and enhanced the institutional mission and goals. For this reason, library administrators and staff should use more direct language that identifies how the library contributes the shared mission and goals throughout the institution.

Figure 6

Frequency of themes coded in provost interviews

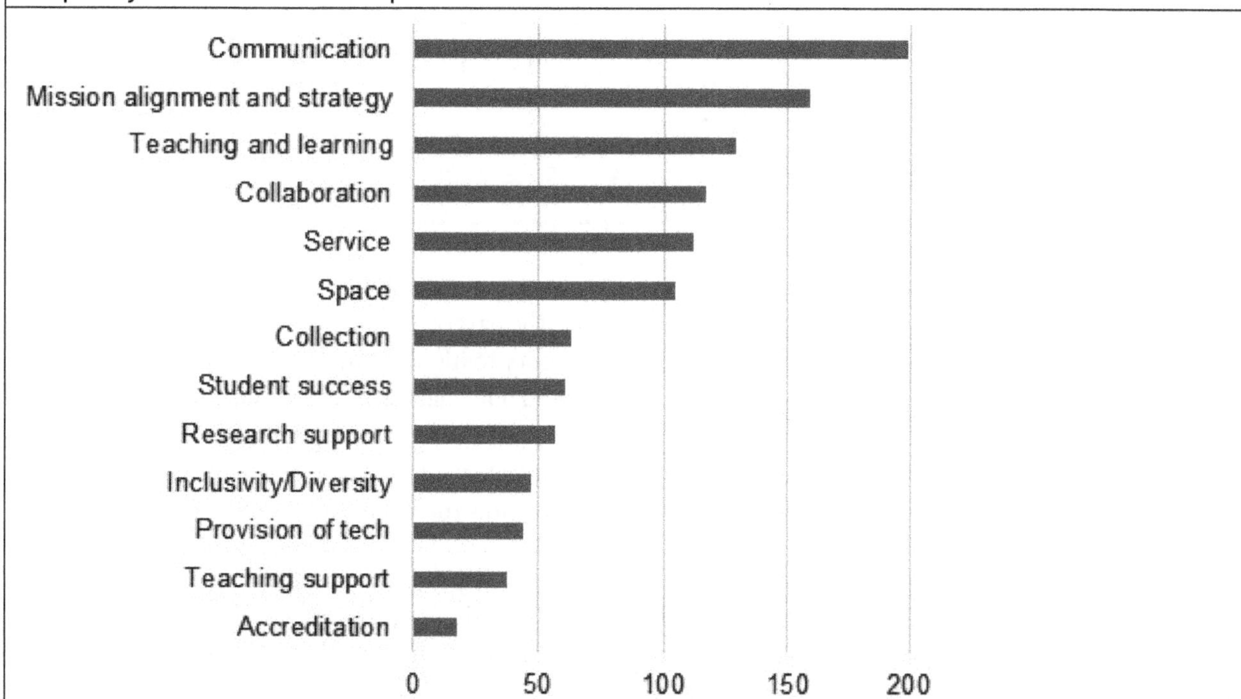

Library administrators and staff should continue to collaborate with the main stakeholders in their institutions by sharing space with them. As indicated by figure 6, provosts discussed space often. For instance, the provost who previously shared a "not helpful" anecdote regarding how librarians should communicate went on to discuss the strongest ways for the library to communicate its value, noting: "A library has so many resources to help with the mission of the university.... But you have to woo in faculty and students and staff... the space is important...." (Provost PP04). But space cannot be limited to supporting library collections or services, as stated by another provost:

> If the library gets into turf protection, it is going to lose.... It is going to look and feel like the stereotypical, antiquated repository of knowledge with dusty books that nobody ever pulls off the shelves. (Provost PP01)

Instead, provosts want library administrators and staff to collaborate with others in using space. Library administrators and staff can achieve this collaboration in several ways, from offering space in the library to a writing center to hosting a museum with artifacts of interest to those within and outside the university. For provosts, being able to see individuals using the space leaves an impression of the library as "a hub of student learning" (Provost PP03). According to one provost:

> I think [space] is one of the most effective ways to get the message out. That... might involve, as an example, making meeting rooms in the library more generally available for people to come and do projects. Creating... the library as this sort of center of intellectual activity. (Provost PP09)

Such communication also keys into mission strategy and alignment. If library administrators and staff are actively assessing services, systems, spaces, and so on, then they are naturally having to communicate and collaborate with the administrators and faculty on a regular basis.

> I think [space] is one of the most effective ways to get the message out. That... might involve, as an example, making meeting rooms in the library more generally available for people to come and do projects. Creating... the library as this sort of center of intellectual activity.
>
> —Provost PP09

Essential to provosts is the contribution libraries can make to the larger institutional mission and goals. Provosts indicate that communication and collaboration-based efforts on the part of library administrators and staff must be tied to the larger institutional mission and goals to sell the library to higher education administrators: "... if it can help a university-wide initiative, that's going to be helpful. Find out what the provost is very interested in, and then try to find a way that the library can help support that initiative" (Provost PP04). Given that these missions vary, it is imperative that library administrators and staff communicate with the provost to identify critical issues and then use language recognized by the provost when explaining how the library can address these issues.

The outcomes of these issues remain unknown to provosts, especially considering the result of the 2016 US presidential election. Library administrators and staff can respond to this uncertainty by communicating some of the new approaches to library assessment and evaluation that address these issues. For instance, they can articulate the importance of systematically integrating information literacy courses beyond a one-time session into the course curriculum and provide teaching and learning responses to address this integration, such as curriculum development and faculty training. Further, they can collaborate with the information technology (IT) department to devote resources to an increasing need for media and digital literacy.[104]

One provost provided a rich, detailed anecdote concerning the importance of library administrators and staff linking communication and collaboration efforts to the institutional mission and goals:

> We are a science and technology university. There is no way on God's green earth that our faculty are ever going leave the peer-review-journal conference-proceedings world. And yet we have got a couple of very bright, very interesting, very cool young library faculty, who when you talk to them, you can tell that they have no idea who their audience is here. They have very exciting ideas. But the kind of stuff they are interested in, and they're wondering why they don't get more response and that sort of thing, this is just not the kind of institution where they are going to get a lot of response. Then you get into this kind of weird situation where you've got these incredibly bright people who are out there talking to other librarians about ideas that are very important to librarians, and that librarians as a body agree are important. But the engineers do not think it is important and the biologists do not think it is important because they are all still very much grounded in the standard grants, peer-review publication, citation count. And so, for me, in that kind of a situation, what is compelling is not, "You should be interested in open-source because it's, A, a moral good, B, we get to stick it to the evil publication company." What is compelling is, "Did you know that on average, faculty members who post the early version of their papers in their university's repository see a 15 percent increase in their citations?" (Provost PP09)

In this example, the provost recognizes the value of practices in which library administrators and staff are engaged. However, she points out that the way library administrators and staff communicate these practices may exhibit disconnection from what provosts value. Library administrators and staff should continue to communicate with provosts to determine what provosts value and develop effective strategies for communicating how these practices contribute to this value. Further, this provost's account, especially her conclusion, should not be interpreted as provosts emphasizing direct outcomes as indicators of library value. Provosts recognized that the influence of the library often is indirect, which has been suggested in older literature supported by the provosts' discussion of teaching and learning (16%, *n*=44) and exemplified by the following quote:[105]

> One thing librarians are great at is collecting metrics on what they are doing, and who is using this and that and so forth, and then trying to adjust their services to meet the development and demands and so forth. You know, the problem, of course, is that there are a lot of less tangible kinds of benefits that the library brings to a campus, in terms of being a place where people meet to exchange ideas, and to develop projects, and things like that.... And use the resources in less visible ways than can always be tracked by these kinds of use metrics. (Provost PP02)

Rather than library administrators and staff concerning themselves with whether an impact is direct or indirect, they should instead connect these effects strategically to the overarching institutional mission and goals (Provost PP14).

Comparing Three Data Sources

Figure 7 compares the percentage of themes across all three data sources: the literature review of selected higher education and LIS documents, focus group transcript, and provost semi-structured individual interview transcripts.

Figure 7
Percentage of themes coded for all three data sources

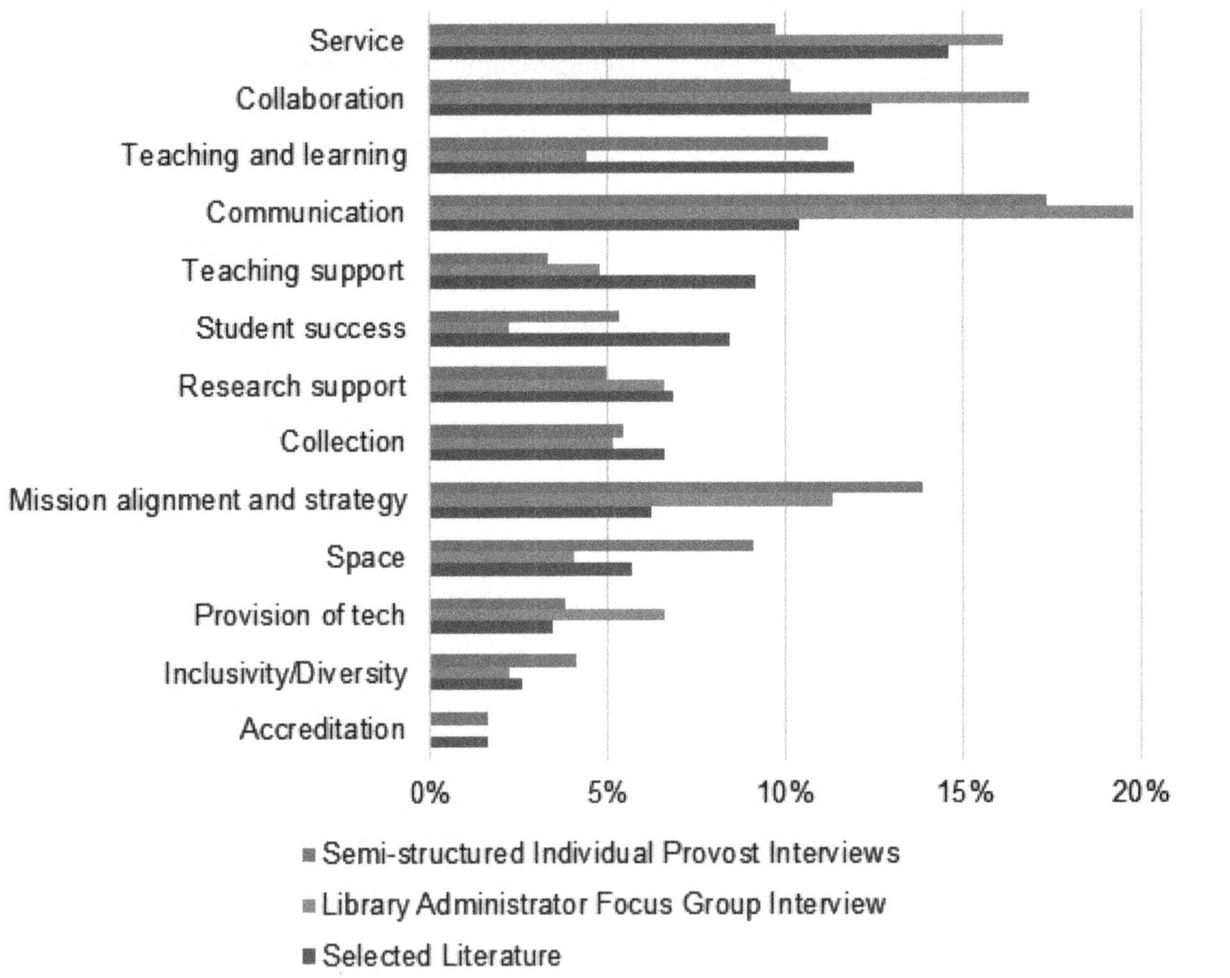

When comparing all three data sources, we can draw some differences among the themes prevalent in each. Literature review documents discussed student success more than the advisory group or provost interviews and communication less. Advisory group members discussed teaching and learning less than the selected literature documents and provost interviews. Provosts discussed space more than the participants of the focus group interview or in the selected literature and service less. Finally, documents from the selected literature examined mission alignment and strategy less than the provosts, whereas provosts focused less on teaching support than the selected literature.

Discussion

The *Findings* section above provided empirical evidence for the identification of themes critical in the selected literature to library administrators and to provosts, as well as for comparisons made between these data collection sources and within data sources (theoretical and research). This section summarizes the three data sources collected and analyzed.

One finding that might be surprising is that all three data sources mention accreditation either infrequently or not at all. In higher education, one cannot overstate the importance of accreditation because "almost every relationship a college has with an external party… is contingent on accreditation."[106] In addition to regional accreditation, which usually applies to the entire institution, programs, departments, and individual schools may also receive more specialized accreditation.[107] Because of accreditation's importance, we note discussion of the topic in literature and interview data, and the occasional appearance of accreditation in the three data sources does not signify its lack of importance. Instead, as conveyed by brainstorming sessions in which we disseminated initial report findings for discussion, advisory group members suggested that few mentions of accreditation may reflect its required, boilerplate nature. As one member stated, librarians at her institution consider accreditation the "least common denominator" when examining student-centered outcomes given that the library does not make or break accreditation decisions. "No institution will fail because of the library," she explained (Advisory Group Member LM07). Another point that was brought up in the focus group was that accreditation currently falls back on collections, but by collaborating with faculty members, librarians might be able to demonstrate their support for these activities using other resources. However, it is also possible that while the library's contribution to regional accreditation efforts is commonplace, the difference in the lack of literature on accreditation and increased discussion in the interviews about the library's contribution to more specialized accreditation suggests that more work on the latter type of accreditation may be warranted.

> [V]iewing the library concerning simply its services may not be an effective communicator of value. While it is likely that library administrators and staff address other issues besides service in their work environments, the fact that this excessive focus also was found in the focus group session suggests that they should consider focusing on other library resources outside of service, such as space, events, and other library offerings.
>
> —Provost PP13

Another key finding is that librarians, as indicated both by the literature review and by the focus group interview, are concerned with service as an indicator of value. Funding for higher education has decreased overall since 2010, and it has affected academic library budgets.[108] The literature and advisory group members might have frequently mentioned service because of stagnant or reduced funding, since it can be cost-effective. Further, service data are easy to collect and analyze and constitute an everyday practice for library administrators and staff. However, as suggested by comparing the higher education literature to the LIS literature, and as discussed in the provost interviews, higher education stakeholders and administrators are not as concerned with service as library administrators and staff seem to be. Instead, as suggested by one provost's comment (see Provost PP13 in the previous section), viewing the library concerning simply its services may not be an effective communicator of value. While it is likely that library administrators and staff address other issues besides service in their work environments, the fact that this excessive focus also was found in the focus group session suggests that they should consider focusing on other library resources outside of service, such as space, events, and other library offerings. Further, they should carefully consider language related to services. Do they mean *service*, or can they use a more directed term, such as *customer service* or *programs*? Library administrators and staff must continue to craft their terms carefully to align them with those used by provosts and considered as indicative of value by them.

As indicated by the frequency of themes coded in the provost interviews, higher education administrators consider space to be a significant library resource. The importance of space is reflective of a larger cultural perspective regarding the importance of libraries as community and technology centers. However, space is not as frequently discussed in the focus group interview when compared to the provost interviews and the analysis of the selected LIS literature. Space might not be addressed by library administrators and staff because they may associate space with costs, such as renovations and additions. However, it also could be that library administrators and staff do not want to call attention to the amount of space allocated to libraries, especially if they have dedicated the space to shelving for materials. They may be involved in—or wanting not to become involved in—turf wars and may be reticent to share their space with groups outside the library. The LIS literature has addressed space and provides an excellent resource for library administrators and staff considering space issues and changes within academic libraries.[109]

Library administrators and staff must not be reticent to collaboratively share space with groups within and outside the institution (i.e., those within the institution but not part of the library; those outside the institution, such as the community). An effective way to communicate value to provosts is for them to see how the library is serving various groups, which is reflected by their use of space.[110] For instance, library administrators and staff can invite provosts to use the library for meeting space so that they might see how students and faculty are using the space for activities beyond checking out books. This value also might be considered more significant with the increase of distance learning, as noted by one provost:

> Well I think space could be fantastic [for] on-campus students who want to gather together. This is my biggest concern, is that the students are not coming together. The library can be that place, that nexus, the crossroads where students can come to study together. So, yes, everything is posted online and they can do this alone, but there is a hunger within our undergraduate student population at least to, to actually socialize. And I think the library can… has always been that crossroads for campuses. It could serve in this capacity, pulling students together. (Provost PP04)

While this provost was the only one to mention virtual space, this is an area that should be considered and addressed, particularly as online learning offerings increase. Library administrators and staff should continue to create virtual spaces that possess the collaborative and programmatic characteristics of physical places. Several examples exist of work from user experience (UX) librarians, who focus on virtual environments. Findings from their work may be used to inform the production, development, and maintenance of virtual space.[111] Further, there is a need for research that assesses these efforts.[112]

However, this provost's account should not be interpreted to mean that library administrators and staff can demonstrate value solely by sharing space—either physically or virtually. When we shared analysis of provost interviews with advisory group members during the brainstorming session at the ALA Midwinter Meeting, advisory group members cautioned that, while space constitutes an important area in which the library can demonstrate value, library administrators and staff must go beyond envisioning space in the physical sense. Instead, they must consider the potential for programmatic integration of library space with complementary value initiatives. According to one advisory group member: "Only sharing space, such as with a writing or computer lab, is low level. There needs to be cooperative programming and interaction" (Advisory Group Member LM06). For example, if the library shares space with a writing center, as is common, both the library and the writing center must increase their shared strategic planning, assessment, training, and communication.[113] Therefore, library administrators and staff must envision space as intersecting with other facets of great contributions to student learning and success, including collaboration and communication.

Results from analysis of provost interviews show that provosts view the library as an essential component of the academic enterprise and recognize some of the larger challenges it faces in demonstrating value linked to student learning and success. However, provosts also contend that library administrators and staff can do better in communicating this demonstration by systematically integrating resources beyond service, such as space, into the lives of its primary users and stakeholders. Further, provosts say that library administrators and staff must be mindful of university-wide initiatives of importance to provosts and align library resources with these initiatives. While these efforts will vary by context, library administrators and staff must keep abreast of larger national and international trends shaping higher education and devote appropriate resources to them, which can be communicated effectively to provosts.

Specifically, library administrators and staff need to connect collaboration, as well as communication, to mission alignment and strategy outcomes.[114] Mission alignment and strategy is addressed more in theoretical pieces from the literature review and is important to provosts; it is less frequently discussed in studies from the literature review and by librarian administrators in the focus group interview. This observation supports the argument that in theory library administrators, library staff, researchers, practitioners, and students recognize the importance of mission alignment and strategy within higher education, but they do not address it in practice. This observation also is supported by a large-scale survey of provosts' perceptions of library value and how library administrators and staff should communicate it.[115] In this survey, provosts stated the perception of library administrators and staff being somewhat involved in initiatives such as retention, student success, and faculty productivity, and less concerned with enrollment. Therefore, it is essential that library administrators and staff market and link their service offerings to the institutional mission and goals in a way that is visible to provosts and other key stakeholders.

> Thinking of how these new learning environments work, and how the library would enhance students' and faculty's ability to access and process knowledge, data, [and] information in those particular kinds of environment[s]... that is what libraries need to do to be successful.
>
> —Provost PP02

The way that library administrators and staff can make this link seems to be contextually bound because of their dependency on the mission and goals unique to their institution. The large-scale survey of provosts mentioned above also supports this finding, which indicates differing communication trends by institution type.[116] The following provost account exemplifies the importance of context in shaping how librarians communicate value:

> There is not one specific thing a library can do, because the environments are so different. Thinking of how these new learning environments work, and how the library would enhance students' and faculty's ability to access and process knowledge, data, [and] information in those particular kinds of environment[s]... that is what libraries need to do to be successful. (Provost PP02)

What library administrators and staff can take away from this account is that they must continue to pay close attention to the unique mission and goals of their institution and link these to broader, higher education trends to effectively communicate to provosts their library's value.

Aside from being abreast of context by linking library value to the mission and goals of one's institution, library administrators and staff also need to consider the contextual nature of their relationships with higher education administrators.[117] As conveyed by one focus group participant:

> I think one of the challenges of building relationships is, if you look at the average tenure of a provost or another chief academic officer, which is something, it's less than five years. So sometimes you're fostering relationships that—maybe key relationships—that you know are going to change over the time when you've established these relationships. We had a plan a year ago to build out a model for successful tutoring center that included peer tutoring. We have one in our science library and we're going to do a more cross-campus one, but those plans had to get set aside.... We had to put them to the side until things settled down at the upper level. So I think being able to work in an environment where you are going to be prepared to learn... to forge a relationship with new players, and to wait for those times when that idea that you had laid the groundwork for previously, you can start laying that groundwork again when you have new players in some of those positions. (Advisory Group Member LM06)

People [are] talking about the problems of educating people to be citizens more, with this election being indicative of that. This is a hard thing to confront right now because we are going to have an administration that doesn't think that's important at all.
—Provost PP02

Provosts, some of whom were interviewed before and some after the 2016 US Presidential election, discussed the need to impart critical literacy skills to students so they can differentiate between facts and fiction—skills that will reverberate outside of the academy.[118] As stated by one provost:

> People [are] talking about the problems of educating people to be citizens more, with this election being indicative of that. This is a hard thing to confront right now because we are going to have an administration that doesn't think that's important at all. (Provost PP02)

Critical literacy skills also have been identified as one of the top trends in higher education.[119] Academic librarians and staff are experts in teaching information literacy and could lead this initiative on campuses, as exemplified by a collaboration between library administrators and staff, IT staff, instructional designers, and faculty at Purdue University.[120] Bringing visibility to such collaborations provides library administrators and staff with the ability to articulate the library's value by connecting the library with the university's story.[121]

If not already aware of the challenges associated with higher education funding, library administrators and staff should become more aware of and involved in its broader landscape.[122] There's more uncertainty among those in higher education as to what the fate of funding will be with the results of the 2016 presidential election. As stated by the same provost:

> The election yesterday, and I think that... Trump winning the presidency may further call into question, higher ed, expenses and value and so forth, and that, again, had really broad impacts on us. [It can be difficult to justify research, and that] hits places like us that want to have a research piece and a teaching piece. Apparently, it is an art because people do not understand the role of research in a university and there would be all kinds of cries for more efficiency. And then by "efficiency," they mean faculty teaching more students. And the more students they are teaching, the less research they're going to do. So that's a really simple equation. (Provost PP02)

So far, this discussion has touched on some important themes that library administrators and staff need to address when demonstrating value, namely, mission alignment and strategy, space, communication, and collaboration. According to evidence from both the focus group and the semi-structured individual interviews, these latter three categories must reflect the mission alignment and strategy theme by keying into the institutional mission and goals. Library administrators and staff can align the library with institutional goals and mission by focusing on the lack of awareness at the institutional level of the new approaches to library assessment and evaluation within the LIS field.

> The election yesterday, and I think that... Trump winning the presidency may further call into question, higher ed, expenses and value and so forth, and that, again, had really broad impacts on us.
>
> —Provost PP02

As conveyed by other reviews of the assessment and evaluation literature, library administrators and staff perceive a demand to link value-based initiatives to direct outcomes.[123] AiA studies employ a heightened use of mixed and multiple methods, and measures—for example, correlation—to demonstrate this value. The analysis of the AiA projects and interview and brainstorming sessions with advisory group members showed that library administrators and staff are aware of and open to the potential for integrating more diverse data points. As conveyed by one advisory group member:

> I think that in order to really truly be able to look at, and be able to tell those stories, and to come up with those snippets of information that will resonate with other leaders, we have to be willing to do types of data collection that libraries have shied away from in the past. And I think that involves tracking user behavior in a way that we've seen in a couple of the different studies that have looked at retention. But I think that there are ways of extrapolating and growing that out a little bit more so that we are dealing with large datasets, and we could... we could still keep it anonymous when we look at it in aggregate, right? I think that we have to be able to be willing to have conversations on campus about tracking user behavior in ways that libraries just haven't done. (Advisory Group Member LM14)

In this account, the library administrator recognizes new approaches to capture direct outcomes and demonstrate the library's effect on student learning and success. However, there appears to be a lack of awareness at the institutional level regarding these methods and the ability of library administrators and staff to employ them. Consider the following quote from the provost at the library administrator's institution: "We have never linked anything happening in the library to retention or graduation rates as we have done with the academic unit. We assume there are indirect effects" (Provost PP14).

One implication of this provost's lack of awareness of how and what student-centered outcomes librarians can capture is the importance of communicating with provosts, such as by having face-to-face meetings.[124] However, this strategy may not be feasible to those outside of library administration. For this reason, another strategy that library administrators and staff can utilize is to focus on the institutional mission and goals that are most relevant to the institution's administration and to determine appropriate library resources that can address those topics and ways to measure them. As an example, six of the fourteen provosts brought up inclusivity and diversity topics as essential areas underlying their institutional mission and goals. These provosts stated the importance for libraries to identify students who may not have comfort and familiarity with libraries, such as distance or transfer students, and marshal collections, services, and spaces to address the barriers these students face.

Another way library administrators and staff can contend with context is by using mixed or multiple methods (see *Appendix A: Glossary* for the explanations of these terms). As discussed above in the *Methods* section, mixed methods are the use of both quantitative and qualitative methods. For instance, the research design for this study employed mixed methods by engaging in qualitative data collection (selected literature review and semi-structured individual interviews), qualitative analysis (content analysis), and quantitative analysis (basic and inferential statistics). It also employed multiple methods, also referred to as triangulation, defined as the use of two or more methods for data analysis and collection.[125] The benefit of using mixed and multiple methods is that they strengthen the validity of the observations being made.[126] Within the context of provost interviews and observations previously made, the use of mixed and multiple methods also addresses the multifaceted context that influences how higher education administrators view and interpret different outcome measures. The AiA projects provide some exemplars for how to use mixed and multiple methods, as these studies disproportionately employ these approaches when compared to non-AiA projects.

Another positive attribute of AiA projects is that they focus on space as an important theme, reflecting the importance assigned to this theme by provosts. These studies also include a variety of populations both regarding institutions (more diverse geographical locations, institution types, and sector affiliations when compared to non-AiA projects) and groups (more diverse concerning studying undergraduates, graduates, and other groups). Like using multiple methods, collecting data from varying populations also enhances the researcher's observations and provides contextually based examples to others who may wish to study a particular population. Therefore, library administrators, library staff, researchers, practitioners, and students can benefit from collaborating across institutions since collaboration can further enhance study findings by rendering them more generalizable across populations. The need for collaboration also is evidenced by the provost interviews when discussing limited resources, as well as from other, reported work.[127] Library administrators and staff can achieve these collaborations within consortia by not only collaborating in collection development and shared collections, but also working on curriculum design or co-teaching courses, sharing research data and teaching materials, and fostering joint research and communication-based projects that demonstrate library value.[128]

This discussion of the findings identified in the project data collection and analysis has aided the development of priority areas for further research, which will provide the framework for the research agenda. The findings have also informed the identification of exemplary practices, studies, and research designs for aligning with and impacting student learning and success with institutional goals and objectives.

Priority Areas for Future Research and Effective Practices

We based the priority areas for future research on the findings of the selected literature review, the advisory group interview, and the provost semi-structured individual interviews. These priority areas intentionally are broad to foster discussion and input from library administrators, library staff, researchers, practitioners, and students. This section links these empirical findings to the identification of and justification for the priority areas for future research. It also explains how these findings informed our selection of exemplary studies and effective practices for each priority area. We follow these studies and practices by a discussion of how we identified specific, future-focused research questions and suggested research designs, again for each priority area.

Identifying the Priority Areas

The most important factor for identifying the priority areas was to discover which themes occurred most frequently in each data source (see table 4). The RFP explicitly stated that the project would "Begin with a high-level look at the trends in higher education that concern academic librarians in the broader context of academia and identify current academic library responses [in the form of resources] to the trends," which is why we included these trends as themes in the codebook.[129] However, we did not include individual library resources in the form of specific collections, spaces, and services in the codebook. While we coded library resources as a theme, these codes were not included in the top five themes since each priority area addresses all three resource types. We decided on six themes because the RFP suggested five to ten examples, and the project proposal specified that "5–10 exemplar cases [would] be categorized by the trends and themes, context, level of effort and impact, populations studied, effectiveness, etc., as identified in the literature."[130] Table 4 shows how we identified five of the six total priority areas—by examining the most frequently coded themes from all three data sources.

Table 4. Top five themes per data source

Selected literature	Library administrator focus group interview	Provost semi-structured individual interviews
• Collaboration (12%) • Teaching and learning (12%) • Communication (10%) • Teaching support (9%) • Student success (8%)	• Communication (20%) • Collaboration (17%) • Mission alignment and strategy (11%) • Research support (7%) • Provision of tech (7%)	• Communication (17%) • Mission alignment and strategy (14%) • Teaching and learning (11%) • Collaboration (10%) • Student success (5%)

Across all three data sources, the most frequently coded themes were communication, collaboration, mission alignment and strategy, teaching and learning, and student success. Another area that was not included as a thematic code, but is important for library administrators and staff to consider when evaluating how the library affects student learning and success, is learning analytics. The importance of this topic, and especially how it relates to privacy, was mentioned in the feedback for the initial report draft, in advisory group brainstorming sessions, and by recent ACRL initiatives, such as the Learning Analytics e-Learning webcast series and ARL's Statistics Data Analytics.[131] Based on the most frequently coded themes, feedback, and ACRL initiatives, the priority areas are as follows:

1. **Communicate the library's contributions.**
2. **Match library assessment to the institution's mission.**
3. **Include library data in institutional data collection.**
4. **Quantify the library's impact on student success.**
5. **Enhance teaching and learning.**
6. **Collaborate with educational stakeholders.**

Identifying Effective Practices

In addition to the priority areas, the report's RFP also asked for an identification of effective practices. Effective practices represent actions library administrators and staff should take under each priority area to impact student learning and success and to align with institutional goals and objectives. We examined the data from all three data sources coded under each theme that corresponded to one or more priority areas to identify these effective practices. We looked for instances where researchers, library administrators, and provosts identified an action that was useful in demonstrating the library's value to higher education stakeholders. We then categorized these activities into broader practices that libraries within various contexts (e.g., community colleges, universities) can adopt for each priority area. These practices are more specific than the actions described in the *Introduction* section because we contextualized them within the three data sources.

Identifying Exemplary Studies

Based on feedback from the advisory group, we decided that identifying exemplary studies, or success stories, would also be helpful in suggesting innovative ways that library administrators and staff can align with and impact student-centered outcomes, as well as communicate this impact to higher education stakeholders. The visualization component shows which documents we identified as exemplary studies so that library administrators, library staff, researchers, practitioners, and students can view more details about them. In addition to these exemplary studies for each priority area, the studies listed in *Appendix L: AiA Studies with Exemplary Design Elements,* which have at least one exemplary research design component, also are tagged as exemplary in the visualization component.

We determined that an exemplary study should be relevant to the priority areas and demonstrate an effective research design. We derived five criteria for assessment: the number of themes discussed, the type of institution where the study occurred, the use of various data collection and analysis methods, whether the study impact resonates outside the library, and the populations studied. For a detailed explanation of how we used these criteria to assign a score to each document, see *Appendix K: Detailed Scoring Scheme for Exemplary Research Designs and Practices.*

Identifying Research Questions

The research questions identified represent future-focused, outstanding research questions that remain essential for library administrators, library staff, researchers, practitioners, and students to explore going forward. Based on our analysis of the existing literature and interviews with library administrators and provosts, these questions define gaps where library administrators, library staff, researchers, practitioners, and students must integrate the library's activities with institutional mission and goals and alignment. Therefore, the questions represent promising lines of inquiry to make a case for impact to higher education stakeholders.

Identifying Research Designs

We identified studies corresponding to each priority area that had exemplary research designs. We evaluated each of the following study components contributing to the research design: context, topic or problem, design, data sampling, data collection, data analysis, discussion, future work, and reporting.[132]

The studies we selected had one or two exemplary components corresponding to each priority area. For instance, we assessed the data collection rationale and procedures for each study based on the appropriateness of the method, whether the study authors employed mixed and multiple methods, and the extent to which the method ensured user privacy or confidentiality. Each priority area includes a study or two that exemplify one or more selected components. We recognize that this evaluation system is highly contextual. For this reason, *Appendix L: AiA Studies with Exemplary Design Elements* lists studies that have exemplary design components to assist researchers, practitioners, and students in developing their research.

There are a variety of resources that cover the general steps in the research process and suggest exemplary design principles.[133] Connaway and Radford provide a detailed overview of research design, including its applications to qualitative, mixed, and quantitative methods.[134]

ACRL Research Agenda for Student Learning and Success

Now that we have discussed how we identified the priority areas for the research agenda, as well as the effective practices, exemplary studies, research questions, and proposed research designs for each, we present the research agenda. This agenda outlines the priority areas and related components. Each priority area is discussed in five sections: (1) general discussion, (2) effective practices, (3) exemplary studies, (4) research questions, and (5) proposed research designs.

Communicate the Library's Contributions

General Discussion

Communication was identified as important in the RFP and the project plan; this was one of the main reasons that we created the advisory group. It allowed library administrators to connect with provosts at their institutions and provide data on how library administrators and staff can communicate the value the library brings to the academic community. As a theme, its definition was "Librarians communicate impact or other aspects of value with stakeholders."

As academic libraries strategically evolve to support student learning and success, library administrators and staff must effectively communicate the library's value to those outside of the library and high in the institution's hierarchy to compete for resources within funding and governance structures both within and outside the academic institution.

Communication was the most commonly identified theme in the selected literature and interview data analyzed for the agenda. The other five priority areas support this priority area. If library administrators and staff better align the library with the institutional mission and goals, understand how the library contributes to learning, teaching, and student success indicators, and collaborate more, then communicating the library's impact will be easier and more productive.

The increasing presence of communication as a theme in the selected literature indicates that as more research saturates this area, more questions arise. A significant difficulty in suggesting best practices for communication between different groups is the variability of factors that can affect with whom to communicate and how. In other words, communication is highly contextual. Our data analysis reflected this finding, demonstrating an overemphasis on service within the LIS literature and advisory group interview. Such overemphasis does not necessarily mean that provosts perceive library services as redundant and not proactive. It shows that library administrators and stakeholders are not clearly communicating the impressive breadth of services they offer and how these services are valuable.

To address this lack of clarity, those involved in this research area should explore ways to effectively communicate both up and out, regarding both the message and the method. Provosts can offer a bird's-eye view of what the library should be doing, to what extent it is succeeding, and the terminology library administrators and staff should use when communicating the library's value.[135] By communicating with provosts, library administrators and staff can also make them feel invested in and a part of the library, which can influence them to become advocates for and supporters of the library.

Effective Practices to Implement at the Library

We identified the following effective practices for this priority area:

- *Communicate with those outside of the library and high in the institution's administration because they can offer a bird's-eye view of what the library should be doing and be advocates for and supporters of the library if they feel invested in and a part of the library.* According to the results of this study, the institution's administration often directly or indirectly influences financial and other resources allocated to libraries. For this reason, it is essential that library administrators and staff communicate with these administrators to determine how to best demonstrate the library's value. Researchers, practitioners, and students should further investigate how provosts and similar administrators perceive the library, as there exist few published studies that include participants from these groups.[136]
- *Determine the terminology used by provosts to communicate the library's value and adopt this terminology in subsequent communications.* To communicate with provosts and similar administrators, library administrators and staff must be familiar with the terminology they use and its alignment with how these stakeholders communicate. One way that library administrators and staff can learn what language their provosts and similar administrators use is by familiarizing themselves with the higher education publications that these administrators read. Further, they may also consider publishing in these venues, which provide a direct line of communication to provosts and similar administrators (Advisory Group Member LM14).

- *Make the provost aware of library participation in various efforts, particularly as they pertain to the institutional mission and goals.* According to both advisory group members and provosts, making provosts aware of the linkage between the library's efforts and the institutional mission and goals is essential. One way library administrators and stakeholders can engender this awareness is by presenting at meetings the provost holds (Advisory Group Member LM14). To get presentation time, library administrators and stakeholders need to identify efforts related to the institutional mission and goals and get involved in them (Provost PP03). Such involvement can also lead to one-on-one face time, which both advisory group members and provosts identify as crucial (Advisory Group Member LM14, Provost PP03). Other ways that library administrators and stakeholders can obtain provost involvement is by creating targeted stories featuring faculty and students that discuss the benefit of library initiatives (Advisory Group Member LM13) and inviting the provost to library events (Provost PP02).
- *Become involved in cross-departmental and divisional efforts to engage in meetings and conversation with leadership among various departments.* Such collaboration facilitates communication of the library's value using "one big megaphone instead of five little ones" (Advisory Group Member LM13). Library administrators and staff can become involved, for example, by attending faculty senate meetings (Provosts PP03, PP14) and monthly meetings of college deans (Provost PP03), participating in curriculum committees (Provost PP03), and forming a library committee to connect directly with faculty (Provost PP01).
- *Use library space to provide central meeting grounds for programs across departments to give a visual indication of the library's value.* According to the provost interviews, library space represents a resource that library administrators and staff do not communicate enough. They should communicate favorable reviews the library receives for events and initiatives using its space. However, they cannot advance communication solely via a newsletter or e-mail. Rather, they must programmatically integrate key stakeholders within the library space to best communicate its value. One way to achieve this integration is bringing administrative leadership into the library by inviting campus meetings and gatherings to occur in library buildings (Advisory Group Member LM08, Provost PP09).
- *Cultivate relationships with leadership by looking for opportunities for informal meetings. Interviews with provosts for this report show the importance of library administrators and staff having close relationships with provosts.* Personal relationships are important. The provost must know and trust those at the administrative levels of the library to approve initiatives that will advance the library's value (Provost PP09). Networking is essential for library administrators and staff to build these relationships (Provost PP12). While such networking must involve the careful development of institutional and community relationships, library administrators and staff should also prepare for serendipitous moments, such as having an elevator speech ready should they run into their provost at a local coffee shop (Advisory Group Member LM14).
- *Recruit individuals to advocate on the library's behalf. Recruitment can occur by providing excellent services, space, or collections.* Advisory group members noted the importance of having students and faculty champion their efforts. Some ways to recruit faculty and students to promote library resources include cultivating relationships with new faculty (Advisory Group Member LM03) and becoming involved in an embedded librarian program (Advisory Group Member LM12).
- *Consider how different groups of stakeholders envision effective communication emanating from various forms of media and position the library accordingly.* Communication is contextual. A mode of communication that might be successful in one context might fail in another. For instance, one advisory group member noted that social media works well with students, but not with faculty (Advisory Group Member LM09). Regardless of context, library administrators and staff must consider how higher education administrators prefer their information disseminated (Advisory Group

Member LM08). They might consider assigning one librarian to be responsible for communication (Advisory Group Member LM09). Provosts recommend being innovative and giving them a "different style of data" (Provost PP11). This innovation could include guerrilla marketing, such as making short videos (Provost PP01).

- *Work to dismantle "pigeonholed" perceptions of the library (e.g., as just providing collections) by thinking out of the box and providing new services, spaces, and collections.* As shown by the provost interviews, key stakeholders within their academic institutions believe several myths about the library. As a result, provosts indicated the importance of library administrators and staff communicating "how they bring people in touch with knowledge in various ways" (Provost PP02). One provost suggested that library administrators and staff could dispel these myths by inviting these stakeholders into the library. Specifically, they could hold a town hall meeting to address the question "What is the role of the library today?" Attendees could formulate an institution-specific response to this issue, which can yield buy-in from all those attending (Provost PP04).
- *Look at how other departments, and not just the academic ones, are communicating their value.* As an example, one advisory group member noted that his library administration and staff have taken notice of the fitness center and how it makes a value-based case. They have used these observations to inform their own assessment-related work.
- *Take advantage of the fact that, unlike other departments, the library serves all students and majors.* One of the questions we asked provosts was what library administrators and staff would need to do to enhance the possibility of the provost accepting a modest funding request. Four provosts stated that the library was at an advantage when making this request. As one provost said, the library is in an advantageous position when it comes to funding requests since it has "impacts beyond borders" (Provost PP01). Library administrators and staff can take advantage of this impact by articulating how they benefit key institutional stakeholders when making a funding request.
- *Keep communication regular and consistent.* Share news and events with the provost, faculty, and students on a regular basis using different channels, such as social media, conversation in the coffee shop and other places on campus, and library marketing materials and venues. Library administrators and staff do not need a lot of face time to highlight the library's staff and services and advertise upcoming events and programs using different modes of communication.

Exemplary Studies

Few studies published since 2000 have looked at how administrators perceive the library and its collections, spaces, and services.[137] One study from 2007 found that according to multiple administrators at six American universities, the library's functional role outweighed its symbolic role as the heart of the university. As a result, the library needed to "connect what it does to the values and mission of the university."[138] A later study of nine Canadian provosts found that the participants most valued information access provided by the library and envisioned the library evolving into more of a learning space.[139] The third study we identified as exemplary is Fister's survey of 134 administrators, which covered the highest number of themes (n=11) and received the highest score of all the studies using the scoring system explained in *Appendix K: Detailed Scoring Scheme for Exemplary Research Designs and Practices* (17 points).[140]

Research Questions Requiring Further Study

1. How can library administrators and staff communicate their contributions to student outcomes more effectively with institutional stakeholders (e.g., administrators)?

2. What types of library services, collections, and spaces matter to institutional stakeholders?
3. To what extent do institutional stakeholders recognize library administrators' and staff's contributions to teaching and learning? What factors affect levels of recognition?
4. How do faculty envision the integration of library services, collections, and spaces for teaching and learning?
5. How can libraries support the information needs of stakeholders related to teaching activities?
6. How are other units effectively communicating with stakeholders?
7. What factors influence librarian communication with academic library users and potential users?
8. How can library administrators and staff leverage social media to increase student engagement?
9. What are the main barriers to communication between library administrators and staff and educational stakeholders (e.g., students, faculty, administrators)?

Proposed Research Design

The exemplary studies discussed above demonstrate the importance of understanding context and identifying the topic or problem in the research design process. When considering the context of the study, researchers, practitioners, and students must recognize the knowledge, experience, and possible bias that they bring to the project.[141] They also need to consider and describe their environment, which includes their library and their parent institution. The environment can influence the priorities,[142] opportunities, and challenges of the study. Perhaps most importantly, researchers, practitioners, and students must consider the audience for their research.[143] Some important audience distinctions include whether it consists of librarians or non-librarians and whether they are external or internal to the researcher's institution. Hahn and Jaeger provide more information on possible audiences, types of publications, and venues for publication.[144] The audience also influences how the researcher reports study findings. For instance, researchers, practitioners, and students should be careful to frame the research so that it is relevant to the intended reader's interests and avoid using library jargon when reporting to non-librarians.[145]

Questions for Researchers: Context

1. Who is the audience?
2. What knowledge, experience, and possible bias might the researcher bring to the research?
3. How might the institutional and library environments affect the research?

When identifying the topic or problem, researchers, practitioners, and students must consult past work and literature in the area and craft their research questions based on this previous research and their context. The theoretical and methodological aspects of earlier work provide the researcher with examples of how to study a topic. Fisher, Erdelez, and McKechnie provide a detailed overview of LIS theories and examples of using these theories in research, which can help researchers, practitioners, and students identify how to study various LIS topics and problems.[146]

The existing literature identifies topics that warrant further or initial research. Researchers identify their topic or problem based on contextual considerations and past work, and these elements influence the research questions for the study. In general, research questions should be open rather than closed.[147] Open questions usually begin with *what, how,* or *why.* Closed questions usually begin with *does* and can be answered with a yes or no. Wildemuth provides more information on crafting compelling research questions.[148]

For the three exemplary communication studies discussed above, the researchers realized potential audiences for library value research could extend beyond librarians and that administrators are an important population in any institution of higher education. Because the literature reviewed had few studies that included this population, the three exemplary studies began with research questions that addressed and engaged a variety of academic administrators.

Questions for Researchers: Topic or Problem

1. What do past work and literature say about the topic?
2. What gaps exist in the research on this subject, and how could this research design bridge those gaps?
3. To what extent are the research questions open-ended rather than closed?

Match Library Assessment to Institution's Mission

General Discussion

The definition for this theme was "Institutionally identified student outcomes (can be co-coded with learning and success)." It appeared in the top five themes in the advisory group and provost interviews, but it was the seventh theme in the analysis of selected literature. Moreover, there was a statistically significant difference between the higher proportion of this theme reported in theoretical documents and lower in research documents, which signifies that the theme likely is being discussed more than empirically tested. This finding means that while library administrators, library staff, researchers, practitioners, and students recognize the importance of integrating institutional mission, goals, and alignment with library assessment in theory, they do not seem to address this integration in practice.

Although provosts and other academic administrators develop institutional plans, supervise libraries and other institutional units, and allocate funds, few studies published since 2000 have investigated administrator perceptions of library collections, spaces, and services.[149] In fact, the number of research studies from LIS and higher education journals in the areas of accreditation and institutional mission, goals, and alignment has fallen from 2010 to 2016. One reason for the lack of research on this topic may be the gap between how higher education administrators and library administrators and staff perceive the library's role in mission strategy and alignment. While interviews with provosts from around the United States showed their concern with mission strategy and alignment, a recent study of 722 library directors indicates that they feel less aligned strategically with their supervisors and less valued by their administration, financially and otherwise.[150] Further, analysis of the LIS literature selected for this research agenda and from our focus group interview with library administrators shows that these two sources mention service more frequently than the provosts interviewed. This finding also suggests a mismatch between library administrators and staff and higher education administrators regarding perceptions of the library's role related to enhancing student learning and success outcomes.

While provosts, academic librarians, and current LIS and higher education literature do not often discuss accreditation, this finding does not signify that it is unimportant. Rather, higher education stakeholders perceive accreditation as a necessary task that the institution can accomplish with or without libraries. For this reason, library administrators and staff must communicate how they contribute to accreditation standards and their importance in meeting these standards.

Library administrators and staff can support student learning and success by strategically aligning their programs, offerings, spaces, and collections to support institutional objectives in these areas. This strategic alignment might include measuring the library's support of nontraditional priorities for libraries, such as student recruitment.[151] Library administrators, library staff, researchers, practitioners, and students doing research in this area should go outside of the library to collect data and suggest possible collaborations around common issues. They also should take care to use terminology similar to that used by others within the academic institution. Further, by working with faculty and staff members from teaching and learning support services, library administrators and staff can build a culture of assessment that adequately demonstrates library alignment with their institutional mission and goals.

Effective Practices to Implement at the Library

We have identified the following effective practices for this priority area:

- *Go outside of the library to collect data and to suggest possible collaborations around common issues.* As noted by advisory group members and provosts, these partnerships should be advantageous to fostering the institutional mission and goals. By getting involved in these partnerships, library administrators and staff will have opportunities for face time with the provost. For instance, Provost PP03 stated that she was made aware of the value-based efforts by library administrators and staff because some sit on the education council and the core educational requirements team.
- *Work with teaching and learning support services and directly with faculty and students to build a culture of assessment using both qualitative and quantitative data for collection, analysis, and reporting.* Provosts and advisory group members gave several examples of how a culture of assessment can be created. For instance, several suggest that library administrators and staff align with the research mission of their institution by creating open access institutional repositories for the work of faculty and students (Advisory Group Members LM06, LM07; Provost PP04). To assess the research productivity of the faculty and students, library administrators and staff could build a reputation cloud that summarizes their current research efforts (Advisory Group Member LM03). Data from this cloud and the institutional repository could feed into how library administrators and staff articulate their contribution to the institution's research mission.
- *Be open to adopting less traditional roles for services, collections, spaces, and staff to fulfill the strategic mission of the university.* While specific activities will vary based on institutional context, one advisory group member recounted an example of how the administrators and staff at her library began sponsoring three-minute research video competitions among graduate students (Advisory Group Member LM03). This action supported the research mission of the university and drew attention to the library's role in advancing this mission because students and faculty shared the videos. The provost from this advisory group member's institution also brought up this initiative as an effective practice (Provost PP03).
- *Be aware of student and faculty demographics and respond to their needs and characteristics.* Provost PP09 states the importance of library administrators and staff knowing their customer. She suggests that library administrators and staff marshal resources and design events that interest people. To develop interest, they must uncover a need and demonstrate how the library can satisfy this need. Provosts identified several approaches that library administrators and staff could take to exercise this awareness and response. Provost PP04 suggests that library administrators and staff

offer hours in the library space where students can come and work with a tutor. In the context of the provost's institution, this action assists the students in a state where six-year, rather than four-year, graduation rates are prevalent. Provost PP08 identifies the importance of diversity and inclusivity within higher education by contending that library administrators and staff should accommodate students with low socioeconomic statuses to demonstrate the importance of the "university as a gateway to a better life."

Exemplary Study

Lombard's 2012 study at Gannon University had a short write-up but was an exemplar in several ways.[152] First, it looked at the library's influence on recruitment, which has been studied in higher education research documents addressing student outcomes, but rarely appears in library research documents. The data collection method, which relied on an online survey of students, also was interesting because the survey was posted on various non-library online spaces, meaning that it may have reached those who do not use the library. It also collected and analyzed qualitative data from interviews with fourteen admissions professionals from various institutions and, based on survey and interview findings, makes suggestions for ways library administrators and staff can collaborate with admissions departments.

Research Questions Requiring Further Study

1. In what ways has the support by library administrators and staff of the institution's mission and specific goals affected student learning and success outcomes?
2. How do libraries fit into the broader array of institutional resources and programs (e.g., writing centers, tutoring)?
3. How do libraries compare to other support units in demonstrating their impact on the institutional mission and goals?
4. How are budget constraints affecting the support by library administrators and staff of the institution's mission and specific goals related to student learning and success outcomes?
5. How do library administrators and staff support accreditation efforts, and are these efforts recognized by the institution?

Proposed Research Design

The exemplary study for matching library assessment to the institution's mission demonstrates the importance of designing a study to include quantitative, qualitative, and mixed methods as appropriate. Just as context and past work influence the study's research questions, so does the study's design affect the data's sampling, collection, and analysis. Qualitative, quantitative, and mixed designs each offer different ways of studying the topic.

Qualitative designs are interpretivist in nature and take an inductive or bottom-up approach. In other words, the researcher assumes that individuals tend to interpret reality differently and uses "collection, analysis, and interpretation of interview, participant observation, and document data to understand and describe meanings, relationships, and patterns."[153]

Quantitative designs are (post)positivist in nature and take a deductive or top-down approach. In other words, the researcher assumes that individuals tend to interpret reality similarly and "use measurements and statistics to transform empirical data into numbers and to develop mathematical models that quantify behavior."[154] Robust quantitative designs often include a model that clearly delineates the factors concerning the topic of inquiry and their relationship to one another.

Although qualitative and quantitative designs offer different viewpoints, mixed methodologies assume that these positions can be complementary rather than polarizing.[155] A strong mixed-methods design must explain and justify what aspects of data sampling, collection, analysis, and interpretation are qualitative and which are quantitative. Creswell and Clark suggest six possible mixed-methods designs.[156] Their book contains guidance on how to choose the best mixed model; instructions for how to collect, analyze, interpret, and write about mixed-methods studies; and detailed examples of studies for each type of design. Despite its challenges, the use of mixed methods tends to lead to a stronger research design because using both qualitative and quantitative approaches can provide a complete look at the data, which constitutes the basis for data triangulation.[157]

Using more than one data collection and analysis method, otherwise known as using multiple methods,[158] is another way to triangulate data. The exemplary study in this priority area uses multiple methods to collect and analyze data from two types of participants: survey data from students, and survey and interview data from admissions professionals.

Questions for Researchers: Design

1. What elements of qualitative and quantitative research can help answer the research questions?
2. How can triangulation using mixed or multiple methods create a more complete picture of the phenomenon studied by the researcher?
3. Is there a clear explanation as to why the researcher chose the selected approach instead of the alternatives?

An excellent study should clearly explain the methods used to sample, collect, and analyze the study's data. *Data sampling* refers to the method researchers use to select the study data or participants from the available data or total study population.[159] The most important data sampling consideration is whether the data or participants are intended to represent a typical case, which is often the case in quantitative designs, or a range of possible cases, which is often the case in qualitative designs.

One issue in many LIS studies, primarily qualitative ones, is the use of convenience or availability sampling, in which participants are willing to participate or nearby, respectively.[160] Also known as accidental samples, convenience sampling is when the researcher selects the cases at hand until the sample reaches a desired size. For instance, researchers might select library users to participate in a study based on who walks through the door.[161] Another related sampling issue is the recruitment of library study participants in library spaces, both in the physical and digital library. As a result of this sampling technique, researchers might disproportionately represent library users in LIS studies and ignore potential library users; these potential users provide different perceptions of library collections, spaces, and services. The exemplary study for this priority area offers one solution to these sampling issues by posting links to the survey on non-library websites. Another way to reach potential library users is by sending the recruitment notice through official channels, such as departmental administrative assistants or departmental chairs and asking them to forward to the faculty, staff, and students on their Listservs.[162] For more information on different sampling types and methods, see Wengraf.[163]

Questions for Researchers: Data Sampling

1. Who would be willing and able to participate in the study and provide the most useful data?
2. How can potential library users, who might not be using the collection, space, or service being considered by the researcher, be recruited?
3. Are there any gatekeepers who would be able and willing to forward the recruitment notice to relevant populations?

Include Library Data in Institutional Data Collection

General Discussion

Although learning analytics did not have a thematic code, documents such as ACRL's "Top Trends in Academic Libraries" and ACRL initiatives, such as the e-learning webcast series "Learning Analytics," identified learning analytics as an important area.[164] Learning analytics involve "data about learners and their contexts, for purposes of understanding and optimizing learning and the environments in which it occurs."[165] While research in this area is relatively new, three of the fourteen provosts interviewed for this agenda described data components that could track student progress on a variety of institutional, programmatic, and course levels. The range of data represented by these components offers library administrators and staff the opportunity to triangulate their data with those from other departments and to make these library data more visible to other departments, administrators, and provosts.

Research in this area mirrors that on analytics and privacy or confidentiality in other areas; for instance, one study assesses what analytics researchers can collect related to the reading behaviors of individuals when they are reading mass-market e-books versus scholarly journals.[166] Library administrators and staff need to inform themselves about how other academic stakeholders are using learning analytics, how librarians can integrate library data into these components, and what safeguards need to be implemented to ensure student privacy or confidentiality.

Those doing research in this area should strategically collect data to integrate into learning analytics software. As previously mentioned, library administrators and staff also should advocate for the inclusion of library data in the volumes of data collected from multiple systems within the academic institution that stakeholders statistically analyze to predict and facilitate student success.

Effective Practices to Implement at the Library

We have identified the following effective practices for this priority area:

- *Measure, collect, analyze and report "data about learners and their contexts, for purposes of understanding and optimizing learning and the environments in which it occurs."*[167] Library data should be included in the volumes of data collected from multiple systems within the academic institution and statistically analyzed to predict student success. In addition to the exemplar studies in this priority area and the previous priority area, several other research studies from the fields of LIS and higher education exist that discuss privacy and confidentiality and how to implement policies for both.[168]

- *Use the data environment employed by senior leadership.* This practice was suggested by Advisory Group Member LM13. It ties into a key finding from our review of all three data sources that a gap exists between how provosts and library administrators and staff communicate the library's value. Implications of this finding for library administrators and staff are to ensure that they are using the same terminology employed by their provosts. This effective practice builds on this implication by suggesting that nonverbal forms of communication, such as the visual presentation of quantitative data, must also be presented in a way that is recognized by provosts.
- *Pull the sort of data to track user behaviors that library administrators and staff have shied away from in the past.* Provosts suggest that library administrators and staff must collect data on the holistic student experience including longitudinal metrics related to the student experience during and after graduation (Provosts PP03, PP11). One provost noted that library administrators and staff could be informed of new metrics to collect by referring to those obtained by independent, for-profit institutions (Provost PP14). An advisory group member suggested that library administrators and staff can initiate conversation with provosts about the types of user data they can collect categorized by departments (Advisory Group Member LM14).

Exemplary Study

Jantti and Heath's 2016 study describes the use of learning analytics at the University of Wollongong in Australia.[169] In addition to collecting library-related data in a repository called the Library Cube, this library collects and analyzes more sources of institutional data than any other. These data sets come from course management software called Moodle, student administration, tutorials, and data measuring student support service use.

Research Questions Requiring Further Study

1. How can library administrators and staff connect their data with student outcomes? To do this effectively, will library administrators and staff need to begin collecting different or additional data?
2. How are other stakeholders in higher education using analytics to affect the areas of teaching and learning and student success, and how can library administrators and staff contribute to these efforts?
3. What types of data do faculty and staff in institutional research offices or units collect that would supplement the data assembled by library administrators and stakeholders to measure the impact of courses, events, and so on, on student learning and success?
4. How can library administrators and staff use triangulated data to demonstrate the impact of library resources and programs on student learning and success?
5. How can library administrators and staff employ mixed methods or multiple methods to demonstrate how student usage of library collections affects retention?
6. How can library administrators and staff balance concerns about maintaining user privacy with the use of individual student data to measure learning and success outcomes?
7. What factors affect librarian decisions regarding the level of confidentiality or privacy of student data?

Proposed Research Design

The exemplary study for including library data in institutional data collection describes how to collect and store a variety of data ethically. When collecting data for a research study, the most important consideration is whether the methods are appropriate for the study's design. Qualitative methods are useful when researchers are developing a hypothesis, while quantitative methods can be used by researchers to test these hypotheses. In other words, qualitative methods take a deep dive into a particular context, and researchers can utilize them to identify a research problem, develop knowledge claims, and begin to develop a hypothesis, while using quantitative methods to test this hypothesis and generalize it across various contexts. While qualitative methods take a deep dive into inductively analyzing data from smaller samples (e.g., focus group and individual interviews), quantitative methods deductively analyze data from larger samples (e.g., log or usage data, demographic data) to test hypotheses and knowledge claims. However, qualitative and quantitative methods should not be viewed as mutually exclusive. Rather, these methods overlap for both data collection (e.g., observation and survey data can be qualitative or quantitative) and analysis. For the latter, researchers can use mixed and multiple methods, which employ both quantitative and qualitative approaches to enhance the rigor of analysis and strengthen the research claims.[170]

Another important consideration regarding data collection is whether the data should be anonymous, confidential, or neither. Anonymous data means that the researcher does not know the identity of the participant, and confidential implies that the researcher knows the identity of the participant but takes steps to ensure that the audience will not. If the library staff collect user data, as in the exemplary study, they can ensure that library usage data, such as checkout and request history, is not accidentally forwarded to other units, such as offices of institutional research. LIS research methods books by Connaway and Radford and Wildemuth provide more information on how to choose a data collection method, guidance on collection procedures, and examples of different types of collection methods.[171]

Questions for Researchers: Data Collection

1. What are the possible ways that the data collected can be triangulated to give a more complete picture of what phenomenon the researcher is studying?
2. Is the rationale for the type of data collected clearly explained and justified?
3. How does one ensure the collection of relevant and critical data?

Quantify the Library's Impact on Student Success

General Discussion

We define student success as the more objective, usually quantifiable, indicators of learning. These outcomes are related to a particular assignment or semester, such as grades or GPA. It could also be related to whether the student re-enrolled or graduated.[172]

Impact on student success has become the most significant way for institutions and their composite units to demonstrate their value to funding and governance boards. These outcomes relate to objective indicators of learning, which include assignment and semester grades and persistence to graduation.

In this report, the proportion of LIS and higher education literature analyzed related to student success peaked in 2013. By 2016, this theme was present in only about half of the documents examined. Based on the analyses conducted for this agenda, we attribute much of this decline to the lack of established best practices and standards regarding student privacy.[173] However, recent research from the University of Minnesota and the University of Wollongong has developed suggested data collection and analysis methods that facilitate user confidentiality and can be used by library administrators, library staff, researchers, practitioners, and students to re-engage with research that quantifies student success.[174]

Those doing research in this area should identify the quantifiable student success indicators at the individual and aggregate levels. These indicators include enrollment in postsecondary education, grades, persistence to the sophomore year, length of time to degree, and career after graduation. When focusing on the individual student, library administrators and staff can partner with other educational stakeholders, including those from other institutions, to identify factors that affect student success before the student begins his or her education at a college or university. Library administrators and staff also can partner with outside stakeholders, such as businesses, to identify factors that affect student success following undergraduate education.

It also is important that library administrators and staff select student success indicators that consider the diverse experiences of students. Six of the fourteen provosts interviewed identified diversity and inclusivity as important trends facing higher education. As the mode for dissemination of higher education changes (e.g., increase in online learning), so does the composition of students engaged in higher education (e.g., nontraditional students, such as military students and online-only students). Interviews with provosts suggest it is essential for library administrators and staff to consider how nontraditional students may or may not engage with library collections, services, and spaces and how this engagement corresponds to their student success outcomes. The success of interventions, such as partnering with community colleges to meet the needs of incoming transfer students, must be measured along with more traditional success factors.

Effective Practices to Implement at the Library

We have identified the following effective practices for this priority area:

- *Work with academic services and faculty to develop ethical collection and reporting methods for individual-level student data that retain individual privacy and confidentiality.* Library administrators, faculty, and staff should familiarize themselves with topics related to student privacy and confidentiality. While few examples of best practices exist, library administrators, library staff, researchers, practitioners, and students should combine their knowledge of their institutional review board's policies and LIS guidelines to create data collection and management systems that advance research in this area while upholding professional standards.[175]
- *Engage with faculty and students for librarian inclusion in developing academic and everyday life support services for students.* This effective practice also builds on the priority areas related to communication and collaboration. Library administrators and staff must collaborate with other departments and stakeholders to nurture student development in higher education and increase student-centered outcomes, such as the likelihood of graduation. Further, these administrators and staff should communicate their contributions to student development. For instance, by collaborating with other departments and stakeholders to nurture student development, the library helps increase likelihood of graduation.[176]
- *Select student success indicators that consider the diverse experiences of students.* Library administrators and staff need to be creative in identifying outcomes that address the needs of nontraditional students. For example, a possible outcome might include the use of library services, collections, and spaces by nontraditional students or the cost savings identified for students by the development of a LibGuide for open-access resources.

Exemplary Study

Soria, Fransen, and Nackerud's 2013 study found empirical evidence that first-time, first-year undergraduate students who used the library were more likely to re-enroll for the second semester and to have higher GPAs than those who did not use the library at the thirteen library access points covered in the data collected.[177] While this study has one of the strongest findings empirically, it was not given as many points using the scoring system explained in *Appendix K: Detailed Scoring Scheme for Exemplary Research Designs and Practices* as other exemplary studies. This lack of points awarded illustrates the difficulty of setting evaluative criteria. As a result, the team solicited additional exemplary studies from advisory group members and other relevant stakeholders. While these individuals did not offer many exemplary studies, they did provide several examples of effective practices, which are noted throughout this report.

Research Questions Requiring Further Study

1. How do library resources and programs (e.g., courses, events, etc.) impact indicators of student success?
2. Does access to library collections impact student retention? If so, how?
3. How do library spaces support student enrollment?
4. How does library instruction affect job placement and salary the first year after graduation? Five years after graduation?
5. What effects do libraries have on success outcomes for different types of students?
6. What are the effects of library instruction on success outcomes for diverse student populations (e.g., military students, non-US students, English language learners, nonresidential students, online-only students, etc.)?
7. How are library administrators and staff implementing continuous assessment to facilitate equal access to information for diverse student populations?
8. How can library administrators and staff supplement the data collected by other university departments (e.g., tutoring and writing centers) to document student learning and success?
9. How does library instruction at the secondary or earlier level affect information competencies at the postsecondary level?
10. How have library administrators and staff updated instruction based on the ACRL Framework for Information Literacy?[178]
11. What factors affect library contributions to positive student learning outcomes?
12. How can academic, public, and school libraries work together to develop connected informal and formal learning opportunities that lead to measurable student success outcomes (e.g., retention, grades, time to graduation) for community college, four-year college, and university students?

Proposed Research Design

The exemplary study for quantifying libraries' impact on student success empirically and statistically demonstrated a correlation between library usage and student retention and success. In addition to collecting data from a variety of sources, which also makes this study a good example of data collection, the exemplary study provides an excellent example of data analysis. The most important criterion for judging data analysis is whether the results answer the research questions.[179] If not, the study's design, which includes the data sampling, collection, and analysis, may have to be modified and the study repeated. As with data collection, the data analysis method should reflect the study's design. Quantitative analysis methods determine whether the data are statistically similar or different using tests based on the general linear model (e.g., regression, cluster analysis) or analysis of variance (ANOVA).[180] Qualitative methods, which include content and discourse analysis, do not have to be statistical or numerical in nature. Descriptive statistics and counts are numerical but do not assume a relationship between factors as in statistical analysis. One criterion for judging the goodness of a study's data analysis is whether the results are replicable.[181] For quantitative data, this could entail sharing the data set so that other researchers are able to replicate the statistical tests. For qualitative data, this could require having another person code or analyze a portion of the data to see if he or she identifies the same themes or counts in the data. Charmaz provides more information on how to analyze qualitative, especially interview, data and formulate grounded theories based on the data.[182] Denzin and Lincoln give more in-depth guidance on qualitative data analysis, and Garson's Statistical Associates publications provide the same for quantitative data.[183] Wildemuth and Connaway and Radford also provide information, overviews, and guidelines on analyzing various types of data.[184]

Questions for Researchers: Data Analysis

1. Do the results of the analysis answer the research questions? If not, which aspect of the research design needs to be modified and what part of the study repeated?
2. Are the data analysis methods appropriate for the qualitative and quantitative data collected?
3. Does the data analysis reporting meet the necessary (e.g., qualitative, quantitative, statistical) standard?

Enhance Teaching and Learning

General Discussion

The definition for this theme was "the less objective concepts of learning, such as critical thinking. Usually not tied to a specific graded assignment or graduation." In contrast to student success, we used this code to identify the less tangible or indirect effect of the library on students.

Teaching refers to the instruction that students receive in classrooms. Library administrators and staff have traditionally collaborated with course instructors at varying levels of involvement to enhance learning outcomes related to the instruction received. At the most basic level, library administrators and staff introduce students to the collections, spaces, and services that the library offers. At the highest level, they function as co-instructors. Teaching is grouped with learning because teaching activities have direct effects on student learning, which can cover a broad range of student-related activities and outcomes.

An established outcome related to student learning is engagement. In the last few years, faculty and staff have increasingly focused on creating more engaged students in school and more engaged citizens upon graduation. Activities that support these outcomes include undergraduate research and training students to identify credible information.[185] These outcomes relate to the less objective concepts of learning, such as critical thinking, instead of being tied to a result, such as an assignment grade or graduation.

Given their experience in information literacy instruction, library administrators and staff have an opportunity to lead the effort in creating more informed citizens. While LIS research from the last six years indicates that research in this area has increased, interviews with provosts from around the United States shows that student learning outcomes are more likely to be associated with library collections, spaces, and services than student success outcomes. At the same time, provosts were much less inclined to associate libraries with providing teaching support than the LIS literature reviewed.

These data suggest that library administrators and staff need to articulate better their support of teaching and learning outcomes, particularly those related to instructional support. One way to incorporate these areas would be to engage teaching faculty and students in the process of making library resources and services more integrated into the academic community's workflows.[186] Those doing research in this area should engage with faculty and students to develop academic (e.g., research and writing workshops) and everyday life (e.g., extending hours and providing stress-relieving programs during final exam periods) support services for students.[187] Library administrators, staff, researchers, practitioners, and students can identify effective practices for collaboration between academic librarians, instructors, and teaching support staff to enhance teaching and learning.

Effective Practices to Implement at the Library

We have identified the following effective practices for this priority area:

- *Engage with faculty and students for librarian inclusion in developing academic and everyday life support services for students.* Librarians can partner with writing centers and teaching faculty to develop services that can support students through all stages of the research process. They can also partner with groups within and outside the institution to provide security and staffing to create safe and open spaces for studying, and services such as therapy dogs and massages during exam periods.[188] This effective practice also builds on the priority areas communication and collaboration.
- *Support student engagement with library services, spaces, and collections by aligning with related programs that require them.* Library administrators and staff should collaborate across departments to leverage library services, spaces, collections, and expertise to assist students in first-year experience programs (Advisory Group Member LM06, Provost PP08). Advisory group members and provosts mentioned the importance of such programs to advancing the institutional mission and goals. Given that these programs are cross-departmental, the library can provide centralized grounds for students in these programs to learn and collaborate.
- *Keep abreast of higher education trends.* As mentioned in the *Discussion* section, one way that library staff and administrators can contextualize their contributions to student learning and success is by showing how these contributions address emerging trends and issues in higher education and libraries. Some of the trends identified by provosts include fostering critical competency skills (Provosts PP03, PP10), supporting continuing learning and educating students to become "informed citizens" (Provosts PP06, PP14), and changing people's perceptions of the library as a storehouse for collections (Provost PP02).

Exemplary Study

Brown-Sica's 2013 study of space redesign at Auraria Library offers one way for various groups to provide multiple types of input and otherwise engage with the library.[189] The Auraria Library serves the University of Colorado Denver, the Metropolitan State College of Denver, and the Community College of Denver. Students were involved in all stages of the study, from formulating the questions to ask, to analyzing the data and offering suggestions based on the results. This study was a high-scoring example (using the scoring system explained in *Appendix K: Detailed Scoring Scheme for Exemplary Research Designs and Practices*) of learning in college because, although not tied to an objective outcome such as student retention or GPA, this study gave students a voice in the project and facilitated unexpected collaborations with faculty. It also touched on library space, which was a library resource that provosts mentioned more frequently than library administrators.

Research Questions Requiring Further Study

1. What is the role of library administrators and staff in evaluating teaching and student learning outcomes?
2. What are the most common difficulties faced by library administrators and staff in measuring teaching and learning outcomes?
3. How do library administrators and staff measure the impact of library instruction on student learning outcomes?
4. How can library administrators and staff increase engagement among students?
5. How are library spaces (online or physical) affecting engagement among students?
6. In what ways have library administrators and staff implemented a continuous improvement process to support engaged student learning?
7. How are library administrators and staff implementing new models of outcomes-based measurement to assess the effectiveness of informal (e.g., Greek life, intramural sports) and formal learning opportunities?
8. Where do students go to discover information (e.g., answers to questions, resources for their needs)? If this is not library websites or online catalogs, what can library administrators and staff do to integrate library discovery systems into academic users' workflows?

Proposed Research Design

The exemplary study for enhancing teaching and learning also included the discussion section in the conclusion, which indicates that there is a lot of flexibility in how researchers can organize the discussion, future work, and conclusion of the study report. Clarity and relevance are the most important criteria for evaluating these aspects. The discussion should reiterate the findings from the data analysis and compare and relate them to past work and literature. A more detailed list of considerations for writing a useful discussion section is in Connaway and Radford.[190] The exemplary study included data from numerous data sources, and the author included several pictures and figures that broke up the text. The conclusion section lists the improvements that took place because of the study and contrasts the results of the study with ACRL's challenges in library design LibGuide.[191] See the table in *Appendix L: AiA Studies with Exemplary Design Elements* for examples of studies with exemplary discussion sections.

Questions for Researchers: Discussion

1. Are the most relevant findings clearly stated?
2. What is the best way to reiterate and frame the findings?
3. How do the findings of the study compare and relate to past work and literature?

Collaborate with Educational Stakeholders

General Discussion

Collaboration is an important theme because of the academic library's primary mission as a research and teaching support unit.[192] The AiA projects explicitly required librarians to collaborate with at least two people outside the libraries.[193] As a theme, it is defined here as, "Library administrators and staff work[ing] with other institutional departments to influence student outcomes or with other institutions."

The primary mission of the academic library is to support an institution's research and teaching, which necessitates collaboration with other educational stakeholders. Such collaboration includes all librarian efforts to work with those inside and outside their institution to influence student learning and success outcomes.[194]

Findings from the agenda indicate that library administrators, library staff, researchers, practitioners, students, and others in higher education are collaborating at an increasing rate. The proportion of documents in the selected literature related to collaboration has more than doubled between 2010 and 2016. The provosts discussed collaboration numerous times in their individual interviews, which underscores the importance of these types of activities across all types of academic institutions. The library administrators in the advisory group also mentioned several collaborative efforts and the importance of communicating the library's role in supporting student learning and success to faculty and administrators.

In AiA projects that ACRL and IMLS supported, nearly 200 research teams collaborated with a variety of university units that also support research and teaching.[195] This report also summarizes how these units (e.g., offices of assessment, institutional research, student affairs, and information or educational technology) collaborate to support each other and students, as well as relevant programs, in bolstering student learning and success, such as study abroad.[*] Internal collaboration is not the only opportunity available. Library administrators and staff also can collaborate with other public institutions such as museums, libraries, and archives. A recent study found that public library staff support students in their learning because students will use public libraries if they know the staff or otherwise feel comfortable going there.[196]

Collaborative research can include studies of how library administrators and staff modified their services and collections to better support other departments, and it also can lead to joint publications in other fields.[197] Those doing research in this area should understand that there are different types and levels of collaboration and consider looking at literature from related fields to see what outside researchers say about libraries and information-related topics. Library administrators, library staff, researchers, practitioners, and students also should work with academic and regional stakeholders, which include administrators, academic services staff, faculty, students, alumni, and other members of their local communities to identify mutual areas of research interest and to initiate collaborative research projects.

Effective Practices to Implement at the Library

We have identified the following effective practices for this priority area:

- *Understand that there are different types and levels of collaboration, and consider looking at literature from other related fields to see what it says about libraries and issues that libraries are facing or may face.* Collaboration can exist on individual, course, departmental, and program levels. It can also relate to the level of involvement. Concerning information literacy, a lower level of collaboration

* See section Measuring Student Learning and Success outside the Library.

between a librarian and a course instructor could include a librarian giving a single session, the next level could include the librarian teaching multiple sessions on information literacy, and a higher level could include the librarian co-teaching the course.

- *Work with academic administrators, academic services, faculty, students, alumni, and other members of the regional and local communities.* The AiA projects offer several examples of how various educational stakeholders have collaborated with librarians.[198] Some examples include projects that collaborated with a student-athlete academic success program, military campus program, professional development center, and advising center for students with disabilities.[199]
- *Identify needs of students and partner with related departments to meet them—think outside of the box.* As advised by one provost, library administrators and staff must "reach across a variety of disciplinary areas and identify those particular areas that might benefit from a cooperative activity because the library must work with everyone. I think that's the biggest challenge—to reach across a variety of disciplinary areas" (Provost PP10). Several provosts gave examples of how library administrators and staff could accomplish such cooperative activity. One example we identified as also exhibiting thinking outside the box is to have library administrators and staff provide or support efforts such as career counseling (Provost PP05).
- *Use library space to provide central meeting grounds for programs across departments.* As suggested by one provost quoted in the *Discussion* section, library staff and administrators should not engage in "turf wars," but rather promote the programmatic integration of other departments into the library space (Provost PP01). This integration can be accomplished by housing a cross-disciplinary program and allowing spaces for students to learn and work (Advisory Group Member LM03), creating a teaching commons for faculty to engage in programs to improve instruction (Advisory Group Member LM13), and engaging in interdisciplinary work by bringing different departments into the space (Provosts PP03, PP08), among other activities.
- *Partner with other departments to reach shared institutional goals.* One provost provided a detailed account of how library administrators and staff could achieve this partnership. She suggested that library administrators and staff engage everyone in the community in redefining the library's role by hosting a town hall meeting and asking, "What is the role of the library today?" By collaborating with other departments, library administrators and staff can formulate an institution-specific response to that question, which gets buy-in from everyone (Provost PP04).
- *Partner with institutions outside the university or college, such as government and commercial institutions.* It is important for library administrators and staff not only to collaborate with those internal to the institution, but also to bring in those external to it. As an example, one provost suggested that library administrators and staff allow community groups from outside the institution to come into the library and give them space in which to engage (Provost PP13). This practice also aligns with a higher education trend identified by provosts, which relates to the growing decentralization of students from their physical institutions due to factors such as the increase in distance learning and the rising importance of continuing education. For these reasons, integrating the outside community into the institution can engender buy-in from those not geographically linked to the institution.

Exemplary Studies

The 2015 study by Hess, Greer, Lombardo, and Lim at Oakland University Libraries is exemplary because it documents the libraries' efforts to collaborate with other departments in support of student success and persistence.[200] The documented and suggested collaborations cover a broad range of services and collections. Another notable collaboration was between Wolfe, an assistant professor in the behavioral and social sciences at Hostos Community College (CUNY), and her college's librarians. Wolfe published in a higher education journal the results of a study that incorporated information literacy into a class assignment. We assigned one of the highest scores to this document, which we retrieved from a higher education database.[201]

Research Questions Requiring Further Study

1. How can library administrators and staff collaborate with staff and faculty members from other academic institutions to increase student learning and success?
2. How can library administrators and staff collaborate with staff and faculty from other academic departments within the same academic institution to increase student learning and success?
3. What can library administrators and staff learn from institutional units that have increased student learning and success? How can library administrators and staff use this information to accomplish these increases and communicate their efforts?
4. What types of collaboration are the most effective in facilitating student learning and success outcomes?
5. How do collaborations between library administrators and staff and other libraries affect contributions to student success outcomes?
6. How can library administrators and staff contribute to areas that demonstrate the most promise for benefiting from library collaboration to increase positive student learning outcomes?

Proposed Research Design

The exemplary studies for collaborating with educational stakeholders also provide good examples of developing future work and reporting the findings. Future work suggests how other research can build on the findings and other aspects of the current study. The limitations and implications of the study help identify how researchers can extend the work in future studies. Since the study results inform future work, implications, and limitations, these elements sometimes are combined. A more detailed list of considerations for organizing and presenting research is in Connaway and Radford.[202] The 2015 study by Hess and colleagues provides several suggested collaborations that involve a broad range of library services and collections and does an exemplary job of suggesting how librarians can collaborate with stakeholders in their institutions.[203] See the table in *Appendix L: AiA Studies with Exemplary Design Elements* for additional examples of studies with exemplary future work sections.

Questions for Researchers: Future Work

1. How can the limitations of the study be clearly stated?
2. How can the implications of the work be connected to suggestions for future research?

When reporting a study, the researcher should report what is appropriate based on format (e.g., poster, paper, presentation) and audience. Like the discussion and future work sections of the research process, the only real criterion for identifying exemplary reporting in studies is how precisely the study presents this information and how relevant it is to the audience. The Wolfe study that we identified as exemplary for this priority area was published by the author in a non-LIS journal. This action is a useful reminder that LIS conferences, journals, and other venues are not and possibly should not be the only sites for sharing LIS research.

Questions for Researchers: Reporting

1. What non-LIS venues should researchers consider for sharing LIS research?
2. Is the information clearly reported?
3. Is the information being shared relevant to the audience?

Visualizing Academic Library Impact: The ACRL/OCLC Literature Analysis Dashboard

To aid researchers, practitioners, and students in answering the research questions above, or library administrators and staff in using the priority areas for the development of effective programs and examples of student learning and success, we created a visualization component. Findings from the data analysis and collection portion of this project informed the development of the component, consisting of a literature search tool and a charts and graphs tool.* Visualizing Academic Library Impact: The ACRL/OCLC Literature Analysis Dashboard is a web application providing two primary functions:

1. A literature search tool for searching through the database of documents analyzed for this report and compiling and sharing reference lists for further study.
2. A charts and graphs tool for producing and sharing visualizations and graphics from data within the document database as well as user-uploaded data.

The literature search tool and the charts and graphs tool both protect the database metadata related to the literature review of this report. We made these data immutable and read-only to protect them from accidental harm. However, regular users can upload their studies, data, and metadata. This uploaded data will be visible only to the uploading user and cannot impact the experience of others. Some modifications to the global, underlying database can be made by Super Users (such as website administrators) so that the database can be kept up to date.

Unlike most web applications, both the visualization backend and its frontend are written in a single strongly typed free and open-source programming language (Scala; http://scala-lang.org). Use of the Scala language enforces software correctness and quality to provide a seamless user experience. Several open-source technologies power the visualization component. These technologies are

- Scala.js (client-side JavaScript generation; http://www.scala-js.org)
- Play Framework (backend application; https://playframework.com)
- H2 database engine (database persistence; http://h2database.com/html/main.html)

* For recognition and usability purposes, we chose to name the tool "charts and graphs." However, we recognize that the tool fulfills the functions of a graph as defined by the Merriam-Webster dictionary as "a diagram (such as a series of one or more points, lines, line segments, curves, or areas) that represents the variation of a variable in comparison with that of one or more other variables." See *Merriam-Webster Dictionary Online*, s.v. "graph," accessed July 1, 2017, https://www.merriam-webster.com/dictionary/graph.

Literature Search Tool

Figure 8

Literature search tool interface

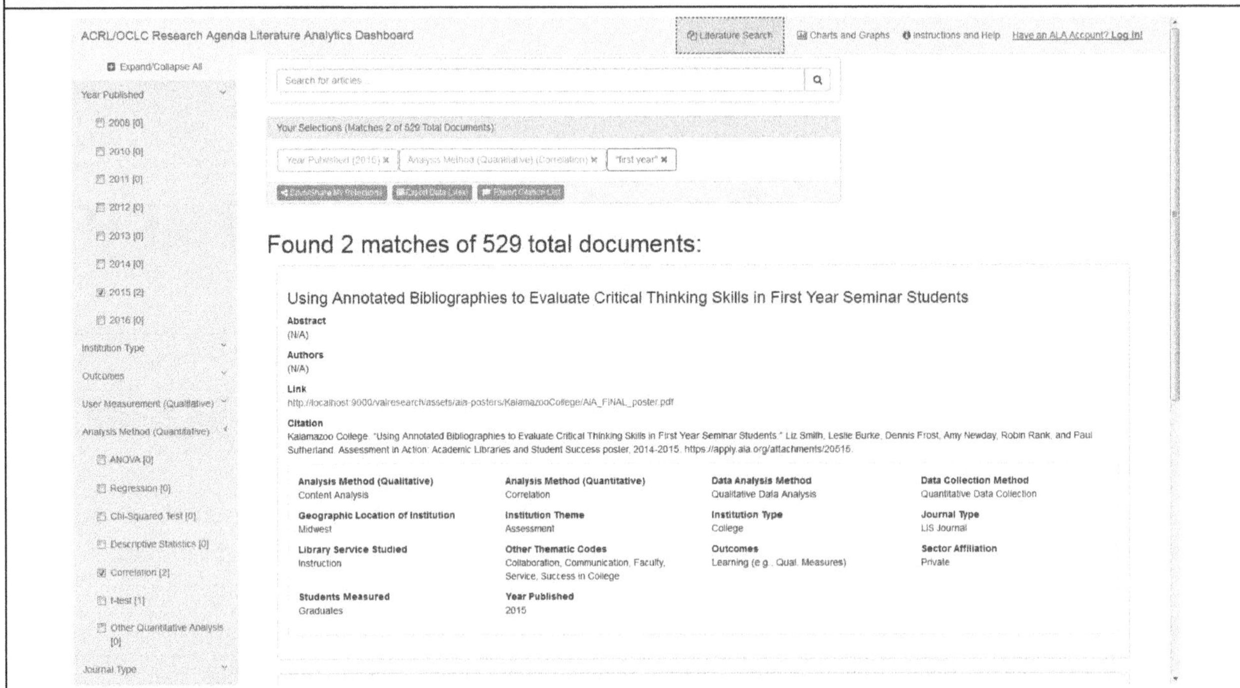

The literature search tool allows library administrators, library staff, researchers, practitioners, and students to search the 535 selected LIS and higher education documents analyzed for the *Literature Review* section of this report. To reiterate, the selection criteria for LIS and higher education documents reviewed are (1) indexed by LIS or higher education databases or identified by the project team or ACRL (e.g., ACRL AiA projects, Ithaka S+R surveys; see *Relevant ACRL Documents* section), (2) published between 2010 and 2016, (3) containing themes identified in the 2010 *VAL Report*, and (4) published in the United States, except for studies outside the United States deemed relevant by the project team.

The tool provides faceted search (i.e., a category-based search) and text search to help users quickly navigate through the document database and find items of interest. It also allows users to save and share reference lists through persistent URLs that can be copied and pasted easily.

Faceted Search

The left navigation bar of the literature search tool features a collection of "search facets." These facets represent areas of interest to search identified by us and reflected in the Thematic and Research Document Characteristics Coding Schemes (see *Appendix D: Codebook*). Facets (i.e., study-related categories) appear as organized checkboxes that filter the document database in real time. As facets are selected, documents are either filtered away or added to the current list of pertinent documents. The currently selected set of facets and text filters is displayed using a breadcrumb metaphor under the Selected Document Attributes panel shown in figure 8. We were inspired by the design of the Zappos website (http://www.zappos.com) and WorldCat Fiction Finder (http://experimental.worldcat.org/xfinder/fictionfinder.html) when designing this feature.

Text Search

Figure 9
Text search with real-time feedback

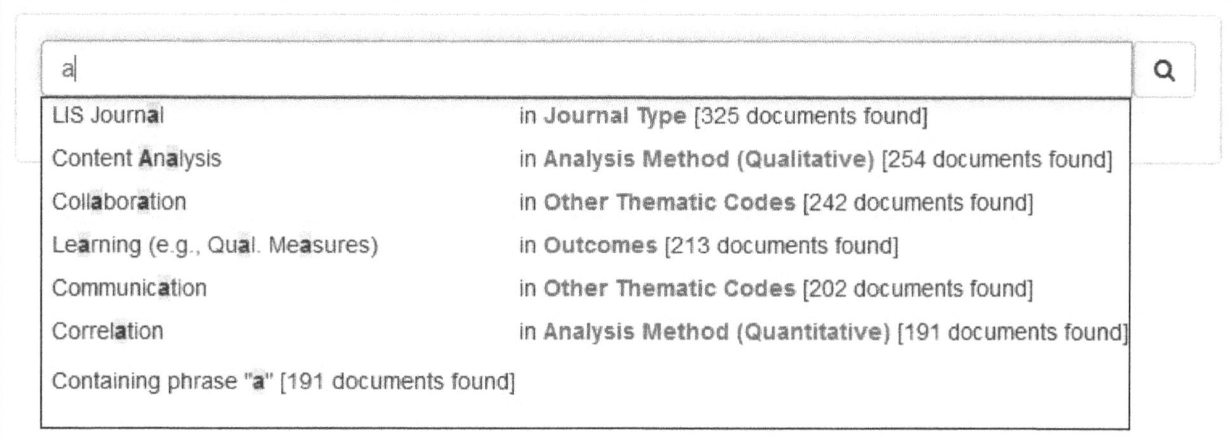

The text search function (figure 9) provides real-time feedback on available documents as a user enters text. This function can help searchers get a sense for the thematic and research document characteristics codes available in the database, as well as other document categorizations. The search function transparently supports basic Boolean queries using *and*, *or*, *not*, and phrase-based search.

Charts and Graphs Tool

Figure 10
The charts and graphs tool

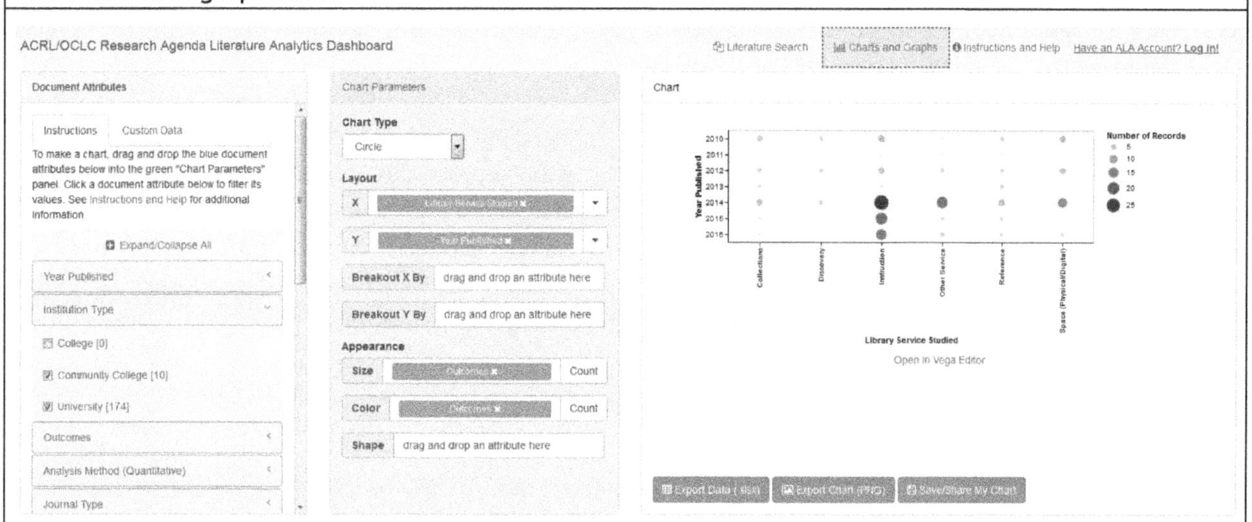

The charts and graphs tool (figure 10) emulates Tableau software (http://www.tableau.com/Tableau-Software), which is sometimes used to generate visualizations both within and outside LIS, by providing a Tableau-like drag-and-drop interface for constructing visualizations and graphics.[204] We have populated this tool with the same documents and metadata from the 535 selected LIS and higher education documents included in the literature search tool. Like the literature search tool facets, the metadata used by the charts and graphs tool has been derived by the team from the Thematic and Research Document Characteristics Coding Schemes (see *Appendix D: Codebook*). While this document database is the default data source for the charts and graphs tool, users can import additional data in supported columnar formats (e.g., Excel tables).

A significant strength of this tool is its use of a powerful visualization grammar called Vega Lite. This grammar is very expressive and can be used to create detailed charts with support for advanced user interaction, streaming data, and chart layering, among other things. However, it is currently available only as grammar, meaning that an individual must understand how to write in this grammar to use these powerful features. For this reason, the charts and graphs tool uses a bidirectional compiler that consumes and generates visualization specifications conforming to the Vega Lite visualization grammar. In other words, users get some of the features of Vega Lite without the learning curve. Only a relatively small number of Vega Lite features are exposed to preserve the simplicity of the user interface. Advanced users with specific needs (such as animation, or "brushing and linking"[205] that associates two or more charts, so that interacting with one chart will highlight data items in the other charts) can export their charts in Vega Lite format and enhance them with these advanced features using the online Vega Lite Editor (https://vega.github.io/new-editor/?mode=vega-lite).

When users finish editing a chart, they can export the chart as an image to share with colleagues or stakeholders. Also, the chart can be saved within the web application so that users can edit it later. An additional feature that we added following feedback from usability testing allows users to download data as a Microsoft Excel document. As we learned from usability testing (detailed below), some users prefer the familiarity of that tool when creating visualizations and graphics.

Administration and Sandboxed Content Tagging

One of the chief objectives of the visualization component is to give users access to the database and related metadata from the *Literature Review*, while also allowing users to upload their data and generate metadata. For these reasons, the visualization component provides standard role-based access control to endow user accounts with special administrator privileges. These privileges will allow a database maintainer to fix typos in the database, edit existing data, or add or delete data.

The typical user can create a set of tags (analogous to "labels" used in Gmail[206]) for labeling existing documents, allowing the user to create personalized metadata. Users can also upload documents to the database. This action is sandboxed, meaning it is reflected only in the user's particular database and not across the visualization component tools. These users can also perform some other sandboxed augmentations to the document database. Since the team has sandboxed these augmentations, there will be no way for a user to affect another user's view of the database, and a non-administrator user cannot harm the database contents.

Usability Testing

A prototype of the visualization component was usability tested in the OCLC Usability Lab in early March 2017. Six participants were recruited to assess the tool. The participants represented academic librarians and administrators, and LIS researchers and students. They varied in their usage of the ACRL AiA tool (https://apply.ala.org/aia/public). The team compared this tool to the visualization component prototype in a post-evaluation interview question.

Participants performed four tasks:

1. a search-related task requiring only faceted search within the literature search tool
2. another search-related task requiring text and keyword search
3. a third search combining both faceted and text and keyword search
4. a fourth task requiring the user to use the charts and graphs tool to create a histogram graph of document data

By observing users and soliciting feedback early in the design and implementation phase of the project, we could pivot to improve the visualization component and acquire empirical assurance that user expectations are satisfied as they interact with the tool. This feedback helps to ensure that users' interactions with the visualization component software and interface are positive and have as little friction as possible.

Searching the Visualization Component Using the Priority Areas

To illustrate how to use the visualization component tools, consider two sample scenarios posed to the usability testing participants.

For the first scenario, imagine being a librarian at a community college who wants to examine how the library impacts the inclusivity and diversity of the student body. Before beginning this study, the librarian wants to get an idea of what recent literature exists on the topic.

To generate a reference list of studies about inclusivity and diversity at community colleges, one could use the literature search tool. The user can accomplish this task by using facets. Specifically, the user could check the Diversity/Inclusivity and Community College facets. Doing so will display a list of references from the 535 documents indexed in the tool's database that we have labeled with these facets. If the user has added additional documents and labeled them with this metadata, the tool also displays those documents in the references list (figure 11).

Figure 11
Screenshot of documents with selected Diversity/Inclusivity and Community College facets

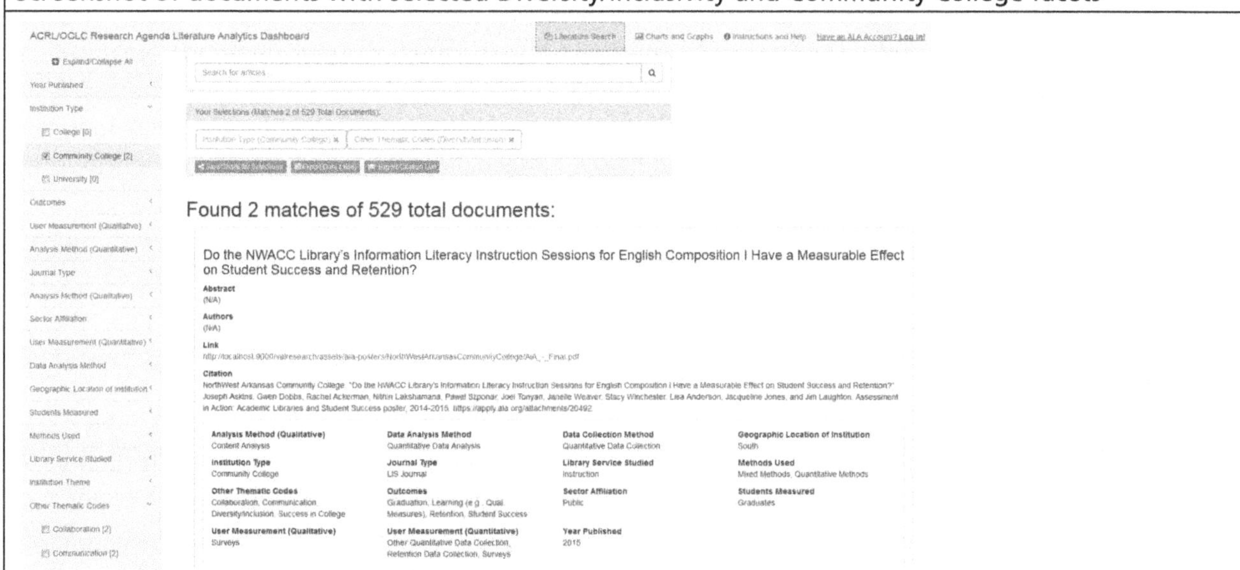

For the second scenario, imagine being a library director who has an upcoming meeting with the provost. The director wants to demonstrate to the provost that correlation is considered a viable means through which to demonstrate the library's impact. To make this demonstration, the director wants to create a bar chart that displays the increase in studies that use correlation over time.

One could use the charts and graphs tool to generate a bar graph showing the number of studies using correlation from 2010 to 2016. The user can assign the Year Published facet to either the *x*- or *y*-axis and the aggregate field COUNT, which generates a count of the number of document records corresponding to the desired query, to the other axis. This action will display a graph illustrating the number of studies indexed in the database. To then show the number of studies using correlation over time, the user could filter the results by checking the Correlation facet so that the resulting graph displays only results tagged as Correlation. Finally, if the graph does not present as a bar, the user can change the display by choosing Bar from the Marks menu (figure 12).

Figure 12

Screenshot of bar chart displaying number of studies using correlation by year

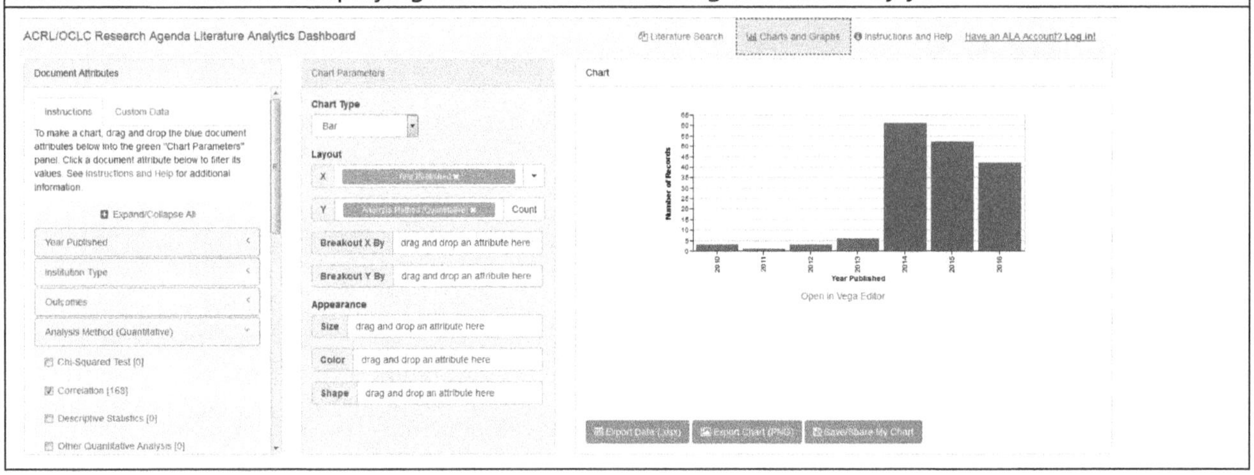

A significant strength of the visualization component is that its document database was developed based on data collection and analysis informed by our expertise and feedback from the ACRL board, VAL committee, and advisory group members. For these reasons, the documents in the database and their metadata correspond to the agenda's priority areas. *Appendix J: Examples of Research Questions That Can Be Addressed Using the Visualization Component, Organized by Priority Area* includes a list of sample research questions, organized by priority area, which can be approached using the visualization component. These questions are more specific than the research questions listed under each priority area in the body of the report because they integrate context, such as the institution type or population studied. A key benefit of the visualization component is the facilitation of targeted research questions.

Limitations

The research report and priority areas are the basis for the research agenda. The exemplary studies and visualization component are the foundation for the identification of the data collection and analysis methods that researchers can use to address the research questions. Although the report, agenda, and visualization component were developed and informed by methods that are systematic and grounded in research theory and practice, as with any project, we must address some limitations. These limitations indicate which conclusions one can draw from the project findings and which one cannot draw.

We divide the limitations of the project into the areas of data collection and analysis. The data collection provides a US-centric perspective of issues related to library assessment and evaluation. The selection criteria for the literature mainly are focused on documents from the United States, and all advisory group members and provosts who participated in the interviews were from United States institutions.

Another limitation in data collection relates to the selection of data sources. Selected LIS and higher education documents may reflect trends from two or more years prior to publication, especially the research documents, given the time it takes to complete a research project, write up the results, submit it for review for publication, and have it accepted for publication and published. The literature disproportionately represents studies addressing public sector universities and institutions, as opposed to colleges and community colleges and institutions in the private sector. The selection of advisory group members, who also are the focus group interview participants, from a variety of institutional settings, with representation from all three institutional types, both public and private sectors, and secular and nonsecular institutions, was intentional to provide a broader perspective on the project.

Since the sample of documents indexed in databases was nonrandom, we may have missed some documents that would be relevant to the literature review (e.g., gray literature, such as other research agendas). We minimized this missed selection by soliciting feedback from the ACRL board and members, as well as the advisory group, regarding what studies we should add to the content analysis of selected LIS and higher education documents.

The selection of the advisory group members and their institutions' provosts provides only an indication of important themes from a high-level administrative perspective. Since the interview participants and the literature samples are purposive and not random, the findings reported do not represent all professional librarians', high-level administrators', and researchers' perspectives on the themes. However, we can draw some conclusions by examining the overlaps between the smaller sample of administrators and the larger sample of the literature.

Due to our purposive sample of all three data sources, our research methodology did not capture the everyday practices and areas of research explored by academic libraries. For this reason, we suggest that a future research direction for libraries is to pursue further study and survey of effective practices beyond what the literature review, advisory group members, provosts, and ACRL board and VAL committee indicated.

Finally, comparing three data sources using the same coding scheme, which was generated deductively from relevant ACRL literature, may have stifled the emergence of other themes. In an attempt to mitigate this limitation, we inductively added codes to the coding scheme when they emerged from the data. These codes included inclusivity/diversity and privacy.

The charts and graphs tool within the visualization component is designed with a tradeoff between simplicity of user interaction and support for Vega Lite features. Usability testing in the OCLC Usability Lab indicated that the interface should favor simplicity over expressive power. Thus, some kinds of graphics that are expressible in Vega Lite cannot be expressed using the charts and graphs tool. However, the Vega Lite source code of graphs within the charts and graphs tool can be exported, edited, and rendered using the Vega Lite online editor. Additionally, users who are comfortable in Excel can export an Excel workbook file for producing visualizations.

Conclusion

This research agenda responded to two areas that ACRL identified as essential for library administrators, library staff, researchers, practitioners, and students to address in future research and practice. These areas are (1) how libraries align with and impact institutional effectiveness related to student learning and success, and (2) how library administrators and staff best communicate this alignment and impact in a way that resonates with higher education stakeholders. This agenda relied on empirical analysis of three data sources to inform the identification of six priority areas for future research, with exemplary studies, practices, research designs, and future-focused research questions under each area. Further, we created a visualization component to facilitate inquiry into these areas and research questions.

The empirical research informing this agenda consisted of our analysis of three data sources: (1) 535 documents from the LIS and higher education literature, (2) focus group interview and brainstorming sessions with an advisory group comprised of academic library administrators, and (3) semi-structured individual interviews with provosts from advisory group members' institutions. The selection criteria for LIS and higher education documents were (1) indexed by LIS or higher education databases or identified by the project team or ACRL (e.g., ACRL AiA projects, Ithaka S+R surveys); (2) published between 2010 and 2016; (3) containing themes identified in the 2010 *Value of Academic Libraries* (VAL) report; and (4) published in the United States, except for studies outside the United States deemed relevant by the project team.

Findings from analysis of selected literature show that it focuses on the themes of collaboration, teaching and learning, and library service. Theoretical documents (e.g., literature reviews, research agendas) discussed the mission alignment and strategy theme more than research documents, which signifies that library administrators, library staff, researchers, practitioners, and students are not addressing this important topic in their work. Documents from the higher education literature examined service less than those within the LIS literature, suggesting a disproportionate focus on this theme among library administrators, library staff, researchers, practitioners, and students.

Findings from the focus group interview with advisory group members, who are library administrators, showed an emphasis on the themes of collaboration, communication, and library service. These findings confirm those from the analysis of selected literature in suggesting that library administrators, library staff, researchers, practitioners, and students may focus on service as a library resource at the expense of the other resources related to space and collection. Building on the analysis of selected literature's emphasis on the theme of collaboration, advisory group members contextualized the need to link both collaboration and communication to the institutional mission and goals, rather than isolate both themes within the library.

Provosts valued the themes of communication, mission alignment and strategy, and space as a library resource. Provosts' valuing communication aligns with the priorities of the ACRL AiA studies and advisory group members. However, provosts discussed mission alignment and strategy to a greater degree than the other data sources. Provosts further emphasized the importance of librarians communicating how the library contributes to institutional goals by marketing, customer service, and sharing space with other groups, both on and off campus.

Relying on three data sources to inform this agenda strengthens the comparisons that can be made between the sources to determine similarities and differences in how each discussed student learning and success. This comparison guided the development of the priority areas by identifying emerging areas related to student learning and success that require future investigation. Library administrators and staff should use the priority areas to influence and guide their efforts in developing academic programs and offerings focused on student learning and success. Researchers, practitioners, and students should use the research questions as a catalyst for the study of college and university student learning and success. The visualization component aids these researchers, practitioners, and students in addressing the identified priority areas and research questions, as well as providing the flexibility to pursue related areas.

Suggested Topics of Interest for Communicating with Academic Administrators

- Inform the provost of a newly created library position. (LM14)
- Get the provost's permission to attend meetings with the student affairs director. (LM14)
- Get involved in efforts related to institutional mission and alignment, which includes face time with the provost. (PP03)
- Create targeted stories featuring faculty and students that discuss the benefit of library initiatives. (LM13)
- Invite the provost to library events. (PP02)
- Run into the provost at a coffee shop and informally discuss the library's value. (LM14)
- Communicate to leadership favorable reviews the library receives for events and initiatives. (LM12)

Appendix A: Glossary

Assessment: Research on the effectiveness of a program, product, or service to facilitate its ongoing improvement; is driven in part by scrutiny on the affordability of higher education. For more information, please see the discussion on Assessment and Evaluation in this report's *Literature Review* section.

Codebook: Documentation of themes derived from coding, their definitions, and examples.

Coding: Placing data in categories, or themes, for organization and analysis.[207]

Communication: Conveying impact or other aspects of value to stakeholders.

Collaboration: Working with other units to influence student outcomes. Collaboration can be intra-institutional (e.g., with mission alignment and strategy unit, faculty) or inter-institutional (e.g., with multiple institutions).

Evaluation: Research on the effectiveness of a program, product, or service that tends to be more holistic,[208] occur on a larger scale, focus on more generalized end results, and be written for a wider audience than assessment. In other words, an evaluation perspective will take a big picture or helicopter view of a collection, space, or service in a larger (e.g., institutional) context. For more information, please see the discussion on Assessment and Evaluation in this report's *Literature Review* section.

Learning analytics: "Data about learners and their contexts, for purposes of understanding and optimizing learning and the environments in which it occurs."[209]

Teaching and learning: An outcome focused on the less objective concepts of learning, such as critical thinking. These encompass the outcomes not covered by the "student success" theme, which the team defines as "quantifiable student attainment indicators, such as enrollment in postsecondary education, grades, persistence to the sophomore year, the length of time to degree, and graduation."[210] Usually not tied to a particular graded assignment or graduation. For more information, please see the discussion on Learning and Success in this report's *Literature Review* section.

Method: "Any procedure employed to attain a certain end"; used to address a research-related goal or goals.[211]

Mixed methods: The use of qualitative collection or analysis and quantitative collection or analysis methods. All mixed methods are multiple methods.

Multiple methods: More than one type of method, but can be two or more qualitative methods or two or more quantitative methods. All mixed methods are multiple methods, but not all multiple methods are mixed.

Student success: An outcome focused on the more objective, usually quantifiable, indicators of learning, or "quantifiable student attainment indicators, such as enrollment in postsecondary education, grades, persistence to the sophomore year, the length of time to degree, and graduation."[212] These outlines relate to a specific assignment or semester, such as grades or GPA. This outcome could also be related to whether the student re-enrolled or graduated. For more information, please see the discussion on Learning and Success in this report's *Literature Review* section.

Appendix B: Provost Semi-structured Interview Protocol

1. Do you have any questions before we begin?
1. How do the specific people that you meet with articulate what they are doing and how well they are doing it?
    a. [Probes: Trying to find out how academic departments/units communicate their activities. If the interviewee mentions them, they are memorable to the administrator.]
2. What information do you or your institution use to measure the effectiveness/impact of different academic departments/units?
    a. [Probes: Trying to identify how the interviewer measures success/impact.]
3. How do you find out about the library's/libraries' activities?
    a. [Probes: Trying to find out how the library communicates its services and activities to the campus and the community. How does the library staff make you aware of services?]
4. How does your institution measure the effectiveness/impact of the library's/libraries' services?
    a. [Probes: How involved is your institution's academic library with each of the following high impact practices: first-year seminars and first-year experiences; common intellectual (curricular or co-curricular) experiences; learning communities; writing-intensive courses; collaborative assignments and projects; undergraduate research; diversity and global learning; service learning and community-based learning; internships; capstone courses and projects.]
    b. [Probes: Are there specific library services, resources, or practices that stand out as evidence of involvement with the high-impact practices we just discussed?]
5. Suppose your institution's library dean or director approached you with a moderate (noncapital) funding request, such as for new positions or an increase in the collections budget, that competed with funding requests from other (revenue-generating) academic units. What data types would influence you to prioritize the library's funding request over those of the other academic units?
6. What challenges do you see in the way the library staff communicates with the academic community, including students, faculty, and administration?
7. What do you think would facilitate communication between the library staff and your academic community, including students, faculty, and administration?
    a. [Probes: What are the most effective modes of communicating each evidence of value that you just mentioned?]
8. What changes do you envision in higher education in the next five years?
9. In what ways can the library be a major contributor to this new higher education environment?
10. If you could create an ideal academic environment, what would that look like? How could the library/libraries enhance or support this environment?
11. Based on your knowledge of our project and the topics we have just covered, is there anything I did not ask you that you think I should have asked?

Appendix C: Provosts' Titles and Carnegie Class for Provosts' Universities

Advisory Group Member Code	Title	Carnegie Classification: Basic
PP01	Associate Provost and Associate Dean of Faculty	Baccalaureate Colleges: Arts & Sciences Focus
PP02	Provost	Doctoral Universities: Higher Research Activity (R2)
PP03	Vice Provost for Education	Doctoral Universities: Highest Research Activity (R1)
PP04	Teaching Professor in Biological Sciences	Doctoral Universities: Highest Research Activity (R1)
PP05	Associate Provost for Undergraduate Affairs	Associate's Colleges: High Transfer-Mixed Traditional/ Nontraditional
PP06	Assistant Dean of Arts and Sciences	Doctoral Universities: Highest Research Activity (R1)
PP07	Assistant Provost for Assessment	Doctoral Universities: Highest Research Activity (R1)
PP08	Chancellor	Doctoral Universities: Higher Research Activity (R2)
PP09	Associate Vice President for Undergraduate Education	Doctoral Universities: Highest Research Activity (R1)
PP10	Associate Provost for Faculty Affairs	Doctoral Universities: Higher Research Activity (R2)
PP11	Associate Provost for the Advancement of Teaching and Learning	Doctoral Universities: Highest Research Activity (R1)
PP12	Vice Provost and Associate Vice Chancellor for Undergraduate Education	Associate's Colleges: High Transfer-Mixed Traditional/ Nontraditional
PP13	Interim Vice President for Learning	Doctoral Universities: Moderate Research Activity (R3)
PP14	Associate Provost for Student Success and Accreditation	Master's Colleges & Universities: Larger Programs (M1)

Appendix D: Codebooks

Theme Coding Scheme

Identify the appropriate library resource (collection, service, or space) discussed and that can be inferred based on the codebook definitions.

All trends and studies in this report deal with student outcomes. However, trends may involve other stakeholders as indicated below.

Library Resources

Service: Ways that the library interacts with users or facilitates use of its spaces or collections (e.g., reference, information literacy instruction)

Space: Areas where users can interact with library services and collections in a physical or digital environment (e.g., physical facilities, seating, library's Facebook page)

Collection: The library's physical and digital holdings (e.g., books, periodicals, microfiche)

Higher education trend	Trend defined	Example of library resources related to trend
Students		
Teaching and learning (and beyond)	Outcome is focused on the less objective concepts of learning, such as critical thinking. These encompass the outcomes not covered by the student success theme, which are "quantifiable student attainment indicators, such as enrollment in postsecondary education, grades, persistence to the sophomore year, length of time to degree, and graduation."[a] Usually not tied to a specific graded assignment or graduation. For more information, please see the discussion on Learning and Success in this report's *Literature Review* section.	Service: Library instruction Space: Collaborative working space for students Collections: Repository of online tutorials not linked to a specific class
Student success (for multiple student groups)	Outcome is focused on the more objective indicators of learning, or "quantifiable student attainment indicators, such as enrollment in postsecondary education, grades, persistence to the sophomore year, length of time to degree, and graduation."[b] These tended to be linked to a specific assignment/semester, such as grades/GPA. Outcome could also be related to whether the student re-enrolled or graduated. For more information, please see the discussion on Learning and Success in this report's *Literature Review* section.	Collections: Physical collections Collections: Digital collections Space: Study spaces Service: Library instruction Service: Collection discovery

Higher education trend	Trend defined	Example of library resources related to trend
Students/Faculty		
Research support	Outcome was tied to research or other use of the library's collections that was not explicitly tied to a class.	Collections: Physical Collections: Digital Service: Data storage Service: Consultation Service: Teach data management Service: Teach data mining methods Service: Collection discovery Space: Research (as opposed to learning) commons
Faculty		
Teaching support	Outcome was viewed from an instructor perspective, and it deals with a specific course.	
Institution		
Accreditation	Accreditation-related student outcomes	Service: Help institutions meet federal guidelines/requirements
Assessment (driven in part by affordability of higher ed)	Institutionally identified student outcomes (can be co-coded with learning and success)	Service: Educate library and other employees Service: Align with institutional mission and goals
Provision of technology	Outcome also dealt with hardware/software that affect student outcomes	Service: Provide expertise for data management Space: Provide hardware and software in makerspaces
Other thematic codes (does not have to align with library service, space, or collection)		
Inclusivity	(Possibly) marginalized groups	First-generation college students; People of color; Commuters; Distance learners; English as a second language; Lower socioeconomic level
Collaboration	Librarians work with other institutional departments to influence student outcomes or with other institutions.	Collaboration could be intra-institutional (e.g., with mission alignment and strategy unit; faculty) or inter-institutional (e.g., with multiple institutions)
Communication	Librarians communicate impact or other aspects of value with stakeholders	

a. George D. Kuh, Jillian Kinzie, Jennifer A. Buckley, Brian K. Bridges, and John C. Hayek, What Matters to Student Success: A Review of the Literature, Commissioned Report for the National Symposium on Postsecondary Student Success: Spearheading a Dialog on Student Success (Washington, DC: National Postsecondary Education Cooperative, 2006), 5, https://nces.ed.gov/npec/pdf/kuh_team_report.pdf.
b. Ibid.

Research Document Characteristics Coding Scheme

Code name	Code definition	Values
Year	Year study was published.	2010–2016
Geographic location	Major geographic regions as defined by census at https://www2.census.gov/geo/pdfs/maps-data/maps/reference/us_regdiv.pdf or outside of the United States where the study was performed. Do not code if institutions were in different regions.	Northeast; Midwest; Outside the US; South; West
Type	Type of institution where the study was performed. Do not code if multiple institution types were studied.	College; Community college; University
Sector affiliation	Whether institution was public, private, secular, or nonsecular. Do not code if multiple institutions are not the same.	Private; Public
Multiple institution	Code if study involved multiple institutions.	Multiple institutions
Outcomes	Specific student outcomes that are tied to a more objective qualitative or quantitative indicator of learning for a specific assignment, class, or graduation.	Enrollment; Graduation; Learning; Retention; Student engagement; Student success
Library service	Library service studied.	Collections; Discovery; Instruction; Reference; Space (physical or digital)
Library measurement	How the library service was measured.	Usage; Attendance
User measurement—Qualitative	How the user data were collected via qualitative methods. Interviews include individual and group interviews. Reference interviews are considered content analysis.*	Interviews; Surveys; Other
User measurement—Quantitative	How the user data were collected via quantitative methods. Interviews include individual and group interviews.	GPA; Persistence; Pre/post test; Retention; Survey; Rubric; Other
User measurement—Student type	Status of participants. Other includes faculty/staff.	Undergraduate; Graduate; Other
Analysis method—Qualitative	How the data were analyzed via qualitative methods.	Content analysis; Other
Analysis method—Quantitative	How the data were analyzed via quantitative methods.	ANOVA; Regression; X2; Descriptive statistics; Correlation; Other

* Note: When the researchers use a rubric to evaluate student work, the analysis method is considered quantitative only if they discuss the numerical values assigned to student work. If they report qualitative findings (e.g., themes) from the student work, then the qualitative analysis method may also be used (e.g., content analysis).

Appendix E: Literature Analyzed Bibliography*

Abbasi, Neda, Hisham Elkadi, Anne Horn, and Sue Owen. "TEALS Project: Evaluating Physical Library Spaces." In *Proceedings of the 2012 Library Assessment Conference: Building Effective, Sustainable, Practical Assessment.* Edited by Steve Hiller, Martha Kyrillidou, Angela Pappalardo, Jim Self, and Amy Yeager, 229–38. Washington, DC: Association of Research Libraries, 2012.

ACRL Research Planning and Review Committee. *Environmental Scan 2015.* Chicago: Association of College and Research Libraries, 2015. http://www.ala.org/acrl/sites/ala.org.acrl/files/content/publications/whitepapers/EnvironmentalScan15.pdf.

———. "Top Trends in Academic Libraries: A Review of the Trends and Issues Affecting Academic Libraries in Higher Education." *College and Research Libraries News* 75, no. 6 (2014): 274–81. http://crln.acrl.org/content/75/6/294.full.

ACRL VAL Committee. "VAL CMTE Trends Analysis 2016." Accessed May 25, 2017. http://www.acrl.ala.org/value/wp-content/uploads/2016/04/VAL-Cmte-Trends-Analysis-2016.pdf.

Alamuddin, Rayane, Martin Kurzweil, and Daniel Rossman. *Higher Ed Insights: Results of the Fall 2015 Survey.* New York: Ithaka S+R, February 22, 2016. http://www.sr.ithaka.org/wp-content/uploads/2016/02/SR_Report_Higher_Ed-Insights_Fall2015Survey_022216.pdf.

Albert, Amanda B. "Communicating Library Value: The Missing Piece of the Assessment Puzzle." *Journal of Academic Librarianship* 40, no. 6 (2014): 634–37. doi:10.1016/j.acalib.2014.10.001.

Allen, Laurie, Neal Baker, Josh Wilson, Kevin Creamer, and David Consiglio. "Analyzing the MISO Data: Broader Perspectives on Library and Computing Trends." In *Proceedings of the 2010 Library Assessment Conference: Building Effective, Sustainable, Practical Assessment.* Edited by Steve Hiller, Kristina Justh, Martha Kyrillidou, and Jim Self, 427–36. Washington, DC: Association of Research Libraries, 2010.

Archambault, Susan Gardner. "Charting Your Course: Using Curriculum Mapping to Enhance Information Literacy." In *Proceedings of the 2014 Library Assessment Conference: Building Effective, Sustainable, Practical Assessment.* Edited by Sarah Durso, Steve Hiller, Martha Kyrillidou, and Angela Pappalardo, 260–64. Washington, DC: Association of Research Libraries, 2014.

Ard, Constance. "Beyond Metrics: The Value of the Information Center." *Information Outlook* 16, no. 5 (2012): 16–18.

Asher, Andrew. "Who's Asking What? Modelling a Large Reference Interaction Dataset." In *Proceedings of the 2014 Library Assessment Conference: Building Effective, Sustainable, Practical Assessment.* Edited by Sarah Durso, Steve Hiller, Martha Kyrillidou, and Angela Pappalardo, 52–62. Washington, DC: Association of Research Libraries, 2014.

Asher, Andrew, and Lynda Duke. "Ethnography as an Assessment Tool: The ERIAL Project." In *Proceedings of the 2010 Library Assessment Conference: Building Effective, Sustainable, Practical Assessment.* Edited by Steve Hiller, Kristina Justh, Martha Kyrillidou, and Jim Self, 461–68. Washington, DC: Association of Research Libraries, 2010.

Askew, Consuella, and Marissa Ball. "Telling the Whole Story: A Mixed Methods Approach to Assessing Roaming Reference Services." In *Proceedings of the 2012 Library Assessment Conference: Building Effective, Sustainable, Practical Assessment.* Edited by Steve Hiller, Martha Kyrillidou, Angela Pappalardo, Jim Self, and Amy Yeager, 89–100. Washington, DC: Association of Research Libraries, 2012.

Asogwa, Brendan Eze. "Libraries in the Information Age: A Measure of Performance, Competencies and Constraints in Academic Libraries in Nigerian Universities." *Electronic Library* 32, no. 5 (2014): 603–21. doi:10.1108/EL-07-2012-0097.

* Please note that this represents a comprehensive list of the literature reviewed to this point in the project.

Association of College and Research Libraries. *Academic Library Contributions to Student Success: Documented Practices from the Field.* Prepared by Karen Brown. Contributions by Kara J. Malenfant. Chicago: Association of College and Research Libraries, 2015. http://www.ala.org/acrl/sites/ala.org.acrl/files/content/issues/value/contributions_report.pdf.

———. *Documented Library Contributions to Student Learning and Success: Building Evidence with Team-Based Assessment in Action Campus Projects.* Prepared by Karen Brown with contributions by Kara J. Malenfant. Chicago: Association of College and Research Libraries, 2016. http://www.ala.org/acrl/sites/ala.org.acrl/files/content/issues/value/contributions_y2.pdf.

———. *Standards for Libraries in Higher Education.* Chicago: Association of College and Research Libraries, 2011. http://www.ala.org/acrl/standards/standardslibraries.

Aversa, Elizabeth, and Steven Maccall. "Profiles in Retention, Part 1: Design Characteristics of a Graduate Synchronous Online Program." *Journal of Education for Library and Information Science* 54, no. 2 (2013): 147–61.

Bailey, Susan, and Claudia Dale. "On Becoming a Process-Focused Library." In *Proceedings of the 2010 Library Assessment Conference: Building Effective, Sustainable, Practical Assessment.* Edited by Steve Hiller, Kristina Justh, Martha Kyrillidou, and Jim Self, 633–42. Washington, DC: Association of Research Libraries, 2010.

Bailey, Susan, and Megan Slemons. "Halt! Who Goes There? Assessing Library Use with Turnstile Data." In *Proceedings of the 2014 Library Assessment Conference: Building Effective, Sustainable, Practical Assessment.* Edited by Sarah Durso, Steve Hiller, Martha Kyrillidou, and Angela Pappalardo, 406–12. Washington, DC: Association of Research Libraries, 2014.

Bakkalbasi, Nisa, Jason Kopp, Jonathan Paulo, Donna Sundre, Stefanie Warlick, and Sara Williams. "Utilizing Cross-Campus Collaboration to Improve the Assessment of Information Literacy." In *Proceedings of the 2012 Library Assessment Conference: Building Effective, Sustainable, Practical Assessment.* Edited by Steve Hiller, Martha Kyrillidou, Angela Pappalardo, Jim Self, and Amy Yeager, 153–60. Washington, DC: Association of Research Libraries, 2012.

Bakkalbasi, Nisa, and Jocelyn Wilk. "Getting to Know You (and Me!): Assessment and the Archival Metrics Toolkit at Columbia University's Rare Book and Manuscript Library." In *Proceedings of the 2014 Library Assessment Conference: Building Effective, Sustainable, Practical Assessment.* Edited by Sarah Durso, Steve Hiller, Martha Kyrillidou, and Angela Pappalardo, 194–203. Washington, DC: Association of Research Libraries, 2014.

Bakoyéma, Fagdéba Adjola. "Engaging Library Websites Users through Usability Testing and Inquiries Using Morae." In *Proceedings of the 2010 Library Assessment Conference: Building Effective, Sustainable, Practical Assessment.* Edited by Steve Hiller, Kristina Justh, Martha Kyrillidou, and Jim Self, 547–56. Washington, DC: Association of Research Libraries, 2010.

Balcom, Lesley, Jeff Carter, and James MacKenzie. "A Usable Movable Feast: Usability and the Mobile Library Website." In *Proceedings of the 2010 Library Assessment Conference: Building Effective, Sustainable, Practical Assessment.* Edited by Steve Hiller, Kristina Justh, Martha Kyrillidou, and Jim Self, 359–68. Washington, DC: Association of Research Libraries, 2010.

Ball, Matt, and Meridith Wolnick. "You Don't Say? Students at the University of Virginia Come Clean When Asked, 'What Are You Doing and How Can We Help?'" In *Proceedings of the 2010 Library Assessment Conference: Building Effective, Sustainable, Practical Assessment.* Edited by Steve Hiller, Kristina Justh, Martha Kyrillidou, and Jim Self, 181–94. Washington, DC: Association of Research Libraries, 2010.

Baudino, Frank, and Carolyn Johnson, eds. *Brick and Click: An Academic Library Conference.* Proceedings of Brick and Click Conference, November 7, 2014. Maryville: Northwest Missouri State University, 2014. http://files.eric.ed.gov/fulltext/ED549163.pdf.

Baumgart, Steve, Erin Carillo, and Laura Schmidli. "Iterative Chat Transcript Analysis." In *Proceedings of the 2014 Library Assessment Conference: Building Effective, Sustainable, Practical Assessment.* Edited by Sarah Durso, Steve Hiller, Martha Kyrillidou, and Angela Pappalardo, 637–57. Washington, DC: Association of Research Libraries, 2014.

Beard, Colin, and David Bawden. "University Libraries and the Postgraduate Student: Physical and Virtual Spaces." *New Library World* 113, no. 9 (2012): 439–47. doi:10.1108/03074801211273911.

Becnel, Kim, Robin A. Moeller, and Jon C. Pope. "Powerful Partnerships: The Worth of Embedding Masters Level Library Science Students in Undergraduate Classes." *Journal of Education for Library and Information Science Online* 57, no. 1 (2016): 31–42. doi:10.12783/issn.2328-2967/57/1/3.

Belanger, Jackie, Ning Zou, Jenny Rushing Mills, Claire Holmes, and Megan Oakleaf. "Project RAILS: Lessons Learned about Rubric Assessment of Information Literacy Skills." *portal: Libraries and the Academy* 15, no. 4 (2015): 623–44.

Benedetti, Allison, Keith Weimer, and Kornelia Tancheva. "Completing Assessment Projects When It Is Only Part of My Job." In *Proceedings of the 2014 Library Assessment Conference: Building Effective, Sustainable, Practical Assessment*. Edited by Sarah Durso, Steve Hiller, Martha Kyrillidou, and Angela Pappalardo, 658–65. Washington, DC: Association of Research Libraries, 2014.

Bennett, Scott. "Putting Learning into Library Planning." *portal: Libraries and the Academy* 15, no. 2 (2014): 215–31. doi:10.1353/pla.2015.0014.

Bicknell-Holmes, Tracy. "Fitting a Round Peg into a Square Hole: Dickeson's Academic Program Prioritization and Libraries." In *Proceedings of the 2014 Library Assessment Conference: Building Effective, Sustainable, Practical Assessment*. Edited by Sarah Durso, Steve Hiller, Martha Kyrillidou, and Angela Pappalardo, 159–82. Washington, DC: Association of Research Libraries, 2014.

Bielavitz, Tom. "The Balanced Scorecard: A Systemic Model for Evaluation and Assessment of Learning Outcomes?" *Evidence Based Library and Information Practice* 5, no. 2 (2010): 35–46.. http://archives.pdx.edu/ds/psu/7358.

Bietila, David. "Beyond Usability: Building Discovery Tool Requirements through User Stories." In *Proceedings of the 2012 Library Assessment Conference: Building Effective, Sustainable, Practical Assessment*. Edited by Steve Hiller, Martha Kyrillidou, Angela Pappalardo, Jim Self, and Amy Yeager, 425–34. Washington, DC: Association of Research Libraries, 2012.

Bird, Amanda, Kelly Rhodes McBride, and Elizabeth Cramer. "Modeling ACRL's Standards for Libraries in Higher Education." *College and Research Libraries News* 75, no. 11 (2014): 614–16. http://crln.acrl.org/index.php/crlnews/article/view/9228/10243.

Bishop, Bradley, Tony H. Grubesic, and Theresa Parrish. "Collaborative Development and Assessment of Student Learning Outcomes for LIS Electives." *Journal of Education for Library and Information Science Online* 56, no. 4 (2015): 272–82. doi:10.12783/issn.2328-2967/56/4/1.

Bishop, Katie. "Flipping, Collaborating, Assessing: Adopting New Modes of Library Instruction." In *Proceedings of the 2014 Library Assessment Conference: Building Effective, Sustainable, Practical Assessment*. Edited by Sarah Durso, Steve Hiller, Martha Kyrillidou, and Angela Pappalardo, 227–32. Washington, DC: Association of Research Libraries, 2014.

Boeninger, Chad, Deborah Daniels, Jeff Ferrier, Sara Harrington, and Janet Hulm. "Expressing Value in a Changing Budget Climate." In *Proceedings of the 2014 Library Assessment Conference: Building Effective, Sustainable, Practical Assessment*. Edited by Sarah Durso, Steve Hiller, Martha Kyrillidou, and Angela Pappalardo, 413–18. Washington, DC: Association of Research Libraries, 2014.

Bollinger, Stephen, Nina Exner, and Octavious Spruill. "Trying to Measure Success: A Mid-size Academic Library Grapples with Assessing a Popular Tablet Loan Project." In "Mobile Devices: Services with Intention," edited by Rebecca K. Miller, Heather Moorefield-Lange, and Carolyn Meier. *Library Technology Reports* 51, no. 7 (October 2015): 9–15.

Bowen, William G. *Issues Facing Major Research Universities at a Time of Stress AND Opportunity*. Issue Brief. New York: Ithaka S+R, April 12, 2016. http://www.sr.ithaka.org/wp-content/uploads/2016/04/SR_Issue_Brief_Issues_Facing_Major_Research_Universities041216.pdf.

Bowlby, Raynna. "Are We There Yet? Aligning Planning and Metrics, Strategically." In *Proceedings of the 2010 Library As-*

sessment Conference: Building Effective, Sustainable, Practical Assessment. Edited by Steve Hiller, Kristina Justh, Martha Kyrillidou, and Jim Self, 437–48. Washington, DC: Association of Research Libraries, 2010.

Bowlby, Raynna, and Daniel O'Mahony. "Tracking Academic Outcomes: What LibQUAL+(R) Tells Us about How Users View Information Literacy Outcomes." In *Proceedings of the 2012 Library Assessment Conference: Building Effective, Sustainable, Practical Assessment.* Edited by Steve Hiller, Martha Kyrillidou, Angela Pappalardo, Jim Self, and Amy Yeager, 669–84. Washington, DC: Association of Research Libraries, 2012.

Bowles-Terry, Melissa. "Library Instruction and Academic Success: A Mixed-Methods Assessment of a Library Instruction Program." *Evidence Based Library and Information Practice* 7, no. 1 (2012): 82–95. doi:10.18438/B8PS4D.

Bradshaw, Agnes, and Kathryn Crowe. "Shop Your Way to Service Excellence: Secret Shopping for Academic Libraries." In *Proceedings of the 2012 Library Assessment Conference: Building Effective, Sustainable, Practical Assessment.* Edited by Steve Hiller, Martha Kyrillidou, Angela Pappalardo, Jim Self, and Amy Yeager, 101–16. Washington, DC: Association of Research Libraries, 2012.

Britton, Scott. "Mining Library and University Data to Understand Library Use Patterns." In *Proceedings of the 2012 Library Assessment Conference: Building Effective, Sustainable, Practical Assessment.* Edited by Steve Hiller, Martha Kyrillidou, Angela Pappalardo, Jim Self, and Amy Yeager, 633–42. Washington, DC: Association of Research Libraries, 2012.

Broady-Preston, Judith, and Alison Lobo. "Measuring the Quality, Value and Impact of Academic Libraries: The Role of External Standards." *Performance Measurement Metrics* 12, no. 2 (2011): 122–35. doi:10.1108/14678041111149327.

Broussard, Mary J. Snyder. "Using Games to Make Formative Assessment Fun in the Academic Library." *Journal of Academic Librarianship* 40, no. 1 (2014): 35–42. doi:10.1016/j.acalib.2012.12.001.

Brown, Elizabeth. "Game of Clones: Using Analytical Research Data to Identify Institutional Peers and Collections Needs." In *Proceedings of the 2012 Library Assessment Conference: Building Effective, Sustainable, Practical Assessment.* Edited by Steve Hiller, Martha Kyrillidou, Angela Pappalardo, Jim Self, and Amy Yeager, 643–56. Washington, DC: Association of Research Libraries, 2012.

Brown, Jeanne. "Developing a Library Value Indicator for a Disciplinary Population." In *Proceedings of the 2010 Library Assessment Conference: Building Effective, Sustainable, Practical Assessment.* Edited by Steve Hiller, Kristina Justh, Martha Kyrillidou, and Jim Self, 643–52. Washington, DC: Association of Research Libraries, 2010.

———. "Quest for Continuous Improvement: Gathering Feedback and Data through Multiple Methods to Evaluate and Improve a Library's Discovery Tool." In *Proceedings of the 2012 Library Assessment Conference: Building Effective, Sustainable, Practical Assessment.* Edited by Steve Hiller, Martha Kyrillidou, Angela Pappalardo, Jim Self, and Amy Yeager, 603–14. Washington, DC: Association of Research Libraries, 2012.

Brown, Jessie, and Martin Kurzweil. *Breaking the Iron Triangle at the University of Central Florida.* Case Study. New York: Ithaka S+R, August 26, 2015. http://www.sr.ithaka.org/wp-content/uploads/2015/09/SR_Case_Study_Breaking_The_Iron_Triangle_University_Of_Central_Florida082615.pdf.

———. *Collaborating for Student Success at Valencia College.* Case Study. New York: Ithaka S+R, October 29, 2015. http://www.sr.ithaka.org/wp-content/uploads/2015/10/SR_Case_Study_Collaborating_Student_Success_Valencia_College1029151.pdf.

———. *Student Success by Design: CUNY's Guttman Community College.* Case Study. New York: Ithaka S+R, February 4, 2016. http://www.sr.ithaka.org/wp-content/uploads/2016/02/SR_Case_Study_Student_Success_by_Design_Guttman020416.pdf.

Brown, Jessie, and Deanna Marcum. *Serving the Adult Student at University of Maryland University College.* Case Study. New York: Ithaka S+R, June 9, 2016. http://www.sr.ithaka.org/wp-content/uploads/2016/06/SR_Case_Study_Serving_Adult_Student_UMUC_060916.pdf.

Brown, Jessie, and Richard Spies. *Reshaping System Culture at the North Carolina Community College System.* Case Study.

New York: Ithaka S+R, September 10, 2015. http://www.sr.ithaka.org/wp-content/uploads/2015/09/SR_Case_Study_Reshaping_System_Culture_North_Carolina_Community_College_System091015.pdf.

Brown-Sica, Margaret. "Using Academic Courses to Generate Data for Use in Evidence Based Library Planning." *Journal of Academic Librarianship* 39, no. 3 (2013): 275–87. doi:10.1016/j.acalib.2013.01.001.

Brungard, Allison, David Nolfi, Marcia Rapchak, Bridget Euliano, Tracie Ballock, and Joseph Nelson. "Thunderstruck! An 'En-Lightning' Look at Recharging Existing Library Data to Electrify University Administration." In *Proceedings of the 2014 Library Assessment Conference: Building Effective, Sustainable, Practical Assessment*. Edited by Sarah Durso, Steve Hiller, Martha Kyrillidou, and Angela Pappalardo, 419–24. Washington, DC: Association of Research Libraries, 2014.

Brunvand, Amy. "Ask the Expert: Using Expertise Domains for Library Service Assessment." In *Proceedings of the 2010 Library Assessment Conference: Building Effective, Sustainable, Practical Assessment*. Edited by Steve Hiller, Kristina Justh, Martha Kyrillidou, and Jim Self, 571–80. Washington, DC: Association of Research Libraries, 2010.

Burger, Robert H., Paula T. Kaufman, and Amy L. Atkinson. "Disturbingly Weak: The Current State of Financial Management Education in Library and Information Science Curricula." *Journal of Education for Library and Information Science Online* 56, no. 3 (2015): 190–97. doi:10.12783/issn.2328-2967/56/3/2.

Carbery, Alan. "Puzzle Pieces: Assessing Student Work Using Rubrics and Citation Analysis for Dual-Purpose Assessment." In *Proceedings of the 2014 Library Assessment Conference: Building Effective, Sustainable, Practical Assessment*. Edited by Sarah Durso, Steve Hiller, Martha Kyrillidou, and Angela Pappalardo, 233–35. Washington, DC: Association of Research Libraries, 2014.

Carlson, Theresa, and Wendy Holliday. "Creating a Culture of Evidence and Assessment: Building a Daily Practice That Matters." In *Proceedings of the 2014 Library Assessment Conference: Building Effective, Sustainable, Practical Assessment*. Edited by Sarah Durso, Steve Hiller, Martha Kyrillidou, and Angela Pappalardo, 154–58. Washington, DC: Association of Research Libraries, 2014.

Carter, Lisa R. "Articulating Value: Building a Culture of Assessment in Special Collections." *RBM: A Journal of Rare Books, Manuscripts and Cultural Heritage* 13, no. 2 (2012): 89–99. http://rbm.acrl.org/index.php/rbm/article/view/376/376.

Celik, Osman, and Roxanne Peck. "If You Expand, They Will Come: Textbook Affordability through Expansion of Course Reserves: The Case of UCLA Library's Course Reserves via Strategic Partnership with the Campus Independent Bookstore." *Technical Services Quarterly* 33, no. 3 (2016): 268–78. doi:10.1080/07317131.2016.1169788.

Chadwell, Faye A. "Assessing the Value of Academic Library Consortia." *Journal of Library Administration* 51, no. 7–8 (2011): 645–61. doi:10.1080/01930826.2011.601268.

Chan, Diana L. H., and Edward Spodick. "Space Development: A Case Study of the HKUST Library." *New Library World* 115, no. 5–6 (2014): 250–62. doi:10.1108/NLW-04-2014-0042.

Chang, Bertha. "Assessing the Impact of a New Library on Graduate Students' Use of Library Spaces." In *Proceedings of the 2014 Library Assessment Conference: Building Effective, Sustainable, Practical Assessment*. Edited by Sarah Durso, Steve Hiller, Martha Kyrillidou, and Angela Pappalardo, 673–78. Washington, DC: Association of Research Libraries, 2014.

Chang, Bertha, and Honora Eskridge. "Practical Research for Library Space and Service Design." In *Proceedings of the 2012 Library Assessment Conference: Building Effective, Sustainable, Practical Assessment*. Edited by Steve Hiller, Martha Kyrillidou, Angela Pappalardo, Jim Self, and Amy Yeager, 239–50. Washington, DC: Association of Research Libraries, 2012.

Chapa, Kay, Kelly Gonzalez, and Richard Wayne. "Performance Measurement: Organizational Changes and Outcomes Monitoring." In *Proceedings of the 2010 Library Assessment Conference: Building Effective, Sustainable, Practical Assessment*. Edited by Steve Hiller, Kristina Justh, Martha Kyrillidou, and Jim Self, 449–60. Washington, DC: Association of Research Libraries, 2010.

Charles, Leslin H. "Using an Information Literacy Curriculum Map as a Means of Communication and Accountability for Stakeholders in Higher Education." *Journal of Information Literacy* 9, no. 1 (2015): 47–61. doi:10.11645/9.1.1959.

Cheng, Hong. "Turn a Disaster into a Research Opportunity: Assessing Our One-Hour Library Sessions after Hurricane Sandy." In *Proceedings of the 2014 Library Assessment Conference: Building Effective, Sustainable, Practical Assessment.* Edited by Sarah Durso, Steve Hiller, Martha Kyrillidou, and Angela Pappalardo, 236–45. Washington, DC: Association of Research Libraries, 2014.

Chew, Katherine, and Erinn Aspinall. "Serving Multiple Stakeholders: Crafting a 'Blended' Scorecard at the University of Minnesota Health Sciences Libraries." In *Proceedings of the 2010 Library Assessment Conference: Building Effective, Sustainable, Practical Assessment.* Edited by Steve Hiller, Kristina Justh, Martha Kyrillidou, and Jim Self, 335–44. Washington, DC: Association of Research Libraries, 2010.

Chew, Katherine, James Stemper, Mary Schoenborn, and Caroline Lilyard. "User-Defined Valued Metrics for Electronic Journals." In *Proceedings of the 2012 Library Assessment Conference: Building Effective, Sustainable, Practical Assessment.* Edited by Steve Hiller, Martha Kyrillidou, Angela Pappalardo, Jim Self, and Amy Yeager. Washington, DC: Association of Research Libraries, 2012.

Chrzastowski, Tina, Lynn Wiley, and Jean-Louise Zancanella. "Three E-Book Outlooks: What Humanists, Social Scientists and Scientists Want and Predict (A LibValue Study)." In *Proceedings of the 2014 Library Assessment Conference: Building Effective, Sustainable, Practical Assessment.* Edited by Sarah Durso, Steve Hiller, Martha Kyrillidou, and Angela Pappalardo, 520–25. Washington, DC: Association of Research Libraries, 2014.

Clarke, Kathy. "The Role of a Required Information Literacy Competency Exam in the First College Year: What Test Data Can, Cannot, and Might Reveal." In *Proceedings of the 2014 Library Assessment Conference: Building Effective, Sustainable, Practical Assessment.* Edited by Sarah Durso, Steve Hiller, Martha Kyrillidou, and Angela Pappalardo, 246–50. Washington, DC: Association of Research Libraries, 2014.

Colburn, Selene. "Herding Cats, Knitting Fog, and Nailing Pudding to the Wall: Toward a Mixed Methods Approach to Evaluating Social Media Marketing in Libraries." In *Proceedings of the 2012 Library Assessment Conference: Building Effective, Sustainable, Practical Assessment.* Edited by Steve Hiller, Martha Kyrillidou, Angela Pappalardo, Jim Self, and Amy Yeager, 615–24. Washington, DC: Association of Research Libraries, 2012.

Collins, Tim. "The Current Budget Environment and Its Impact on Libraries, Publishers and Vendors." *Journal of Library Administration* 52, no. 1 (2012): 18–35. doi:10.1080/01930826.2012.630643.

Connaway, Lynn Silipigni. "Why Libraries? A Call for Use-Centered Assessment." *Bid* 32 (2014), http://bid.ub.edu/en/32/connaway3.htm.

Cowan, Susanna M. "Information Literacy: The Battle We Won That We Lost?" *portal: Libraries and the Academy* 14, no. 1 (2014): 23–32. doi:10.1353/pla.2013.0049.

Cox, Brian L., and Margie H. Jantti. "Discovering the Impact of Library Use and Student Performance." *EDUCAUSE Review*, July 17, 2012, http://er.educause.edu/articles/2012/7/discovering-the-impact-of-library-use-and-student-performance.

Creaser, Claire, Susanne Cullen, Ruth Curtis, Nicola Darlington, Jane Maltby, Elizabeth Newall, and Valerie Spezi. "Working Together: Library Value at the University of Nottingham." *Performance Measurement and Metrics* 15, no. 1/2 (2014): 41–49. doi:10.1108/PMM-03-2014-0011.

Creaser, Claire, and Valerie Spezi. *Working Together: Evolving Value for Academic Libraries.* Thousand Oaks, CA: Sage Publications, 2012

Crowe, Kathryn. "Assessment = Improved Teaching and Learning: Using Rubrics to Measure Information Literacy Skills." In *Proceedings of the 2010 Library Assessment Conference: Building Effective, Sustainable, Practical Assessment.* Edited by Steve Hiller, Kristina Justh, Martha Kyrillidou, and Jim Self, 147–58. Washington, DC: Association of Research Libraries, 2010.

———. "Libraries and Student Success: A Campus Collaboration with High Impact Educational Practices." In *Proceedings of the 2014 Library Assessment Conference: Building Effective, Sustainable, Practical Assessment.* Edited by

Sarah Durso, Steve Hiller, Martha Kyrillidou, and Angela Pappalardo, 251–55. Washington, DC: Association of Research Libraries, 2014.

Crowe, Kathryn, and Michael Crumpton. "Defining the Libraries' Role in Research: A Needs Assessment; A Case Study." In *Proceedings of the 2014 Library Assessment Conference: Building Effective, Sustainable, Practical Assessment.* Edited by Sarah Durso, Steve Hiller, Martha Kyrillidou, and Angela Pappalardo, 321–33. Washington, DC: Association of Research Libraries, 2014.

Crum, Janet. "Using an Availability Study to Assess Access to Electronic Articles." In *Proceedings of the 2010 Library Assessment Conference: Building Effective, Sustainable, Practical Assessment.* Edited by Steve Hiller, Kristina Justh, Martha Kyrillidou, and Jim Self, 683–702. Washington, DC: Association of Research Libraries, 2010.

Crumpton, Michael, and Kathryn Crowe. "Sustaining an Assessment Mentality to Navigate Library Space Planning." In *Proceedings of the 2014 Library Assessment Conference: Building Effective, Sustainable, Practical Assessment.* Edited by Sarah Durso, Steve Hiller, Martha Kyrillidou, and Angela Pappalardo, 679–83. Washington, DC: Association of Research Libraries, 2014.

Cunningham, Nancy, and Meg Scharf. "Closing the Loop: How Are LibQUAL+(R) Results Being Communicated to Stakeholders?" In *Proceedings of the 2012 Library Assessment Conference: Building Effective, Sustainable, Practical Assessment.* Edited by Steve Hiller, Martha Kyrillidou, Angela Pappalardo, Jim Self, and Amy Yeager, 693–706. Washington, DC: Association of Research Libraries, 2012.

Dabbour, Katherine S., and James David Ballard. "Information Literacy and US Latino College Students: A Cross-Cultural Analysis." *New Library World* 112, no. 7/8 (2011): 347–64. doi:10.1108/03074801111150477.

Dahan, Suziyana Mat, Mohd Yusof Taib, Nurhaizan Mohd Zainudin, and Fadzida Ismail. "Surveying Users' Perception of Academic Library Services Quality: A Case Study in Universiti Malaysia Pahang (UMP) Library." *Journal of Academic Librarianship* 42, no. 1 (2015): 38–43. doi:10.1016/j.acalib.2015.10.006.

Dahlen, Sarah, and Pam Baker. "Assessing Information Literacy and Critical Thinking across the Curriculum." In *Proceedings of the 2014 Library Assessment Conference: Building Effective, Sustainable, Practical Assessment.* Edited by Sarah Durso, Steve Hiller, Martha Kyrillidou, and Angela Pappalardo, 462–69. Washington, DC: Association of Research Libraries, 2014.

Daly, Emily. "What Do We Do Now? Moving beyond Survey Results." In *Proceedings of the 2014 Library Assessment Conference: Building Effective, Sustainable, Practical Assessment.* Edited by Sarah Durso, Steve Hiller, Martha Kyrillidou, and Angela Pappalardo, 397–400. Washington, DC: Association of Research Libraries, 2014.

Daniels, William, Colin Darch, and Karin De Jager. "The Research Commons: A New Creature in the Library?" *Performance Measurement and Metrics* 11, no. 2 (2010): 116–30. doi:10.1108/14678041011064043.

Davidson, Catherine, and Aaron Lupton. "Mining E-Resource Data to Reveal Hidden Assets: How One School Dug Deeper into Its MINES for Libraries (R) Results to Assess the Research Value of E-Resources." In *Proceedings of the 2012 Library Assessment Conference: Building Effective, Sustainable, Practical Assessment.* Edited by Steve Hiller, Martha Kyrillidou, Angela Pappalardo, Jim Self, and Amy Yeager, 575–86. Washington, DC: Association of Research Libraries, 2012.

Davidson, Catherine, Dana Thomas, Martha Kyrillidou, and Terry Plum. "Measuring Use of Licensed Electronic Resources: A Progress Report on the Second Iteration of the MINES for Libraries (R) Survey on Scholars Portal and Other Resources for the Ontario Council of University Libraries." In *Proceedings of the 2010 Library Assessment Conference: Building Effective, Sustainable, Practical Assessment.* Edited by Steve Hiller, Kristina Justh, Martha Kyrillidou, and Jim Self, 395–416. Washington, DC: Association of Research Libraries, 2010.

Davidson, Karen S., Stephanie Havron Rollins, and Ed Cherry. "Demonstrating Our Value: Tying Use of Electronic Resources to Academic Success." *Serials Librarian* 65, no. 1 (2013): 74–79. doi:10.1080/0361526X.2013.800630.

de Jager, Karin. "Demonstrating Library Value: Appropriate Methodologies and Practical Approaches at the University of Cape Town." In *Proceedings of the 2014 Library Assessment Conference: Building Effective, Sustainable, Practi-*

cal Assessment. Edited by Sarah Durso, Steve Hiller, Martha Kyrillidou, and Angela Pappalardo, 545–48. Washington, DC: Association of Research Libraries, 2014.

Dempsey, Lorcan, Constance Malpas, and Brian Lavoie. "Collection Directions: The Evolution of Library Collections and Collecting." *portal: Libraries and the Academy* 14, no. 3 (2014): 393–423. doi:10.1353/pla.2014.0013.

Diep, Kim Chi, and Diane Nahl. "Information Literacy Instruction in Four Vietnamese University Libraries." *International Information and Library Review* 43, no. 4 (2011): 198–206. doi:10.1080/10572317.2011.10762901.

Diller, Karen, and Sue Phelps. "Multiple Methodologies for Space Assessment to Support Learning." In *Proceedings of the 2010 Library Assessment Conference: Building Effective, Sustainable, Practical Assessment*. Edited by Steve Hiller, Kristina Justh, Martha Kyrillidou, and Jim Self, 195–200. Washington, DC: Association of Research Libraries, 2010.

Dollinger, Elizabeth. "Rolling It Up: The Evolution of an Information Literacy Assessment Plan." In *Proceedings of the 2012 Library Assessment Conference: Building Effective, Sustainable, Practical Assessment*. Edited by Steve Hiller, Martha Kyrillidou, Angela Pappalardo, Jim Self, and Amy Yeager, 285–92. Washington, DC: Association of Research Libraries, 2012.

Donahue, Annie. "Charting Success: Using Practical Measures to Assess Student Learning in a Peer2Peer Model." In *Proceedings of the 2012 Library Assessment Conference: Building Effective, Sustainable, Practical Assessment*. Edited by Steve Hiller, Martha Kyrillidou, Angela Pappalardo, Jim Self, and Amy Yeager, 501–12. Washington, DC: Association of Research Libraries, 2012.

Dryden, Nancy H., and Shelley Goldstein. "Regional Campus Learning Commons: Assessing to Meet Student Needs." *Journal of Library Administration* 53, no. 5/6 (2013): 293–322. doi:10.1080/01930826.2013.876822.

Duerr, Larry, and Jodi Eastberg. "Beyond the Annotated Bibliography: Engaging Students with Library Collections." *College and Research Libraries News* 73, no. 8 (2012): 478–80.

Dupont, Christian, and Elizabeth Yakel. "'What's So Special about Special Collections?' Or, Assessing the Value Special Collections Bring to Academic Libraries." In *Proceedings of the 2010 Library Assessment Conference: Building Effective, Sustainable, Practical Assessment*. Edited by Steve Hiller, Kristina Justh, Martha Kyrillidou, and Jim Self, 417–26. Washington, DC: Association of Research Libraries, 2010.

Eaton, Judith. "Higher Education in a New Era of Public Accountability: What Does This Mean for You?" In *Proceedings of the 2012 Library Assessment Conference: Building Effective, Sustainable, Practical Assessment*. Edited by Steve Hiller, Martha Kyrillidou, Angela Pappalardo, Jim Self, and Amy Yeager, 23–26. Washington, DC: Association of Research Libraries, 2012.

Einasto, Olga. "Transforming Library Communication: From Gutenberg to Zuckerberg." *New Library World* 116, no. 5/6 (2015): 247–63. doi:10.1108/NLW-05-2014-0055.

Elmborg, James. "Tending the Garden of Learning: Lifelong Learning as Core Library Value." *Library Trends* 64, no. 3 (2016): 533–55. http://muse.jhu.edu/journals/library_trends/v064/64.3.elmborg.pdf.

Emmons, Mark, and Frances C. Wilkinson. "The Academic Library Impact on Student Persistence." *College and Research Libraries* 74, no. 1 (2011): 128–49. doi:10.5860/crl-74r1.

Entlich, Richard. "Focus on Circulation Snapshots: A Powerful Tool for Print Collection Assessment." In *Proceedings of the 2010 Library Assessment Conference: Building Effective, Sustainable, Practical Assessment*. Edited by Steve Hiller, Kristina Justh, Martha Kyrillidou, and Jim Self, 703–14. Washington, DC: Association of Research Libraries, 2010.

Escobar, Hector, and Heidi Gauder. "Integrated Service Spaces: New Ways of Assessing Collaboration." In *Proceedings of the 2014 Library Assessment Conference: Building Effective, Sustainable, Practical Assessment*. Edited by Sarah Durso, Steve Hiller, Martha Kyrillidou, and Angela Pappalardo, 684–86. Washington, DC: Association of Research Libraries, 2014.

Fagan, Jody Condit. "The Effectiveness of Academic Library Deans and Directors: A Literature Review." *Library Leadership and Management* 26, no. 1 (2012): 1–19.

Farkas, Meredith Gorran. "Building and Sustaining a Culture of Assessment: Effective Practices for Change Leadership." *Reference Services Review* 41, no. 1 (2013): 13–31. doi:10.1108/00907321311300857.

Farkas, Meredith Gorran, and Lisa Janicke Hinchliffe. "Library Faculty and Instructional Assessment: Creating a Culture of Assessment through the High Performance Programming Model of Organizational Transformation." In *Proceedings of the 2012 Library Assessment Conference: Building Effective, Sustainable, Practical Assessment.* Edited by Steve Hiller, Martha Kyrillidou, Angela Pappalardo, Jim Self, and Amy Yeager, 161–70. Washington, DC: Association of Research Libraries, 2012.

Farmer, Lesley. "Programmatic Role of Education Libraries in Informatics to Support Preservice Teacher Preparation Programs." *Teachers College Record* 112, no. 10 (2010): 2603–22. http://www.scopus.com/inward/record.url?eid=2-s2.0-78650404796&partnerID=40&md5=861e2e7ebfdf5351a87158a7a4b288cf.

Fazal, Shafeek. "Library Strategic Planning for Middle States Accreditation: A 10-Year Road to Success." *Journal of Library Administration* 56, no. 1 (2015): 27–40. doi:10.1080/01930826.2015.1105027.

Felix, Elliott. "Designing and Assessing Library Services." In *Proceedings of the 2012 Library Assessment Conference: Building Effective, Sustainable, Practical Assessment.* Edited by Steve Hiller, Martha Kyrillidou, Angela Pappalardo, Jim Self, and Amy Yeager, 251–60. Washington, DC: Association of Research Libraries, 2012.

Fister, Barbara. "Critical Assets: Academic Libraries, A View from the Administration Building." *Library Journal* 135, no. 8 (2010): 24–27.

Fleming-May, Rachel, Regina Mays, and Anne Pemberton. "Academic Libraries' Support for Teaching: A LibValue Project." In *Proceedings of the 2014 Library Assessment Conference: Building Effective, Sustainable, Practical Assessment.* Edited by Sarah Durso, Steve Hiller, Martha Kyrillidou, and Angela Pappalardo, 526–28. Washington, DC: Association of Research Libraries, 2014.

Fleming-May, Rachel A., Regina Mays, and Rachel Radom. "'I Never Had to Use the Library in High School:' A Library Instruction Program for At-Risk Students." *portal: Libraries and the Academy* 15, no. 3 (2015): 433–56. doi:10.1353/pla.2015.0038.Fleming-May, Rachel, and Crystal Sherline. "What Impact Do Academic Libraries Have on Teaching and Learning? A Review of the Literature and Preliminary Taxonomy of Standards." In *Proceedings of the 2010 Library Assessment Conference: Building Effective, Sustainable, Practical Assessment.* Edited by Steve Hiller, Kristina Justh, Martha Kyrillidou, and Jim Self, 485–98. Washington, DC: Association of Research Libraries, 2010.

Fontno, Tiffeni J., and Dianne N. Brown. "Putting Information Literacy in the Students' Hands: The Elementary Learning Centers Approach Applied to Instruction in Higher Education." *College and Research Libraries News* 76, no. 2 (2015): 92–96. http://crln.acrl.org/index.php/crlnews/article/view/9263/10313.

Foster, Nancy Fried. "The Librarian-Student-Faculty Triangle: Conflicting Research Strategies?" In *Proceedings of the 2010 Library Assessment Conference: Building Effective, Sustainable, Practical Assessment.* Edited by Steve Hiller, Kristina Justh, Martha Kyrillidou, and Jim Self, 469–76. Washington, DC: Association of Research Libraries, 2010.

Fox, Robert, and Ameet Doshi. "Longitudinal Assessment of 'User-Driven' Library Commons Spaces." In *Proceedings of the 2010 Library Assessment Conference: Building Effective, Sustainable, Practical Assessment.* Edited by Steve Hiller, Kristina Justh, Martha Kyrillidou, and Jim Self, 63–72. Washington, DC: Association of Research Libraries, 2010.

Franklin, Brinley. "MINES for E-Books." In *Proceedings of the 2012 Library Assessment Conference: Building Effective, Sustainable, Practical Assessment.* Edited by Steve Hiller, Martha Kyrillidou, Angela Pappalardo, Jim Self, and Amy Yeager, 587–602. Washington, DC: Association of Research Libraries, 2012.

———. "Surviving to Thriving: Advancing the Institutional Mission and Goals." *Journal of Library Administration* 52, no. 1 (2012): 94–107. doi:10.1080/01930826.2012.630244.

Friesen, Margaret, Bailey Diers, and Suher Zaher-Mazawi. "Towards Democratizing Library Data: Data Management and Sharing in the Institutional Repository." In *Proceedings of the 2010 Library Assessment Conference: Building*

Effective, Sustainable, Practical Assessment. Edited by Steve Hiller, Kristina Justh, Martha Kyrillidou, and Jim Self, 201–13. Washington, DC: Association of Research Libraries, 2010.

Gan, Laurissa B., and Greg F. Pratt. "Using Library Search Service Metrics to Demonstrate Library Value and Manage Workload." *Journal of the Medical Library Association* 101, no. 3 (2013): 227–29. doi:10.3163/1536-5050.101.3.015.

Gap Analysis Subcommittee. *Final Report to ACRL VAL Committee from Gap Analysis Subcommittee Presented for ALA Annual Conference 2015*. Chicago: Association of College and Research Libraries, 2015. http://www.acrl.ala.org/value/wp-content/uploads/2016/04/VAL-Cmte-Gap-Analysis-FINAL-ALA-Annual-2015.pdf.

———. *A Report to ACRL VAL Committee from the Gap Analysis Subcommittee, Presented for ALA Midwinter 2015*. Chicago: Association of College and Research Libraries, 2015. http://www.acrl.ala.org/value/wp-content/uploads/2016/04/VAL-Cmte-Gap-Analysis-ALA-Midwinter-2015.pdf.

Garcia, Larissa. "Applying the Framework for Information Literacy to the Developmental Education Classroom." *Community and Junior College Libraries* 20, no. 1/2 (2014): 39–47. doi:10.1080/02763915.2014.1013399.

Gardner, Julia, and Leah Richardson. "Beyond the Cabinet of Curiosities: Demonstrating the Impact of Special Collections Instruction." In *Proceedings of the 2014 Library Assessment Conference: Building Effective, Sustainable, Practical Assessment*. Edited by Sarah Durso, Steve Hiller, Martha Kyrillidou, and Angela Pappalardo, 204–11. Washington, DC: Association of Research Libraries, 2014.

Gardner, Susan, and Elisa Slater Acosta. "Using a Rubric to Assess Freshman English Literacy Instruction." In *Proceedings of the 2010 Library Assessment Conference: Building Effective, Sustainable, Practical Assessment*. Edited by Steve Hiller, Kristina Justh, Martha Kyrillidou, and Jim Self, 159–74. Washington, DC: Association of Research Libraries, 2010.

Gariepy, Laura, and Jenny Stout. "Using Rubrics for Programmatic Assessment of Learning Outcomes in Course-Integrated Library Instruction." In *Proceedings of the 2014 Library Assessment Conference: Building Effective, Sustainable, Practical Assessment*. Edited by Sarah Durso, Steve Hiller, Martha Kyrillidou, and Angela Pappalardo, 256–59. Washington, DC: Association of Research Libraries, 2014.

Gazzolo, Paul. "Insider's Perspective: Academic Libraries Take Back the Power." *Information Today* 32, no. 2 (March 2015): 18. http://www.infotoday.com/it/mar15/index.shtml.

Gerke, Jennifer, and Jack M. Maness. "The Physical and the Virtual: The Relationship between Library as Place and Electronic Collections." *College and Research Libraries* 71, no. 1 (2010): 20–31.

Giesecke, Joan. "The Value of Partnerships: Building New Partnerships for Success." *Journal of Library Administration* 52, no. 1 (2012): 36–52. doi:10.1080/01930826.2012.629964.

Gilchrist, Debra. "Leading with Strategy and Evidence." In *Proceedings of the 2014 Library Assessment Conference: Building Effective, Sustainable, Practical Assessment*. Edited by Sarah Durso, Steve Hiller, Martha Kyrillidou, and Angela Pappalardo, 23–30. Washington, DC: Association of Research Libraries, 2014.

Greenwood, Judy T., Alex P. Watson, and Melissa Dennis. "Ten Years of LibQual: A Study of Qualitative and Quantitative Survey Results at the University of Mississippi 2001–2010." *Journal of Academic Librarianship* 37, no. 4 (2011): 312–18. doi:10.1016/j.acalib.2011.04.005.

Griffin, Melanie, Barbara Lewis, and Mark Greenberg. "Data-Driven Decision Making: A Holistic Approach to Assessment in Special Collections Repositories." In *Proceedings of the 2012 Library Assessment Conference: Building Effective, Sustainable, Practical Assessment*. Edited by Steve Hiller, Martha Kyrillidou, Angela Pappalardo, Jim Self, and Amy Yeager, 381–96. Washington, DC: Association of Research Libraries, 2012.

Guo, Shu. "Grade Trend Analysis for a Credit-Bearing Library Instruction Course." *portal: Libraries and the Academy* 15, no. 2 (2015): 251–265. doi:10.1353/pla.2015.0018.

Guthrie, Kevin M., Christine Mulhern, and Martin A. Kurzweil. In *Pursuit of Excellence and Inclusion: Managing Change at Arizona State University*. New York: Ithaka S+R, January 20, 2015. http://www.sr.ithaka.org/wp-content/uploads/2015/08/SR_Report_Managing_Change_ASU_012015.pdf.

Habich, Elizabeth, and Karen Merguerian. "Evaluating the Impact of Library Renovation: A Multiple Methods Approach." In *Proceedings of the 2014 Library Assessment Conference: Building Effective, Sustainable, Practical As-*

sessment. Edited by Sarah Durso, Steve Hiller, Martha Kyrillidou, and Angela Pappalardo, 483–89. Washington, DC: Association of Research Libraries, 2014.

Haddow, Gaby, and Jayanthi Joseph. "Loans, Logins, and Lasting the Course: Academic Library Use and Student Retention." *Australian Academic and Research Libraries* 41, no. 4 (2010): 233–44. doi:10.1080/00048623.2010.10721478.

Hagel, Pauline, Anne Horn, Sue Owen, and Michael Currie. "'How Can We Help?' The Contribution of University Libraries to Student Retention." *Australian Academic and Research Libraries* 43, no. 3 (2012): 214–30.

Hall, Monena. "Roving: Aimless or Purposeful?" In *Proceedings of the 2014 Library Assessment Conference: Building Effective, Sustainable, Practical Assessment*. Edited by Sarah Durso, Steve Hiller, Martha Kyrillidou, and Angela Pappalardo, 425–31. Washington, DC: Association of Research Libraries, 2014.

Hansson, Joacim. "Documentality and Legitimacy in Future Libraries: An Analytical Framework for Initiated Speculation." *New Library World* 116, no. 1/2 (2015): 4–14. doi:10.1108/NLW-05-2014-0046.

Harvey, Diane, Yvonne Belanger, Emily Daly, and Linda Daniel. "Know Thy User: The Duke Libraries User Studies Initiative." In *Proceedings of the 2010 Library Assessment Conference: Building Effective, Sustainable, Practical Assessment*. Edited by Steve Hiller, Kristina Justh, Martha Kyrillidou, and Jim Self, 213–24. Washington, DC: Association of Research Libraries, 2010.

Harvey, Eugene, and Maureen Lindstrom. "LibQUAL+(R) and the Information Commons Initiative at Buffalo State College." In *Proceedings of the 2010 Library Assessment Conference: Building Effective, Sustainable, Practical Assessment*. Edited by Steve Hiller, Kristina Justh, Martha Kyrillidou, and Jim Self, 73–88. Washington, DC: Association of Research Libraries, 2010.

Head, Ronald B. "Evidence-Based Management and Community College Decision-Making." *Journal of Applied Research in the Community College* 22, no. 1 (2015): 25–33.

Hensley, Merinda Kaye. "A Survey of Instructional Support for Undergraduate Research Programs." *portal: Libraries and the Academy* 15, no. 4 (2016): 719–62.

Herman, Matthew, Robert Thomas, and Mario Violich. "Shaping Community: Re-creating Connectivity on Campus through Student Life." *Planning for Higher Education Journal* 43, no. 4 (2015): 26–40.

Hersey, Denise, and Francine De Franco. "Do We Have What It Takes? Assessing Liaison Librarians' Skill Sets to Build Strong Partnerships and Ensure Better Outreach in a Quickly Changing Research and Learning Environment." In *Proceedings of the 2012 Library Assessment Conference: Building Effective, Sustainable, Practical Assessment*. Edited by Steve Hiller, Martha Kyrillidou, Angela Pappalardo, Jim Self, and Amy Yeager, 127–34. Washington, DC: Association of Research Libraries, 2012.

Hess, Amanda Nichols. "Equipping Academic Librarians to Integrate the Framework into Instructional Practices: A Theoretical Application." *Journal of Academic Librarianship* 41, no. 6 (2015): 771–76. doi:10.1016/j.acalib.2015.08.017.

Hess, Amanda Nichols, and James L. Moseley. "Conducting Formative Evaluation Online: From Planning to Execution." *College and Research Libraries News* 77, no. 2 (2016): 66–69. http://crln.acrl.org/index.php/crlnews/article/view/9442/10671.

Hess, Kirk, and Sarah Hoover. "Value of the Online Newspaper Collection at the University of Illinois at Urbana-Champaign Library." In *Proceedings of the 2014 Library Assessment Conference: Building Effective, Sustainable, Practical Assessment*. Edited by Sarah Durso, Steve Hiller, Martha Kyrillidou, and Angela Pappalardo, 292–307. Washington, DC: Association of Research Libraries, 2014.

Hiller, Steve, Kristina Justh, Martha Kyrillidou, and Jim Self, eds. *Proceedings of the 2010 Library Assessment Conference: Building Effective, Sustainable, Practical Assessment*. Washington, DC: Association of Research Libraries, 2010.

Hiller, Steve, and Betsy Wilson. "Making the Case for Institutional Investment in Libraries: The Value of Evidence-Based Narratives at the University of Washington." In *Proceedings of the 2012 Library Assessment Conference: Building*

Effective, Sustainable, Practical Assessment. Edited by Steve Hiller, Martha Kyrillidou, Angela Pappalardo, Jim Self, and Amy Yeager, 345–54. Washington, DC: Association of Research Libraries, 2012.

Hinchliffe, Lisa, and Kara Malenfant. "What Do We Want to Know: Articulating a Research Agenda for the Value of Academic Libraries." In *Proceedings of the 2012 Library Assessment Conference: Building Effective, Sustainable, Practical Assessment.* Edited by Steve Hiller, Martha Kyrillidou, Angela Pappalardo, Jim Self, and Amy Yeager, 27–34. Washington, DC: Association of Research Libraries, 2012.

Hinchliffe, Lisa Janicke, and Meredith Farkas. "Community College Libraries and Culture of Assessment: A Survey of Library Leaders." In *Proceedings of the 2014 Library Assessment Conference: Building Effective, Sustainable, Practical Assessment.* Edited by Sarah Durso, Steve Hiller, Martha Kyrillidou, and Angela Pappalardo, 183–87. Washington, DC: Association of Research Libraries, 2014.

Hinchliffe, Lisa Janicke, and Melissa Autumn Wong. "From Services-Centered to Student-Centered: A 'Wellness Wheel' Approach to Developing the Library as an Integrative Learning Commons." *College and Undergraduate Libraries* 17, no. 2/3 (2010): 213–24. doi:10.1080/10691316.2010.490772.

Hintz, Kimberley, Paula Farrar, Shirin Eshghi, Barbara Sobol, Jo-Anne Naslund, Teresa Lee, Tara Stephens, and Aleha McCauley. "Letting Students Take the Lead: A User-Centered Approach to Evaluating Subject Guides." *Evidence Based Library and Information Practice* 5, no. 4 (2010): 39–52. https://journals.library.ualberta.ca/eblip/index.php/EBLIP/article/view/8663/7523.

Holmes, John, and Kathleen Collins. "Viral Reference in the Writing Center: Using Metrics to Reinvent Library Reference." In *Proceedings of the 2014 Library Assessment Conference: Building Effective, Sustainable, Practical Assessment.* Edited by Sarah Durso, Steve Hiller, Martha Kyrillidou, and Angela Pappalardo, 696. Washington, DC: Association of Research Libraries, 2014.

Hornby, Amanda, Louise Richards, and Jill McKinstry. "Learning in a Library: How Active Learning Classrooms and Informal Learning Spaces Contribute to Student Engagement, Effective Teaching, and Coordinated Assessment." In *Proceedings of the 2014 Library Assessment Conference: Building Effective, Sustainable, Practical Assessment.* Edited by Sarah Durso, Steve Hiller, Martha Kyrillidou, and Angela Pappalardo, 490–506. Washington, DC: Association of Research Libraries, 2014.

Hosseini-Ara, Moe, and Rebecca Jones. "Overcoming Our Habits and Learning to Measure Impact." *Computers in Libraries* 33, no. 5 (2013): 3–7.

Housewright, Ross, and Roger Schonfeld. *Ithaka's 2006 Studies of Key Stakeholders in the Digital Transformation in Higher Education.* Report. New York: Ithaka S+R, August 18, 2008. http://www.sr.ithaka.org/wp-content/uploads/2015/08/4.16.1.pdf.

Housewright, Ross, Roger C. Schonfeld, and Kate Wulfson. *Ithaka S+R US Faculty Survey 2012.* New York: Ithaka S+R, April 8, 2013. http://www.sr.ithaka.org/wp-content/uploads/2015/08/Ithaka_SR_US_Faculty_Survey_2012_FINAL.pdf.

Hsu, Maxwell K., Richard G. Cummings, and Stephen W. Wang. "Business Students' Perception of University Library Service Quality and Satisfaction." *Contemporary Issues in Education Research* 7, no. 2 (2014): 137–44.

Hu, Rachael, and Brian Tingle. "Understanding the User's Mental Model: An Evolving Design and Assessment Strategy for Archival Collection Description." In *Proceedings of the 2012 Library Assessment Conference: Building Effective, Sustainable, Practical Assessment.* Edited by Steve Hiller, Martha Kyrillidou, Angela Pappalardo, Jim Self, and Amy Yeager, 397–414. Washington, DC: Association of Research Libraries, 2012.

Hu, Shouping, and Alexander C. McCormick. "An Engagement-Based Student Typology and Its Relationship to College Outcomes." *Research in Higher Education* 53, no. 7 (2012): 738–54. doi:10.1007/s11162-012-9254-7.

Hufford, Jon R. "Can the Library Contribute Value to the Campus Culture for Learning?" *Journal of Academic Librarianship* 39, no. 3 (2013): 288–96. doi:10.1016/j.acalib.2013.03.002.

———. "A Review of the Literature on Assessment in Academic and Research Libraries, 2005 to August 2011." *portal: Libraries and the Academy* 13, no. 1 (2013): 5–35. doi:10.1353/pla.2013.0005.

Hughes, Hilary. "School Libraries, Teacher-Librarians and Student Outcomes: Presenting and Using the Evidence." *School Libraries Worldwide* 20, no. 1 (2014): 29–50.

Huisman, Rhonda. "The A-Team: Making a Plan Come Together across Campus." In *Proceedings of the 2012 Library Assessment Conference: Building Effective, Sustainable, Practical Assessment.* Edited by Steve Hiller, Martha Kyrillidou, Angela Pappalardo, Jim Self, and Amy Yeager, 513–22. Washington, DC: Association of Research Libraries, 2012.

Hulett, Heather, Jenny Corbin, Sharon Karasmanis, Tracy Robertson, Fiona Salisbury, and Tai Peseta. "Information Literacy at University: A Toolkit for Readiness and Measuring Impact." *Australian Academic and Research Libraries* 44, no. 3 (2013): 151–62. doi:10.1080/00048623.2013.813372.

Hunter, Ben, and Robert Perret. "Can Money Buy Happiness? A Statistical Analysis of Predictors for User Satisfaction." *Journal of Academic Librarianship* 37, no. 5 (2011): 402–8. doi:10.1016/j.acalib.2011.06.004.

Hunter, Jonathan, and Andrew Cox. "Learning over Tea! Studying in Informal Learning Spaces." *New Library World* 115, no. 1/2 (2014): 34–50. doi:10.1108/NLW-08-2013-0063.

Hurst, Susan. "Current Trends in UK University Libraries." *New Library World* 114, no. 9 (2013): 398–407. doi:10.1108/NLW-04-2013-0032.

Huwe, Terence K. "Toward a New Perspective on Library Space." Building Digital Libraries, *Computers in Libraries* 35, no. 8 (October 2015): 9. http://www.infotoday.com/cilmag/oct15/index.shtml.

Iannuzzi, Patricia, and Jeanne M. Brown. "ACRL's Standards for Libraries in Higher Education." *College and Research Libraries News* 79, no. 9 (2010): 486–87.

Information Outlook. "College Librarians Value Role in Information Literacy, But Faculty Demur." *Information Outlook* 15, no. 5 (2011): 5.

Ireland, Ashley. "Time Lords of Instruction: Knowing When to Teach Which Skills in a Major Program from Student and Instructor Feedback." In *Proceedings of the 2014 Library Assessment Conference: Building Effective, Sustainable, Practical Assessment.* Edited by Sarah Durso, Steve Hiller, Martha Kyrillidou, and Angela Pappalardo, 382–85. Washington, DC: Association of Research Libraries, 2014.

Jackson, Brian. "University Rankings: How Well Do They Measure Library Service Quality?" *portal: Libraries and the Academy* 15, no. 2 (2015): 315–30. doi:10.1353/pla.2015.0026.

———. "What Do University Rankings Tell Us about Perceptions of Library Value?" In *Proceedings of the 2014 Library Assessment Conference: Building Effective, Sustainable, Practical Assessment.* Edited by Sarah Durso, Steve Hiller, Martha Kyrillidou, and Angela Pappalardo, 431–37. Washington, DC: Association of Research Libraries, 2014.

Jackson, Heather Lea, and Trudi Bellardo Hahn. "Serving Higher Education's Highest Goals: Assessment of the Academic Library as Place." *College and Research Libraries* 72, no. 5 (2011): 428–42. doi:10.5860/crl-123.

Jacsó, Peter. "The JISC Academic Database Assessment Tool: Virtues and Vices." *Online Information Review* 34, no. 5 (2010): 806–14. doi:10.1108/14684521011084636.

Jaggars, Damon E. "We Can Imagine the Future, but Are We Equipped to Create It?" *portal: Libraries and the Academy* 14, no. 3 (2014): 319–23.

Jaggars, Damon, Gabriela Castro Gessner, Jennifer Rutner, and Kornelia Tancheva. "A 2CUL Collaborative Ethnographic Assessment of Humanities Doctoral Students." In *Proceedings of the 2012 Library Assessment Conference: Building Effective, Sustainable, Practical Assessment.* Edited by Steve Hiller, Martha Kyrillidou, Angela Pappalardo, Jim Self, and Amy Yeager, 301–10. Washington, DC: Association of Research Libraries, 2012.

Janks, Gregory, Mel Lockhart, and Alan S. Travis. "New Metrics for the New Normal: Rethinking Space Utilization within the University System of Georgia." *Planning for Higher Education* 41, no. 1 (2012): 38–63.

Jantti, Margie. "Aspiring to Excellence: Maximising Data to Sustain, Shift and Reshape a Library for the Future." In *Proceedings of the 2014 Library Assessment Conference: Building Effective, Sustainable, Practical Assessment.* Edited by Sarah Durso, Steve Hiller, Martha Kyrillidou, and Angela Pappalardo, 15–22. Washington, DC: Association of Research Libraries, 2014.

Jantti, Margie, and Brian Cox. "Measuring the Value of Library Resources and Student Academic Performance through Relational Datasets." *Evidence Based Library and Information Practice* 8, no. 2 (2013): 163–71.

Jastram, Iris, Danya Leebaw, and Heather Tompkins. "Situating Information Literacy within the Curriculum: Using a Rubric to Shape a Program." *portal: Libraries and the Academy* 14, no. 2 (2014): 165–86.

Jones, Jennifer. "Secret Shoppers in the Library." In *Proceedings of the 2012 Library Assessment Conference: Building Effective, Sustainable, Practical Assessment*. Edited by Steve Hiller, Martha Kyrillidou, Angela Pappalardo, Jim Self, and Amy Yeager, 117–26. Washington, DC: Association of Research Libraries, 2012.

Jubb, Michael, Ian Rowlands, and David Nicholas. "Value of Libraries: Relationships between Provision, Usage, and Research Outcomes." In *Proceedings of the 2010 Library Assessment Conference: Building Effective, Sustainable, Practical Assessment*. Edited by Steve Hiller, Kristina Justh, Martha Kyrillidou, and Jim Self, 311–22. Washington, DC: Association of Research Libraries, 2010.

Kay, David. "Discovering the Pattern, Discerning the Potential: The Role of the Library in Unraveling the Cat's Cradle of Activity Data." In *Proceedings of the 2014 Library Assessment Conference: Building Effective, Sustainable, Practical Assessment*. Edited by Sarah Durso, Steve Hiller, Martha Kyrillidou, and Angela Pappalardo, 269–82. Washington, DC: Association of Research Libraries, 2014.

Ke, Irene, and Christina Gola. "Collaborating with Assessment Services to Evaluate Information Literacy Skills of Graduating Undergraduates." In *Proceedings of the 2012 Library Assessment Conference: Building Effective, Sustainable, Practical Assessment*. Edited by Steve Hiller, Martha Kyrillidou, Angela Pappalardo, Jim Self, and Amy Yeager, 171–80. Washington, DC: Association of Research Libraries, 2012.

Kelly, Betsy, Claire Hamasu, and Barbara Jones. "Applying Return on Investment (ROI) in Libraries." *Journal of Library Administration* 52, no. 8 (2012): 656-71. doi:10.1080/01930826.2012.747383.

Kelly, Madeline. "Applying the Tiers of Assessment: A Holistic and Systematic Approach to Assessing Library Collections." *Journal of Academic Librarianship* 40, no. 6 (2014): 585–91. doi:10.1016/j.acalib.2014.10.002.

Kennedy, Marie. "Cycling Through: Paths Libraries Take to Marketing Electronic Resources." In *Proceedings of the 2010 Library Assessment Conference: Building Effective, Sustainable, Practical Assessment*. Edited by Steve Hiller, Kristina Justh, Martha Kyrillidou, and Jim Self, 721–30. Washington, DC: Association of Research Libraries, 2010.

Kenney, Anne R., and Xin Li. "Rethinking Research Libraries in the Era of Global Universities." Ithaka S+R, July 14, 2016. doi:10.18665/sr.283378.

Kiel, Stephen "Mike," Natalie Burclaff, and Catherine Johnson. "Learning by Doing: Developing a Baseline Information Literacy Assessment." *portal: Libraries and the Academy* 15, no. 4 (2015): 747–66.

Killick, Selena. "Applying Performance Measurement to Safeguard Budgets: Qualitative and Quantitative Measurement of Electronic Journal Packages." In *Proceedings of the 2012 Library Assessment Conference: Building Effective, Sustainable, Practical Assessment*. Edited by Steve Hiller, Martha Kyrillidou, Angela Pappalardo, Jim Self, and Amy Yeager, 731–36. Washington, DC: Association of Research Libraries, 2012.

Kim, Hae Min. "Evaluation of the Applicability of E-S-QUAL for Assessing the Service Quality of Social Media: A Case Study of an Academic Library's Facebook Service." In *Proceedings of the 2014 Library Assessment Conference: Building Effective, Sustainable, Practical Assessment*. Edited by Sarah Durso, Steve Hiller, Martha Kyrillidou, and Angela Pappalardo, 622–35. Washington, DC: Association of Research Libraries, 2014.King, Donald, Ariana Ricci, Carol Tenopir, Ben Birch, and Liz Whitson. "Assessment of the Use, Value and ROI of All Academic Library Services." In *Proceedings of the 2012 Library Assessment Conference: Building Effective, Sustainable, Practical Assessment*. Edited by Steve Hiller, Martha Kyrillidou, Angela Pappalardo, Jim Self, and Amy Yeager, 35–50. Washington, DC: Association of Research Libraries, 2012.

King, Donald W., and Carol Tenopir. "Linking Information Seeking Patterns with Purpose, Use, Value, and Return on Investment of Academic Library Journals." *Evidence Based Library and Information Practice* 8, no. 2 (2013): 153–62.

King, Valery, and Sara Christensen-Lee. "Full-Time Reference with Part-Time Librarians: Dealing with Staffing Realities, Meeting User Needs." *Reference and User Services Quarterly* 54, no. 1 (2014): 34–43. doi:10.5860/rusq.54n1.34.

Kinsley, Kirsten, and Rachel Besara. "Increasing the Impact and Value of a Graduate-Level Research Methods Course by Embedding Assessment Librarians." In *Proceedings of the 2012 Library Assessment Conference: Building Effective, Sustainable, Practical Assessment*. Edited by Steve Hiller, Martha Kyrillidou, Angela Pappalardo, Jim Self, and Amy Yeager, 311–22. Washington, DC: Association of Research Libraries, 2012.

Kiviluoto, Johanna. "Information Literacy and Diginatives: Expanding the Role of Academic Libraries." *IFLA Journal* 41, no. 4 (2015): 308–16. doi:10.1177/0340035215596177.

Koltay, Zsuzsa, and Elena MacGurn. "Cutting the Knot: A Holistic and Pragmatic Framework for Public Services Measures." In *Proceedings of the 2010 Library Assessment Conference: Building Effective, Sustainable, Practical Assessment*. Edited by Steve Hiller, Kristina Justh, Martha Kyrillidou, and Jim Self, 533–38. Washington, DC: Association of Research Libraries, 2010.

Kopp, Maggie Gallup. "Academic Libraries, Institutional Missions, and New Student Recruitment: A Case Study." *Reference Services Review* 41, no. 2 (2013): 192–200. doi:10.1108/00907321311326192.

Krueger, Stephanie, and Anna Perricci. "Evaluating Usage of Non-text Resources within and beyond the Online Environment." In *Proceedings of the 2010 Library Assessment Conference: Building Effective, Sustainable, Practical Assessment*. Edited by Steve Hiller, Kristina Justh, Martha Kyrillidou, and Jim Self, 563–70. Washington, DC: Association of Research Libraries, 2010.

Kurzweil, Martin, Rayane Alamuddin, and Daniel Rossman. *Higher Ed Insights: Results of the Fall 2015 Survey*. Survey Report. New York: Ithaka S+R, February 22, 2016. http://www.sr.ithaka.org/wp-content/uploads/2016/02/SR_Report_Higher_Ed-Insights_Fall2015Survey_022216.pdf.

Kurzweil, Martin, and Daniel Rossman. *Broad-Based and Targeted: Florida State University's Efforts to Retain Every Student*. Case Study. New York: Ithaka S+R, April 28, 2016. http://www.sr.ithaka.org/wp-content/uploads/2016/04/SR_Case_Study_Broad_Based_Targeted_Florida_State042816.pdf.

Kurzweil, Martin, and D. Derek Wu. *Building a Pathway to Student Success at Georgia State*. Case Study. New York: Ithaka S+R, April 23, 2015. http://www.sr.ithaka.org/wp-content/uploads/2015/08/SR_Case_Study_Building_Pathway_Student_Success_042315_0.pdf.

Kyrillidou, Martha. "The Association of Research Libraries Library Scorecard Pilot: Using the Balanced Scorecard in Research Libraries." *Research Library Issues: A BiMonthly Report from Association of Research Libraries, CNI, and SPARC*, no. 271 (2010): 33–35. http://www.arl.org/resources/pubs/rli/archive/rli271.shtml.

Law, Derek. "The World Is Our Lobster: Rethinking Traditional Attitudes." *New Library World* 115, no. 5/6 (2014): 200–210. doi:10.1108/NLW-05-2014-0054.

Lazzaro, Althea Eannance, Shardé Mills, Tami Garrard, Emily Ferguson, Megan Watson, and Dave Ellenwood. "Cultural Competency on Campus: Applying ACRL's Diversity Standards." *College and Research Libraries News* 73, no. 8 (2014): 332–35.

Levine-Clark, Michael. "Access to Everything: Building the Future Academic Library Collection." *portal: Libraries and the Academy* 14, no. 3 (2014): 425–37. doi:10.1353/pla.2014.0015.

Lewellen, Rachel, and Terry Plum. "Assessment of the Usage of Electronic Resources at the University of Massachusetts Amherst: A MINES for Libraries(R) Study Using Tableau Software for Visualization and Analysis." In *Proceedings of the 2014 Library Assessment Conference: Building Effective, Sustainable, Practical Assessment*. Edited by Sarah Durso, Steve Hiller, Martha Kyrillidou, and Angela Pappalardo, 601–14. Washington, DC: Association of Research Libraries, 2014.

Lewis, Janice Steed. "The Academic Library in Institutional Assessment: Seizing an Opportunity." *Library Leadership and Management* 24, no. 2 (2010): 65–77. https://journals.tdl.org/llm/index.php/llm/article/view/1830.

Little, Hannah Byrd. "Prove It! Putting Together the Evidence-Based Practice Puzzle." *Knowledge Quest* 43, no. 3 (2015): 62–68.

Loertscher, David V. "Collaboration and Coteaching: A New Measure of Impact." *Teacher Librarian* 42, no. 2 (2014): 8–19.

Lombard, Emmett. "The Role of the Academic Library in College Choice." *Journal of Academic Librarianship* 38, no. 4 (2012): 237–41. doi:10.1016/j.acalib.2012.04.001.

Long, Matthew, and Roger Schonfeld. "Ithaka S+R's Research Support Services for Scholars: A Disciplinary Approach to Creating Innovative Library Services." In *Proceedings of the 2012 Library Assessment Conference: Building Effective, Sustainable, Practical Assessment.* Edited by Steve Hiller, Martha Kyrillidou, Angela Pappalardo, Jim Self, and Amy Yeager, 331–36. Washington, DC: Association of Research Libraries, 2012.

Lowe, M. Sara, Char Booth, Sean Stone, and Natalie Tagge. "Impacting Information Literacy Learning in First-Year Seminars: A Rubric-Based Evaluation." *portal: Libraries and the Academy* 15, no. 3 (2015): 489–512. doi:10.1353/pla.2015.0030.

Lundrigan, Courtney, Kevin Manuel, and May Yan. "'Feels like You've Hit the Lottery': Assessing the Implementation of a Discovery Layer Tool at Ryerson University." In *Proceedings of the 2012 Library Assessment Conference: Building Effective, Sustainable, Practical Assessment.* Edited by Steve Hiller, Martha Kyrillidou, Angela Pappalardo, Jim Self, and Amy Yeager, 447–68. Washington, DC: Association of Research Libraries, 2012.

Lupton, Aaron, Marcia Salmon, and Dany Savard. "An Implementation of LibQUAL+(R) Triads at York University." In *Proceedings of the 2012 Library Assessment Conference: Building Effective, Sustainable, Practical Assessment.* Edited by Steve Hiller, Martha Kyrillidou, Angela Pappalardo, Jim Self, and Amy Yeager, 685–92. Washington, DC: Association of Research Libraries, 2012.

Lym, Brian, Hal Grossman, Lauren Yannotta, and Makram Talih. "Assessing the Assessment: How Institutions Administered, Interpreted, and Used SAILS." *Reference Services Review* 38, no. 1 (2010): 168–86. doi:10.1108/00907321011020806.

Lynch, Beverly, Susan Parker, Linda Kobashigawa, Sara Pacheco, Jeremy Whitt, Leslie McMichael, and Michael Qui. "A Longitudinal Analysis of 2003–2013 LibQUAL+(R) Survey Results for the UCLA Library." In *Proceedings of the 2014 Library Assessment Conference: Building Effective, Sustainable, Practical Assessment.* Edited by Sarah Durso, Steve Hiller, Martha Kyrillidou, and Angela Pappalardo, 91–124. Washington, DC: Association of Research Libraries, 2014.

MacAyeal, Greg. "A Culture of Assessment: Five Mindsets." *College and Research Libraries News* 75, no. 6 (2014): 311–12.

MacDonald, Karen I., and Wyoma VanDuinkerken. "Libraries Surviving as Entrepreneurial Organizations: A Creative Destruction Perspective." *New Library World* 116, no. 7/8 (2015): 406–19. doi:10.1108/NLW-01-2015-0005.

Mackenzie, Allison. "Revitalising Strategic Planning: Introducing the Balanced Scorecard." In *9th Northumbria International Conference on Performance Measurement in Libraries and Information Services,* 243–48. Heslington, York: University of York, 2012. http://citeseerx.ist.psu.edu/viewdoc/download?doi=10.1.1.297.5043&rep=rep1&type=pdf#page=245.

Mader, Sharon, Tish Hayes, Susan Miller, Leslie Morgan, Nicole Pagowsky, and Donna Witek. "Framework Advisory Report to the Board." In *ACRL MW16 Board Update,* 1–90. Boston: Association of College and Research Libraries, 2016.

Malenfant, Kara, and Karen Brown. "Assessment in Action: Multifaceted Collaboration." In *Proceedings of the 2014 Library Assessment Conference: Building Effective, Sustainable, Practical Assessment.* Edited by Sarah Durso, Steve Hiller, Martha Kyrillidou, and Angela Pappalardo, 377–81. Washington, DC: Association of Research Libraries, 2014.

Marcum, Deanna. *Technology to the Rescue: Can Technology-Enhanced Education Help Public Flagship Universities Meet Their Challenges?* New York: Ithaka S+R, 2014. http://www.sr.ithaka.org/wp-content/uploads/2014/04/SR_BriefingPaper_Marcum_20140421.pdf.

Marcum, Deanna, Christine Mulhern, and Clara Samayoa. *Technology-Enhanced Education at Public Flagship Universities: Opportunities and Challenges.* New York: Ithaka S+R, December 11, 2014. http://www.sr.ithaka.org/wp-content/mig/reports/SR_Technology_Enhanced_Education_Public_Flagship_Universities_121114_0.pdf.

Martell, Charles. "Age of Creative Insecurity: Student-Centered Learning." *Journal of Education for Librarianship* 15, no. 2 (1974): 112–20.

Martinelli, Meredith, and Jennifer Peasley. "One Size Doesn't Fit All? Harnessing Multiple Assessment Frameworks to Build the Value Proposition for the Organisation." In *Proceedings of the 2012 Library Assessment Conference:*

Building Effective, Sustainable, Practical Assessment. Edited by Steve Hiller, Martha Kyrillidou, Angela Pappalardo, Jim Self, and Amy Yeager, 143–52. Washington, DC: Association of Research Libraries, 2012.

Massis, Bruce E. "Information Literacy Instruction in the Library: Now More Than Ever." *New Library World* 112, no. 5/6 (2011): 274–77. doi:10.1108/03074801111136301.

Mathews, Brian. "Librarian as Futurist: Changing the Way Libraries Think about the Future." *portal: Libraries and the Academy* 14, no. 3 (2014): 453–62.

———. "Think Like a Startup." White paper, April 2012. VTechWorks, Virginia Tech. https://vtechworks.lib.vt.edu/bitstream/handle/10919/18649/Think%20like%20a%20STARTUP.pdf.Mathuews, Katy. "Moving beyond Diversity to Social Justice: A Call to Action for Academic Libraries." *Progressive Librarian* 44 (2016): 6–27.

Mathuews, Katy, and Rebekah Kilzer. "Driving Partnerships for Assessment and Engagement." In *Proceedings of the 2014 Library Assessment Conference: Building Effective, Sustainable, Practical Assessment*. Edited by Sarah Durso, Steve Hiller, Martha Kyrillidou, and Angela Pappalardo, 443–46. Washington, DC: Association of Research Libraries, 2014.

Matthews, Graham, and Graham Walton. "Strategic Development of University Library Space: Widening the Influence." *New Library World* 115, no. 5/6 (2014): 237–49. doi:10.1108/NLW-05-2014-0062.

Matthews, Joseph R. "Addressing Organizational Effectiveness: The Role of Frameworks." In *Proceedings of the 2010 Library Assessment Conference: Building Effective, Sustainable, Practical Assessment*. Edited by Steve Hiller, Kristina Justh, Martha Kyrillidou, and Jim Self, 277–98. Washington, DC: Association of Research Libraries, 2010.

———. "Assessing Library Contributions to University Outcomes: The Need for Individual Student Level Data." *Library Management* 33, no. 6/7 (2012): 389–402.

———. "Assessing Organizational Effectiveness: The Role of Performance Measures." *Library Quarterly* 81, no. 1 (2011): 83–110.

———. "Valuing Information, Information Services, and the Library: Possibilities and Realities." *portal: Libraries and the Academy* 13, no. 1 (2013): 91–112. doi:10.1353/pla.2013.0000.

Mays, Regina, and Teresa Walker. "How Library Learning Spaces Contribute to Student Success: A LibValue Project." In *Proceedings of the 2014 Library Assessment Conference: Building Effective, Sustainable, Practical Assessment*. Edited by Sarah Durso, Steve Hiller, Martha Kyrillidou, and Angela Pappalardo, 541–44. Washington, DC: Association of Research Libraries, 2014.

McCarthy, Cheryl, and Danuta Nitecki. "An Assessment of the Bass Library as a Learning Commons Environment." In *Proceedings of the 2010 Library Assessment Conference: Building Effective, Sustainable, Practical Assessment*. Edited by Steve Hiller, Kristina Justh, Martha Kyrillidou, and Jim Self, 89–98. Washington, DC: Association of Research Libraries, 2010.

McClure, Hazel, and Patricia Bravender. "Regarding Reference in an Academic Library: Does the Desk Make a Difference?" *Reference and User Services Quarterly* 52, no. 4 (2013): 302–8.

McCulley, Lucretia. "Sustaining Feedback: Assessment in the Liberal Arts College Library." In *Proceedings of the 2010 Library Assessment Conference: Building Effective, Sustainable, Practical Assessment*. Edited by Steve Hiller, Kristina Justh, Martha Kyrillidou, and Jim Self, 225–34. Washington, DC: Association of Research Libraries, 2010.

McEachron, D. L., C. Bach, and M. Sualp. "Digital Socrates: A System for Disseminating and Evaluating Effective Practices in Education." *Campus-Wide Information Systems* 29, no. 4 (2012): 226–37. doi:10.1108/10650741211253822.

McLure, Merinda, Allison V. Level, Catherine L. Cranston, Beth Oehlerts, and Mike Culbertson. "Data Curation: A Study of Researcher Practices and Needs." *portal: Libraries and the Academy* 14, no. 2 (2014): 139–64. doi:10.1353/pla.2014.0009.

Menchaca, Frank. "Start a New Fire: Measuring the Value of Academic Libraries in Undergraduate Learning." *portal: Libraries and the Academy* 14, no. 3 (2014): 353–67. doi:10.1353/pla.2014.0020.

Mengel, Elizabeth, and Vivian Lewis. "Collaborative Assessment: North American Academic Libraries' Experiences Using the Balanced Scorecard to Measure Performance and Show Value." *Library Management* 33, no. 6/7 (2012): 357–64.

Milbourn, Amanda. "A Big Picture Approach: Using Embedded Librarianship to Proactively Address the Need for Visual Literacy Instruction in Higher Education." *Art Documentation: Bulletin of the Art Libraries Society of North America* 32, no. 2 (2013): 274–83.

Miller, Kelly E. "Imagine! On the Future of Teaching and Learning and the Academic Research Library." *portal: Libraries and the Academy* 14, no. 3 (2014): 329–51.

Mirtz, Ruth. "Spatial Metaphors and Distance Learning Library Services: Why 'Where' Makes a Difference." *Journal of Library Administration* 50, no. 7/8 (2010): 857–66. doi:10.1080/01930826.2010.488984.

Monroe-Gulick, Amalia, and Julie Petr. "Conversations with Students: Assessment Leads to Adjustment." In *Proceedings of the 2012 Library Assessment Conference: Building Effective, Sustainable, Practical Assessment*. Edited by Steve Hiller, Martha Kyrillidou, Angela Pappalardo, Jim Self, and Amy Yeager, 523–32. Washington, DC: Association of Research Libraries, 2012.

Morales, Myrna, Em Claire Knowles, and Chris Bourg. "Diversity, Social Justice, and the Future of Libraries." *portal: Libraries and the Academy* 14, no. 3 (2014): 439–51.

Moser, Mary, Andrea Heisel, Nitya Jacob, and Kitty Mcneill. "A More Perfect Union: Campus Collaborations for Curriculum Mapping Information Literacy Outcomes." In *ACRL 2011 Conference Proceedings*, 330–39. Chicago: Association of College and Research Libraries, 2011.

Most, Linda R., Michelle M. Kazmer, and Paul F. Marty. "Intangible Factors Influencing the Successful Completion of Graduate LIS Coursework by Non-Traditional Students: A Case of Two IMLS-Funded Scholarship Projects." *Journal of Education for Library and Information Science* 54, no. 3 (2013): 205–19. http://files.eric.ed.gov/fulltext/EJ1074133.pdf.

Mulhern, Christine, Richard R. Spies, Matthew P. Staiger, and D. Derek Wu. *The Effects of Rising Student Costs in Higher Education: Evidence from Public Institutions in Virginia*. Report. New York: Ithaka S+R, March 4, 2015. http://www.sr.ithaka.org/wp-content/uploads/2015/08/SR_Report_Effects_of_Rising_Student_Costs_in_Higher_Education_Virginia_030415.pdf.

Murphy, Jennifer. "Marketing the Library in an On-Line University to Help Achieve Information Literacy." *Education Libraries* 36, no. 2 (2013): 17–24.

Murphy, Sarah Anne. "Quality Frameworks in Academic Libraries: Organizing and Sustaining Library Assessment Activities." In *Proceedings of the 2012 Library Assessment Conference: Building Effective, Sustainable, Practical Assessment*. Edited by Steve Hiller, Martha Kyrillidou, Angela Pappalardo, Jim Self, and Amy Yeager, 483–94. Washington, DC: Association of Research Libraries, 2012.

Murray, Adam. "Academic Libraries and High-Impact Practices for Student Retention: Library Deans' Perspectives." *portal: Libraries and the Academy* 15, no. 3 (2015): 471–87. doi:10.1353/pla.2015.0027.

Nackerud, Shane, Jan Fransen, Kate Peterson, and Kristen Mastel. "Analyzing Demographics: Assessing Library Use across the Institution." *portal: Libraries and the Academy* 13, no. 2 (2013): 131–45.

Neurohr, Karen, and Lucy Bailey. "Using Photovoice to Explore Native American Students' Perceptions of the Physical Library." In *Proceedings of the 2014 Library Assessment Conference: Building Effective, Sustainable, Practical Assessment*. Edited by Sarah Durso, Steve Hiller, Martha Kyrillidou, and Angela Pappalardo, 74–89. Washington, DC: Association of Research Libraries, 2014.

Nguyen, Linh Cuong. "Establishing a Participatory Library Model: A Grounded Theory Study." *Journal of Academic Librarianship* 41, no. 4 (2015): 475–87. doi:10.1016/j.acalib.2015.03.018.

Nichols, Jane. "Nuanced and Timely: Capturing Collections Feedback at Point of Use." In *Proceedings of the 2014 Library Assessment Conference: Building Effective, Sustainable, Practical Assessment*. Edited by Sarah Durso, Steve Hiller, Martha Kyrillidou, and Angela Pappalardo, 615–21. Washington, DC: Association of Research Libraries, 2014.

Nichols Hess, Amanda, Katie Greer, Shawn V. Lombardo, and Adriene Lim. "Books, Bytes, and Buildings: The Academic

Library's Unique Role in Improving Student Success." *Journal of Library Administration* 55, no. 8 (2015): 622–38. doi:10.1080/01930826.2015.1085241.

Nicol, Erica Carlson, and Mark O'English. "Rising Tides: Faculty Expectations of Library Websites." *portal: Libraries and the Academy* 12, no. 4 (2012): 371–86.

Nitecki, Danuta. "Space Assessment as a Venue for Defining the Academic Library." *Library Quarterly* 81, no. 1 (2011): 27–59.

Nitecki, Danuta A., and Eileen G. Abels. "Exploring the Cause and Effect of Library Value." *Performance Measurement and Metrics* 14, no. 1 (2013): 17–24. doi:10.1108/14678041311316103.

Noh, Younghee. "A Study Measuring the Performance of Electronic Resources in Academic Libraries." *Aslib Proceedings* 64, no. 2 (2012): 134–53. doi:10.1108/00012531211215169.

Nolfi, David, Maureen Diana Sasso, and Lori Koelsch. "Collaborating with Faculty to Assess Undergraduate Information Literacy in Degree Programs." In *Proceedings of the 2014 Library Assessment Conference: Building Effective, Sustainable, Practical Assessment.* Edited by Sarah Durso, Steve Hiller, Martha Kyrillidou, and Angela Pappalardo, 142–45. Washington, DC: Association of Research Libraries, 2014.

Northam, Sarah, Gail Johnston, Megan Beard, Scott Lancaster, and John Atabaev. "The Stat Solicitor: Proving Academic Value through Statistics." In *Proceedings of the 2014 Library Assessment Conference: Building Effective, Sustainable, Practical Assessment.* Edited by Sarah Durso, Steve Hiller, Martha Kyrillidou, and Angela Pappalardo, 447–54. Washington, DC: Association of Research Libraries, 2014.

Oakleaf, Megan. "Are They Learning? Are We? Learning Outcomes and the Academic Library." *Library Quarterly* 81, no. 1 (2012): 61–82.

Oakleaf, Megan. "Correlating Library Services, Expertise, and Resources with Student Learning." *Information Outlook* 18, no. 2 (2014): 13–16.

Oakleaf, Megan. "Staying on Track with Rubric Assessment: Five Institutions Investigate Information Literacy Learning." *Peer Review* 14, no. 1 (2011): 18–21.

Oakleaf, Megan. "Three Years of Rubric Research: The Take Aways for Information Literacy Teaching, Learning, and Assessment." In *Proceedings of the 2014 Library Assessment Conference: Building Effective, Sustainable, Practical Assessment.* Edited by Sarah Durso, Steve Hiller, Martha Kyrillidou, and Angela Pappalardo, 470–75. Washington, DC: Association of Research Libraries, 2014.

Oakleaf, Megan, and Amy VanScoy. "Instructional Strategies for Digital Reference: Methods to Facilitate Student Learning." *Reference and User Services Quarterly* 49, no. 4 (2010): 380–90.

Odeh, Atif Yousef. "Use of Information Resources by Undergraduate Students and Its Relationship with Academic Achievement." *Libri* 62, no. 3 (2012): 222–32. doi:10.1515/libri-2012-0018.

Pan, Denise, Ignacio J. Ferrer-Vinent, and Margret Bruehl. "Library Value in the Classroom: Assessing Student Learning Outcomes from Instruction and Collections." *Journal of Academic Librarianship* 40, no. 3/4 (2014): 332–38. doi:10.1016/j.acalib.2014.04.011.

Passonneau, Sarah. "Instant Messaging, A Synchronous Virtual Reference Tool That Mirrors Higher Education's Mission and Students' Needs: How Grounded Theory Placed the Library in the Middle of the Mix." In *Proceedings of the 2010 Library Assessment Conference: Building Effective, Sustainable, Practical Assessment.* Edited by Steve Hiller, Kristina Justh, Martha Kyrillidou, and Jim Self, 581–92. Washington, DC: Association of Research Libraries, 2010.

Pellegrino, Catherine. "But What Did They Learn? What Classroom Assessment Can Tell You about Student Learning." In *Proceedings of the 2010 Library Assessment Conference: Building Effective, Sustainable, Practical Assessment.* Edited by Steve Hiller, Kristina Justh, Martha Kyrillidou, and Jim Self, 175–80. Washington, DC: Association of Research Libraries, 2010.

Pemberton, Anne, and Linda Siefert. "Assessing Information Literacy in General Education: A Collaborative Approach Using a Metarubric." In *Proceedings of the 2014 Library Assessment Conference: Building Effective, Sustainable,*

Practical Assessment. Edited by Sarah Durso, Steve Hiller, Martha Kyrillidou, and Angela Pappalardo, 265–68. Washington, DC: Association of Research Libraries, 2014.

Poll, Roswitha. "Can We Quantify the Library's Influence? Creating an ISO Standard for Impact Assessment." *Performance Measurement and Metrics* 13, no. 2 (2012): 121–30. doi:10.1108/14678041211241332.

Porat, Lynne. "Marketing and Assessment in Academic Libraries: A Marriage of Convenience or True Love?" In *Proceedings of the 2010 Library Assessment Conference: Building Effective, Sustainable, Practical Assessment*. Edited by Steve Hiller, Kristina Justh, Martha Kyrillidou, and Jim Self, 743–48. Washington, DC: Association of Research Libraries, 2010.

Radcliff, Carolyn, Megan Oakleaf, and Michele Van Hoeck. "So What? The Results and Impact of a Decade of IMLS-Funded Information Literacy Assessments." In *Proceedings of the 2014 Library Assessment Conference: Building Effective, Sustainable, Practical Assessment*. Edited by Sarah Durso, Steve Hiller, Martha Kyrillidou, and Angela Pappalardo, 801–9. Washington, DC: Association of Research Libraries, 2014.

Radcliff, Sharon, and Elise Wong. "Assessing Argument, Critical Thinking and Information Literacy Learning Outcomes." In *Proceedings of the 2014 Library Assessment Conference: Building Effective, Sustainable, Practical Assessment*. Edited by Sarah Durso, Steve Hiller, Martha Kyrillidou, and Angela Pappalardo, 386–87. Washington, DC: Association of Research Libraries, 2014.

Rawls, Michael. "Can Academic Analytics Tell Us How Libraries Impact Faculty Scholarly Research Productivity in Different Disciplines?" In *Proceedings of the 2014 Library Assessment Conference: Building Effective, Sustainable, Practical Assessment*. Edited by Sarah Durso, Steve Hiller, Martha Kyrillidou, and Angela Pappalardo, 710–20. Washington, DC: Association of Research Libraries, 2014.

———. "Measuring the Impact of Electronic Library Materials on the University's Research Mission." In *Proceedings of the 2012 Library Assessment Conference: Building Effective, Sustainable, Practical Assessment*. Edited by Steve Hiller, Martha Kyrillidou, Angela Pappalardo, Jim Self, and Amy Yeager, 67–76. Washington, DC: Association of Research Libraries, 2012.

Ray, Lauren, and Katharine Macy. "Assessment in Space Designed for Experimentation: The University of Washington Libraries Research Commons." In *Proceedings of the 2014 Library Assessment Conference: Building Effective, Sustainable, Practical Assessment*. Edited by Sarah Durso, Steve Hiller, Martha Kyrillidou, and Angela Pappalardo, 507–16. Washington, DC: Association of Research Libraries, 2014.

Research Libraries UK and the Research Information Network. *The Value of Libraries for Research and Researchers: A RIN and RLUK Report*. London: Research Libraries UK and Research Information Network, March 2011. http://www.rluk.ac.uk/wp-content/uploads/2014/02/Value-of-Libraries-report.pdf.

Richardson, Joanna, Therese Nolan-Brown, Pat Loria, and Stephanie Bradbury. "Library Research Support in Queensland: A Survey." *Australian Academic and Research Libraries* 43, no. 4 (2012): 258–77. doi:10.1080/00048623.2012.10722287.

Riehle, Catherine Fraser, and Sharon A. Weiner. "High-Impact Educational Practices: An Exploration of the Role of Information Literacy, Critical Thinking, and Lifelong Learning." *College and Undergraduate Libraries* 20, no. 2 (2013): 127–43. doi:10.1080/10691316.2013.789658.

Rinto, Erin E., and Elisa I. Cogbill-Seiders. "Library Instruction and Themed Composition Courses: An Investigation of Factors That Impact Student Learning." *Journal of Academic Librarianship* 41, no. 1 (2015): 14–20. doi:10.1016/j.acalib.2014.11.010.

Ritterbush, Jon. "Assessing Academic Library Services to Distance Learners: A Literature Review of Perspectives from Librarians, Students, and Faculty." *Reference Librarian* 55, no. 1 (2014): 26–36. doi:10.1080/02763877.2014.853274.

Robertson, Mark. "Perceptions of Canadian Provosts on the Institutional Role of Academic Libraries." *College and Research Libraries* 76, no. 4 (2015): 490–511. doi:10.5860/crl.76.4.490.

Roy, Abhik, Adwait Khare, Ben S. C. Liu, Linda M. Hawkes, and Janice Swiatek-Kelley. "An Investigation of Affect of

Service Using a LibQUAL+™ Survey and an Experimental Study." *Journal of Academic Librarianship* 38, no. 3 (2012): 153–60. doi:10.1016/j.acalib.2012.03.018.

Rutner, Jennifer. "Still Bound for Disappointment? Another Look at Faculty and Library Journal Collections." In *Proceedings of the 2010 Library Assessment Conference: Building Effective, Sustainable, Practical Assessment.* Edited by Steve Hiller, Kristina Justh, Martha Kyrillidou, and Jim Self, 297–310. Washington, DC: Association of Research Libraries, 2010.

Samson, Sue. "Information Literacy Learning Outcomes and Student Success." *Journal of Academic Librarianship* 36, no. 3 (2010): 202–10. doi:10.1016/j.acalib.2010.03.002.

Santos, Ieda M., Nagla Ali, and Anthony Hill. "Students as Co-designers of a Virtual Learning Commons: Results of a Collaborative Action Research Study." *Journal of Academic Librarianship* 42, no. 1 (2015): 8–14. doi:10.1016/j.acalib.2015.09.006.

Saunders, Laura. "Academic Libraries' Strategic Plans: Top Trends and Under-recognized Areas." *Journal of Academic Librarianship* 41, no. 3 (2015): 285–91. doi:10.1016/j.acalib.2015.03.011.

Saunders, Laura, and Megan Oakleaf. "Assessment of Information Literacy as a Student Learning Outcome: Overcoming Barriers and Achieving Standards." In *Proceedings of the 2012 Library Assessment Conference: Building Effective, Sustainable, Practical Assessment.* Edited by Steve Hiller, Martha Kyrillidou, Angela Pappalardo, Jim Self, and Amy Yeager, 292–300. Washington, DC: Association of Research Libraries, 2012.

Saurina, Elvira, Nick Kelly, Maximiliano Montenegro, Carlos Gonzalez, Magdalena Jara, Rosa Alarcon, and Felipe Cano. "Exploring the Relationship between Undergraduate Students' Use of Library Resources and Learning Outcomes." In *Proceedings of the 2014 Library Assessment Conference: Building Effective, Sustainable, Practical Assessment.* Edited by Sarah Durso, Steve Hiller, Martha Kyrillidou, and Angela Pappalardo, 476–82. Washington, DC: Association of Research Libraries, 2014.

Savage, Devin. "Collaborating across Campus to Articulate the Value of Research Consultations." In *Proceedings of the 2014 Library Assessment Conference: Building Effective, Sustainable, Practical Assessment.* Edited by Sarah Durso, Steve Hiller, Martha Kyrillidou, and Angela Pappalardo, 558–60. Washington, DC: Association of Research Libraries, 2014.

Scales, B. Jane, and Marilyn Von Seggern. "Experiencing the Assessment Cycle: Government Document Instruction to Undergraduates." *DttP: Documents to the People* 38, no. 3 (2010): 22–26. https://journals.ala.org/index.php/dttp/issue/view/584.

Scharf, Meg, and Bob Fox. "The Role of Student Advisory Boards in Assessment." In *Proceedings of the 2014 Library Assessment Conference: Building Effective, Sustainable, Practical Assessment.* Edited by Sarah Durso, Steve Hiller, Martha Kyrillidou, and Angela Pappalardo, 146–48. Washington, DC: Association of Research Libraries, 2014.

Schonfeld, Roger C., and Ross Housewright. *Faculty Survey 2009: Key Strategic Insights for Libraries, Publishers, and Societies.* New York: Ithaka S+R, April 7, 2010. http://www.sr.ithaka.org/wp-content/uploads/2015/08/Faculty_Study_2009.pdf.

Schonfeld, Roger C., Ross Housewright, and Kate Wulfson. "Ithaka S+R US Faculty Survey 2012 (ICPSR 34571." Datasets. Last updated December 21, 2016. doi:10.3886/ICPSR34651.

Schwieder, David, and Lisa Janicke Hinchliffe. "NCES Datasets and Library Value: An Exploratory Study of the 2008 Data." In *Proceedings of the 2012 Library Assessment Conference: Building Effective, Sustainable, Practical Assessment.* Edited by Steve Hiller, Martha Kyrillidou, Angela Pappalardo, Jim Self, and Amy Yeager, 657–68. Washington, DC: Association of Research Libraries, 2012.

Searing, Susan E., and Alison M Greenlee. "Faculty Responses to Library Service Innovations: A Case Study." *Journal of Education for Library and Information Science* 52, no. 4 (2011): 279–94.

Self, James. "Library Assessment: More than Numbers." In *Proceedings of the 2012 Library Assessment Conference: Building Effective, Sustainable, Practical Assessment.* Edited by Steve Hiller, Martha Kyrillidou, Angela Pappalardo, Jim Self, and Amy Yeager, 495–500. Washington, DC: Association of Research Libraries, 2012.

Selingo, Jeffrey J. *2026, The Decade Ahead: The Seismic Shifts Transforming the Future of Higher Education*. Washington, DC: *Chronicle of Higher Education*, 2016.

Shepstone, Carol. "Finding the Library: An Institutional Assessment of the Undergraduate Experience." In *Proceedings of the 2010 Library Assessment Conference: Building Effective, Sustainable, Practical Assessment*. Edited by Steve Hiller, Kristina Justh, Martha Kyrillidou, and Jim Self, 251–60. Washington, DC: Association of Research Libraries, 2010.

Simon, John. "Dollars and Sense: The New Financial Realities of Higher Education." In *Proceedings of the 2012 Library Assessment Conference: Building Effective, Sustainable, Practical Assessment*. Edited by Steve Hiller, Martha Kyrillidou, Angela Pappalardo, Jim Self, and Amy Yeager, 19–22. Washington, DC: Association of Research Libraries, 2012.

Sites, Martha, Donna Tolson, and Anda Webb. "Telling the Story: Library Assessment for University Leadership." In *Proceedings of the 2012 Library Assessment Conference: Building Effective, Sustainable, Practical Assessment*. Edited by Steve Hiller, Martha Kyrillidou, Angela Pappalardo, Jim Self, and Amy Yeager, 337–44. Washington, DC: Association of Research Libraries, 2012.

Sivak, Allison, and Richard Hayman. "Interdisciplinary Collection Assessment Model." In *Proceedings of the 2010 Library Assessment Conference: Building Effective, Sustainable, Practical Assessment*. Edited by Steve Hiller, Kristina Justh, Martha Kyrillidou, and Jim Self, 663–76. Washington, DC: Association of Research Libraries, 2010.

Slight-Gibney, Nancy, and Wendy Ames. "GRAD Connect." In *Proceedings of the 2014 Library Assessment Conference: Building Effective, Sustainable, Practical Assessment*. Edited by Sarah Durso, Steve Hiller, Martha Kyrillidou, and Angela Pappalardo, 555–57. Washington, DC: Association of Research Libraries, 2014.

Smith, Meggan D., and Amy B. Dailey. "Improving and Assessing Information Literacy Skills through Faculty-Librarian Collaboration." *College and Undergraduate Libraries* 20, no. 3/4 (2013): 314–26. doi:10.1080/10691316.2013.829370.

Soria, Krista M., Jan Fransen, and Shane Nackerud. "Library Use and Undergraduate Student Outcomes: New Evidence for Students' Retention and Academic Success." *portal: Libraries and the Academy* 13, no. 2 (2013): 147–64. doi:10.1353/pla.2013.0010.

Spadafora, David. "Short-Term Costs for Long-Term Benefits." *Journal of Library Administration* 52, no. 1 (2012): 108–23. doi:10.1080/01930826.2012.629967.

Speare, Marie. "LibQUAL+(R) Triads Pilot: Results from the University of Manitoba Libraries." In *Proceedings of the 2012 Library Assessment Conference: Building Effective, Sustainable, Practical Assessment*. Edited by Steve Hiller, Martha Kyrillidou, Angela Pappalardo, Jim Self, and Amy Yeager, 707–18. Washington, DC: Association of Research Libraries, 2012.

Staley, David J., and Kara J. Malenfant. "Futures Thinking for Academic Librarians: Higher Education in 2025." *Information Services and Use* 30, no. 1/2 (2010): 57–90. doi:10.3233/ISU-2010-0614.

Steele, Patricia, and Nancy Fried Foster. "Multidisciplinary Rethinking and Redesign of Library Space." In *Proceedings of the 2012 Library Assessment Conference: Building Effective, Sustainable, Practical Assessment*. Edited by Steve Hiller, Martha Kyrillidou, Angela Pappalardo, Jim Self, and Amy Yeager, 261–68. Washington, DC: Association of Research Libraries, 2012.

Stemmer, John, and David Mahan. "Assessing the Library's Influence on Undergraduate Outcomes with Student Usage Surveys." In *Proceedings of the 2012 Library Assessment Conference: Building Effective, Sustainable, Practical Assessment*. Edited by Steve Hiller, Martha Kyrillidou, Angela Pappalardo, Jim Self, and Amy Yeager, 77–88. Washington, DC: Association of Research Libraries, 2012.

Stewart, Christopher. "Measuring Information Literacy: Beyond the Case Study." *Journal of Academic Librarianship* 37, no. 3 (2011): 270–72. doi:10.1016/j.acalib.2011.03.003.

Stewart-Mailhiot, Amy, Mary O'Kelly, and Danielle Theiss. "*Assessment in Action*: A Journey through Campus Collaboration, a Learning Community, and Research Design." In *Proceedings of the 2014 Library Assessment Conference:*

Building Effective, Sustainable, Practical Assessment. Edited by Sarah Durso, Steve Hiller, Martha Kyrillidou, and Angela Pappalardo, 388–90. Washington, DC: Association of Research Libraries, 2014.

Stielow, Fred. "Accreditation, ROI, and the Online Academic Library." *Computers in Libraries* 31, no. 9 (November 2011), http://www.infotoday.com/cilmag/nov11/Stielow.shtml.

Stone, Graham, and Bryony Ramsden. "Library Impact Data Project: Looking for the Link between Library Usage and Student Attainment." *College and Research Libraries* 74, no. 6 (2013): 546–59. doi:10.5860/crl12-406.

Strub, Maurini, and Melissa Laning. "Putting a UX Lens on Library Space Assessment." In *Proceedings of the 2014 Library Assessment Conference: Building Effective, Sustainable, Practical Assessment.* Edited by Sarah Durso, Steve Hiller, Martha Kyrillidou, and Angela Pappalardo, 693–95. Washington, DC: Association of Research Libraries, 2014.

Szentkiralyi, Zoltan. "Patron Usage of Information Commons at SMU." In *Proceedings of the 2014 Library Assessment Conference: Building Effective, Sustainable, Practical Assessment.* Edited by Sarah Durso, Steve Hiller, Martha Kyrillidou, and Angela Pappalardo, 561–65. Washington, DC: Association of Research Libraries, 2014.

Tang, Karen. "Did They Find It? Developing a Revised Materials Availability Survey." In *Proceedings of the 2014 Library Assessment Conference: Building Effective, Sustainable, Practical Assessment.* Edited by Sarah Durso, Steve Hiller, Martha Kyrillidou, and Angela Pappalardo, 706–9. Washington, DC: Association of Research Libraries, 2014.

Tawatao, Christine, Rachel Hungerford, Lauren Ray, and Jennifer L. Ward. "LibGuides Usability Testing: Customizing a Product to Work for Your Users." In *Proceedings of the 2010 Library Assessment Conference: Building Effective, Sustainable, Practical Assessment.* Edited by Steve Hiller, Kristina Justh, Martha Kyrillidou, and Jim Self, 369–86. Washington, DC: Association of Research Libraries, 2010.

Tawatao, Christine, Verletta Kern, Nia Lam, and Robin Chin Roemer. "Watch and Learn: Assessment of Online Video Tutorials." In *Proceedings of the 2014 Library Assessment Conference: Building Effective, Sustainable, Practical Assessment.* Edited by Sarah Durso, Steve Hiller, Martha Kyrillidou, and Angela Pappalardo, 566–70. Washington, DC: Association of Research Libraries, 2014.

Tenopir, Carol. "Building Evidence of the Value and Impact of Library and Information Services: Methods, Metrics and ROI." *Evidence Based Library and Information Practice* 8, no. 2 (2013): 270–74.

———. "Measuring the Value of the Academic Library: Return on Investment and Other Value Measures." *Serials Librarian* 58, no. 1/4 (2010): 39–48. doi:10.1080/03615261003623005.Tenopir, Carol, Lisa Christian, and Donald King. "Scholarly Reading Patterns of US Graduate and Undergraduate Students." In *Proceedings of the 2014 Library Assessment Conference: Building Effective, Sustainable, Practical Assessment.* Edited by Sarah Durso, Steve Hiller, Martha Kyrillidou, and Angela Pappalardo, 535–40. Washington, DC: Association of Research Libraries, 2014.

Tenopir, Carol, Rachel Volentine, and Donald W. King. *UK Scholarly Reading and the Value of Library Resources: Summary Results of the Study Conducted Spring 2011.* Center for Information and Communication Studies, University of Tennessee, February 1, 2012. https://www.jisc-collections.ac.uk/Documents/Reports/UK%20Scholarly%20Reading%20and%20the%20Value%20of%20Library%20Resources%20Final%20Report.pdf.

Teske, Boris, Michael DiCarlo, and Dexter Cahoy. "Libraries and Student Persistence at Southern Colleges and Universities." *Reference Services Review* 41, no. 2 (2013): 266–79. doi:10.1108/00907321311326174.

Theodore-Shusta, Eileen, and Araba Dawson-Andoh. "Engaging the Campus Community in Conversations on Diversity." *College and Research Libraries News* 75, no. 6 (2014): 328–31.

Thomas, Brittney, Sam Van Horne, Wayne Jacobson, and Matthew Anson. "The Design and Assessment of the Learning Commons at the University of Iowa." *Journal of Academic Librarianship* 41, no. 6 (2015): 804–13. doi:10.1016/j.acalib.2015.09.005.

Thomas, Dana, and Kevin Manuel. "'Absolutely Amazing!': A Comparative Study of User Satisfaction with Summon(R)." In *Proceedings of the 2014 Library Assessment Conference: Building Effective, Sustainable, Practical Assessment.* Edited by Sarah Durso, Steve Hiller, Martha Kyrillidou, and Angela Pappalardo, 571–82. Washington, DC: Association of Research Libraries, 2014.

Thorpe, Angie, Ria Lukes, Diane J. Bever, and Yan He. "The Impact of the Academic Library on Student Success: Connecting the Dots." *portal: Libraries and the Academy* 16, no. 2 (2016): 373–92.

Town, J. Stephen. "Value, Impact and the Transcendent Library: Progress and Pressures in Performance Measurement and Evaluation." In *Proceedings of the 2010 Library Assessment Conference: Building Effective, Sustainable, Practical Assessment.* Edited by Steve Hiller, Kristina Justh, Martha Kyrillidou, and Jim Self, 267–76. Washington, DC: Association of Research Libraries, 2010.

Town, J. Stephen, and Martha Kyrillidou. "Developing a Values Scorecard." *Performance Measurement and Metrics* 14, no. 1 (2013): 7–16. doi:10.1108/14678041311316095.

Town, Stephen. "Making Value Measurement a Reality: Implementing the Value Scorecard." In *Proceedings of the 2014 Library Assessment Conference: Building Effective, Sustainable, Practical Assessment.* Edited by Sarah Durso, Steve Hiller, Martha Kyrillidou, and Angela Pappalardo, 721. Washington, DC: Association of Research Libraries, 2014.

Tuamsuk, Kulthida, Kanyarat Kwiecien, and Jutharat Sarawanawong. "A University Library Management Model for Students' Learning Support." *International Information and Library Review* 45, no. 3/4 (2013): 94–107. doi:10.1016/j.iilr.2013.10.002.

Turner, Nancy. "Librarians Do It Differently: Comparative Usability Testing with Students and Library Staff." In *Proceedings of the 2010 Library Assessment Conference: Building Effective, Sustainable, Practical Assessment.* Edited by Steve Hiller, Kristina Justh, Martha Kyrillidou, and Jim Self, 387–94. Washington, DC: Association of Research Libraries, 2010.

Vance, Jason M., Rachel Kirk, and Justin G. Gardner. "Measuring the Impact of Library Instruction on Freshmen Success and Persistence: A Quantitative Analysis." *Communications in Information Literacy* 6, no. 1 (2012): 49–58. http://www.comminfolit.org/index.php?journal=cil&page=article&op=view&path%5B%5D=v6i-1p49&path%5B%5D=144.

Walsh, Taylor. *Unlocking the Gates: How and Why Leading Universities Are Opening Up Access to Their Courses.* Princeton, NJ: Princeton University Press, 2011.

Washburn, Allyson, and Sheila Bibb. "Student Information Seeking Behaviors: A Case Study in Collaboration." In *Proceedings of the 2012 Library Assessment Conference: Building Effective, Sustainable, Practical Assessment.* Edited by Steve Hiller, Martha Kyrillidou, Angela Pappalardo, Jim Self, and Amy Yeager, 323–30. Washington, DC: Association of Research Libraries, 2012.

Watts, John, and Stephanie Mahfood. "Assessing Library Research Consultations: A Mixed-Method Approach." In *Proceedings of the 2014 Library Assessment Conference: Building Effective, Sustainable, Practical Assessment.* Edited by Sarah Durso, Steve Hiller, Martha Kyrillidou, and Angela Pappalardo, 583–89. Washington, DC: Association of Research Libraries, 2014.

Weaver, Margaret. "Student Journey Work: A Review of Academic Library Contributions to Student Transition and Success." *New Review of Academic Librarianship* 19, no. 2 (2013): 101–24. doi:10.1080/13614533.2013.800754.

Weiner, Sharon A., Tomalee Doan, and Hal Kirkwood. "The Learning Commons as a Locus for Information Literacy." *College and Undergraduate Libraries* 17, no. 2/3 (2010): 192–212. doi:10.1080/10691316.2010.484275.

Weiner, Sharon, and Charles Watkinson. "What Do Students Learn from Participation in an Undergraduate Research Journal? Results of an Assessment." In *Proceedings of the 2014 Library Assessment Conference: Building Effective, Sustainable, Practical Assessment.* Edited by Sarah Durso, Steve Hiller, Martha Kyrillidou, and Angela Pappalardo, 338–76. Washington, DC: Association of Research Libraries, 2014.

Willcoxson, Lesley, Julie Cotter, and Sally Joy. "Beyond the First-Year Experience: The Impact on Attrition of Student Experiences throughout Undergraduate Degree Studies in Six Diverse Universities." *Information Research* 20, no. 1 (2015): 331–52. doi:10.1080/03075070903581533.

Wilson, Lizabeth A. "Creating Sustainable Futures for Academic Libraries." *Journal of Library Administration* 52, no. 1 (2012): 78–93. doi:10.1080/01930826.2012.630241.

Wolfe, Kate S. "Emerging Information Literacy and Research-Method Competencies in Urban Community College Psychology Students." *Community College Enterprise* 21, no. 2 (2015): 93–99.

Wolff, Christine, Alisa B. Rod, and Roger C. Schonfeld. *Ithaka S+R US Faculty Survey 2015*. Report. New York: Ithaka S+R, April 4, 2016. http://www.sr.ithaka.org/wp-content/uploads/2016/03/SR_Report_US_Faculty_Survey_2015040416.pdf.

Wong, Shun Han Rebekah, and Dianne Cmor. "Measuring Association between Library Instruction and Graduation GPA." *College and Research Libraries* 72, no. 5 (2011): 464–73. doi:10.5860/crl-151.

Wong, Shun Han Rebekah, and T. D. Webb. "Uncovering Meaningful Correlation between Student Academic Performance and Library Material Usage." *College and Research Libraries* 72, no. 4 (2011): 361–70. doi:10.5860/crl-129.

Wu, Ming-der, and Shih-chuan Chen. "Graduate Students Appreciate Google Scholar, but Still Find Use for Libraries." *Electronic Library* 32, no. 3 (2014): 375–89. doi:10.1108/EL-08-2012-0102.

Yu, Jen-chien. "Show This, Not That: How to Communicate Assessment Results." In *Proceedings of the 2014 Library Assessment Conference: Building Effective, Sustainable, Practical Assessment/* Edited by Sarah Durso, Steve Hiller, Martha Kyrillidou, and Angela Pappalardo, 455–61. Washington, DC: Association of Research Libraries, 2014.

Zaugg, Holt. "Library Impact Study." In *Proceedings of the 2014 Library Assessment Conference: Building Effective, Sustainable, Practical Assessment*. Edited by Sarah Durso, Steve Hiller, Martha Kyrillidou, and Angela Pappalardo, 722–28. Washington, DC: Association of Research Libraries, 2014.

Ziegenfuss, Donna Harp, and Stephen Borrelli. "The Engaged Librarian: Crafting an Effective Assessment Plan to Determine the Impact of a Key Strategic Library Initiative." In *Proceedings of the 2014 Library Assessment Conference: Building Effective, Sustainable, Practical Assessment*. Edited by Sarah Durso, Steve Hiller, Martha Kyrillidou, and Angela Pappalardo, 753–65. Washington, DC: Association of Research Libraries, 2014.

Zucca, Joe. "Data Farms or a Field of Dreams? Libraries Can Build Infrastructure for Collaborative Assessment." In *Proceedings of the 2010 Library Assessment Conference: Building Effective, Sustainable, Practical Assessment*. Edited by Steve Hiller, Kristina Justh, Martha Kyrillidou, and Jim Self, 515–24. Washington, DC: Association of Research Libraries, 2010.

Appendix F: Advisory Group Members' Titles and Institutions' Carnegie Class

Advisory Group Member Code	Title	Carnegie Classification: Basic
LM01	Library Director	Baccalaureate Colleges: Arts & Sciences Focus
LM02	Dean of Libraries	Doctoral Universities: Higher Research Activity (R2)
LM03	Associate Dean & Director of Research & Academic Services	Doctoral Universities: Highest Research Activity (R1)
LM04	Associate Chair, Associate University Librarian	Doctoral Universities: Highest Research Activity (R1)
LM05	Reference Librarian	Associate's Colleges: High Transfer-Mixed Traditional/ Nontraditional
LM06	Associate University Librarian for User Services and Associate Dean of Libraries	Doctoral Universities: Highest Research Activity (R1)
LM07	Vice President for Information Services and University Librarian	Doctoral Universities: Highest Research Activity (R1)
LM08	Associate Dean	Doctoral Universities: Higher Research Activity (R2)
LM09	Dean of Libraries	Doctoral Universities: Highest Research Activity (R1)
LM10	Dean & Director of Library	Doctoral Universities: Higher Research Activity (R2)
LM11	Dean of Libraries	Doctoral Universities: Highest Research Activity (R1)
LM12	Library Director	Associate's Colleges: High Transfer-Mixed Traditional/ Nontraditional
LM13	University Librarian	Doctoral Universities: Moderate Research Activity (R3)
LM14	Dean of Libraries and Educational Technologies	Master's Colleges & Universities: Larger Programs (M1)

Appendix G: Library Administrator Focus Group Interview Protocol

1. Explain or tell me how your academic library/libraries has/have succeeded in supporting the mission and goals of your institution.
2. How do you communicate your library's activities to your larger institution's administration?
    a. [Probe: How do you make the institution's administration aware of the services your library provides?]
    b. [Probe: How do you tie these activities to advancing your institution's mission and goals?]
3. How has your library collaborated with other libraries (both on campus and off campus) and other academic departments? Explain the collaborations (i.e., which academic departments, staff, etc.).
    a. [Probe: How do you communicate/collaborate with students, faculty, and administration?]
    b. [Probe: How did the library initiate these collaborations? Why did the library initiate these collaborations?]
    c. [Probe: Were these collaborations effective? If yes, why and what factors made them effective? If not, why and what factors made them ineffective?]
    d. [Probe: How did these collaborations facilitate communication with your institution's administration?]
    e. [Probe: How did these collaborations impact the students, faculty, or staff at your institution? How were these impacts measured?]
4. What could facilitate improved communication between your library and your larger institution's administration, faculty, and students?
    a. [Probe: What different types of engagement could facilitate communication (i.e., face-to-face or online events, update sessions, new service offerings, etc.)?]
5. What factors hinder communication between your library and your institution's administration?
6. If you had a magic wand, how would you better communicate and make your administration, faculty, and students more aware of the services the library offers and their impact on student learning and success?
7. What else would you like to share about:
    a. How your library supports the mission of your larger institution?
    b. How you communicate this support to your institution's administration?
    c. How you articulate value to your institution's administration?

Appendix H: Further Description of the Coding Process for Data Analysis

Once the two codebooks were developed and revised, the three data sources (i.e., documents from the literature review, focus group interview transcript, provost interview transcripts) were imported into NVivo, a qualitative research environment that facilitates the maintenance and application of codes across various data sources.[213] Specifically, NVivo allows coders to highlight sections of text and label these sections with the relevant codes from the codebook that describe it. If an individual renames or deletes a code, the change will be updated in NVivo. NVivo also keeps track of the number of times an individual applies a code and for which data sources they used the code. This information was used to complete post hoc data analysis.

Another useful feature of NVivo is its ability to determine if team members agreed with one another when labeling sections of text, and the degree of this agreement. Multiple team members engaged in coding and measuring the agreement of this coding, referred to as "inter-coder reliability."[214] For each of the three data sources, at least two project team members coded 20 percent of the data using the thematic codes. For instance, if a data source was ten pages, the team coded two pages of text. Twenty percent of all the literature review documents coded as research also were coded using the research document characteristics codebook. The team reviewed the codes assigned, discussed coding discrepancies, and revised the codebooks to reflect the changes (e.g., making a definition more specific). Based on these actions, inter-coder reliability was calculated for the research document characteristics at 95 percent agreement and 99 percent agreement for the theme coding. The coding of the two team members was compared to a third team member's coding, again discussing any coding discrepancies and revising the codebook to reflect changes. Following this discussion, the team attained 100 percent agreement for both coding schemes on 20 percent of the documents. Two team members coded the remainder of the documents. During this latter phase of coding, team members also labeled portions of the data as being "juicy quotes," which are particularly interesting or notable statements. Use of juicy quotes "brings the research to life and enables the reader to hear the participant's voice, which adds validity to the findings."[215] Another team member then reviewed the codes, amending them as necessary based on the codebooks.

Appendix I: Description of Post Hoc Techniques Used in Report

Below is a description of the three post hoc techniques used in this report. There exist several resources that provide a comprehensive review of post hoc analysis with relevant examples.[216] The three post hoc techniques used in this report are

1. *Linear regression.* To observe and assess trends related to how the proportion of themes coded in the selected documents changed over time. Linear regression (line fitting) was applied and coupled with significance testing via F-tests. By measuring the goodness of fit of a statistically significant linear model to the proportion data and considering the slope of the resulting model, prevalence of a theme could be assessed over time as increasing (positive slope), decreasing (negative slope), or stable (roughly zero slope).
2. *Two-proportion z-tests.* To identify significant differences between the proportions of times that codes were applied among the three data sources. Two-proportion z-tests[217] are ideal for making this determination, as they compare two groups (here, data sources) sampled from separate, independent populations (e.g., from focus group interviews, from a literature search). Some online resources provide examples, as well as Microsoft Excel workbooks containing formulas and worksheets for performing z-tests.[218] In the *Findings* section, we use a significance level of $\alpha = 0.05$ (equivalently, $p < 0.05$) to identify statistically significant differences in proportions. While the p-value is useful in determining whether differences exist between a proportion of codes applied to each data source, it is not the only measure that can be used, and it does not indicate the degree of difference (effect size) or the likelihood of differences occurring (probability). P-values, therefore, should be viewed as indicators that observations are "on the right track." In this analysis, reporting p-values was used to bolster the observation of differences in proportions of each code among the three document sources.
3. *Benjamini-Hochberg procedure.* To ensure that the differences found between the proportions of times that codes were applied among the three data sources were sound. Post hoc analysis must accommodate for multiple comparisons, as the chances of making false discoveries increases with each hypothesis test. The Benjamini-Hochberg procedure was applied to p-values prior to significance testing to adjust for false-discovery rates.[219]

Appendix J: Examples of Research Questions That Can Be Addressed Using the Visualization Component, Organized by Priority Area

Below are examples of research questions that can be addressed using the visualization component. These questions are organized by priority area. *Italicized* words represent facets and metadata labeled using the Theoretical and Research Document Characteristics Coding Schemes. Underlined words represent those identified by the free text search feature.

I. Institutional mission and goals and alignment
   1. What types of diversity/inclusivity outcomes does library instruction support for undergraduate students?
      a. How can library services increase graduate student engagement?
   2. Are writing centers having an effect on student retention in community colleges?
      a. In what ways are writing centers affecting student retention at community colleges?
      b. How do other units track impact on student graduation?
      c. Where do libraries fall in the institutional mission and goals or other strategic planning at four-year colleges?
      d. How are budget constraints affecting libraries at research universities?
   3. To what extent are librarians involved with accreditation?
      a. How have librarians at four-year colleges assisted other departments with accreditation?
      b. How do current accreditation standards affect libraries in the South?

II. Teaching and learning
   1. How are teaching and learning being evaluated at community colleges in the Midwest?
      a. What are the most common difficulties in measuring teaching and learning?
      b. How is the impact of library instruction being measured at public four-year colleges?
   2. How can libraries increase engagement among undergraduate students?
      a. How are library spaces (online or physical) affecting engagement among graduate students?
      b. How have libraries modified their instruction based on undergraduate student feedback?
   3. How will libraries evolve to affect teaching and learning at their institutions?
      a. What have been the unexpected consequences of partnering with others with regard to teaching and learning outcomes in research universities?
      b. Have university libraries enriched student engagement with their communities? If so, how?

III. Student success
   1. How do academic library resources or services impact success outcomes for students?
      a. How do library collections impact student retention for undergraduate students?
      b. How do library spaces support student enrollment?
      c. How does library instruction affect job placement or salary?
   2. How do academic library resources or services impact success outcomes for different students?
      a. What difference in information literacy test scores (test/retest scores) do graduate and undergraduate students exhibit?
      b. How do military students benefit from library instruction?
   3. What outcome data do other departments/units in different institution types collect?
      a. What data do university tutoring centers collect?
      b. What student success and library instruction data do libraries at community colleges collect?
      c. How does library instruction at the primary level affect information literacy in four-year colleges?

IV. Learning analytics
    1. How are analytics being used?
        a. What types of data do offices or units relating to institutional research collect?
        b. What data are being used to correlate resources and services with student success in the Midwest?
    2. How have libraries triangulated data on their resources and services to demonstrate their impact on student success?
        a. How have librarians used (mixed or multiple methods) to demonstrate how undergraduate student usage of library collections affects retention?
        b. What qualitative data collection methods have been used to measure the impact of library instruction on graduate student success?
    3. How have libraries at research universities balanced concerns about maintaining user privacy with correlation studies?
        a. How are administrators monitoring student success?
    4. What data collection methods have LIS researchers used to measure the impact of library instruction on student learning and success?

V. Collaboration
    1. What types of collaboration exist between libraries and other departments that share space in private research universities?
        a. What departments are sharing library space in four-year colleges?
        b. Were libraries sharing space differently in 2010 compared to 2016?
    2. How do libraries collaborate with other units to support teaching and learning in community colleges?
        a. Where do undergraduate students go to discover information?
    3. What affects collaboration at four-year colleges?
        a. How can libraries increase collaboration with faculty when teaching graduate students?
        b. How is collaboration with writing centers measured?
    4. How have collaborative relationships between library administrators and staff, faculty, and staff from different academic departments evolved over time?
    5. How are library contributions to collaborative efforts measured?

VI. Communication
    1. What types of library resources or services matter to administrators?
        a. How do provosts view libraries' contributing to teaching and learning?
    2. What do faculty surveys tell us about how they envision library resources or services?
        a. What types of information do instructors need for teaching?
    3. How can libraries develop better communication?
        a. What are the main barriers to communication for undergraduate students at four-year colleges?
    4. What factors influence library communication with community college users and potential users?
        a. How does the use of social media increase library communication?

Appendix K: Detailed Scoring Scheme for Exemplary Research Designs and Practices

As noted in the *Selected LIS and Higher Education Literature* section, there were 369 research documents coded in this project. To identify the studies that relate to the priority areas and that demonstrated exemplary designs and effective practices, the studies were scored quantitatively. This provided a relatively simple and objective way to identify studies that covered a relatively wide range of higher education trends. To quantitatively score the 369 studies for consideration as exemplar, a method of assigning points to each study was developed. There were five criteria each for which points were assigned. These criteria are:

Number of themes it incorporates (each theme = 1 pt). Covering more themes is desirable since it indicates that the study was based on research, or at least knowledge, of what was going on in higher education.

Context (community college = 1 pt, multiple institutions = 2 pts). Based on evidence from the literature review and feedback from advisory group members and the ACRL board, there exists a lack of research in community colleges. For this reason, studies that took place in this type of institution were awarded a point. Studies between multiple institutions broadened the context of a finding and suggested that the study could be replicated at another institution, so these studies were awarded two points.

Level of effort of data collection and analysis (mixed methods = 2 pts, multiple methods = 1 pt). Use of mixed or multiple methods strengthens the validity of a study's findings. Mixed methods are worth more than multiple methods since they employ qualitative and quantitative approaches.

Level of impact (collaboration/communication/mission alignment and strategy/teaching and learning/student success = 1pt). The level of impact includes whether the research document would resonate with those outside libraries. This translated into codes that involved interactions with those outside the library, specifically collaboration and communication, or evaluative standards from the institution and outside the library, specifically mission alignment and strategy, student learning, and student success.

Population studied (inclusivity = 1 pt). The RFP suggested that the research agenda and report include studies that "include[d] but [were] not limited to studies of defined populations (e.g., economically disadvantaged students, adult learners, or students who are the first in their families to attend college) in a manner that promotes equity mindedness and inclusive excellence."[220] The theme of inclusivity also came up in the provost interviews as a key strength of the libraries because all students were welcome there, and in many ways, the library spaces were more neutral meeting grounds between various academic and institutional units.[221] Therefore, studies that were coded with the inclusivity theme also received a point.

Appendix L: AiA Studies with Exemplary Design Elements

Context

Balci, Leanna F., Ben Crowder, and Nancy Wentworth. "Lost Library Links: Student's Ignore LMS Library Integration." Assessment in Action. Accessed January 5, 2017. https://apply.ala.org/attachments/26857.

Erickson, Sue, Patty Clark, David Dirlam, Denise Wilkinson, Stephen Leist, and Cathal Woods. "Understanding the Liberal Arts through Book Displays at Hofheimer Library." Assessment in Action. Accessed January 5, 2017. https://apply.ala.org/attachments/20599.

Samuel, Judith, and Sally Romero. "Measuring Information Literacy Success: From One-Shot Basic Skills Workshops to Embedded Librarian in California Acceleration Project." Assessment in Action. Accessed January 5, 2017. https://apply.ala.org/attachments/8871.

Tharp, Julie, Lisa Kammerlocher, Ashley Barckett, Kate Frost, and Jeanne Hanrahan. "Bridging the Critical Thinking Gap: Assessing the Integration of Information Literacy into the Curriculum for At-Risk Students." Assessment in Action. Accessed January 5, 2017. https://apply.ala.org/attachments/8866.

Data Collection

Blank, Michelle, Lisa Crumit-Hancock, Nathan Griggs, and Abigail Taylor. "'I Just Use Google': The Role of Information Literacy Skills in Academic Inquiry." Assessment in Action. Accessed January 5, 2017. https://apply.ala.org/attachments/20474.

Carbery, Alan, Ellen Zeman, Josh Blumberg, and Steve Wehmeyer. "Authentic Assessment: Building a Longitudinal Information Literacy Assessment Model Using Student Research Artifacts." Assessment in Action. Accessed January 5, 2017. https://apply.ala.org/attachments/20610.

Epperson, Anne, James Henderson, and Evan Welch. "Designed and Furnished for Success: Fostering an 'Academically Social' Campus Space." Assessment in Action. Accessed January 5, 2017. https://apply.ala.org/attachments/8881.

Ireland, Ashley, Jana Hackathorn, Jamie Mantooth, Aleeah McGinnis, Adam Murray, and Kelley Wezner. "Predictor of Success: The Relationship between Known Library Use and Student Retention at a Regional Public University." Assessment in Action. Accessed January 5, 2017. https://apply.ala.org/attachments/8986.

Massengale, Lisa, Pattie Piotrowski, and Devin Savage. "Galvin Library Assessment." Assessment in Action. Accessed January 5, 2017. https://apply.ala.org/attachments/20544.

Data Sampling

Alexander, Stephanie, Alexis Alabastro, My-Lan Huynh, and Sharon Radcliff. "Impact of IL Instruction on Transfer Student GPA and Use of Library Resources." Assessment in Action. Accessed January 5, 2017. https://apply.ala.org/attachments/27461.

Caldwell, Lesley, Emma Lausen, Courtney Edwards, Zoe Fisher, Erik Gimness, Rachel Goon, Carly Haddon, Robert Johnson, Krissy Kim, Laurie Shuster, Kathy Twart, Beth Thoms, and Shane Agustin. "Plant More One-Shots?

Prune Them Back? Or Plow Them Under?" Assessment in Action. Accessed January 5, 2017. https://apply.ala.org/attachments/20496.

Leung, Sofia, Stephanie Gamble, Ellen Raimond, Anne M. Johnson, and Amalia Monroe-Gulick. "Exploring Undergraduate Student Use of Learning Studio Space at the University of Kansas (KU)." Assessment in Action. Accessed January 5, 2017. https://apply.ala.org/attachments/26824.

Mondschein, Henri, Cia DeMartino, Rodney Reynolds, and Nicole M. Stanoff. "Do Online Learning Modules Have a Role in Information Literacy Instruction?" Assessment in Action. Accessed January 5, 2017. https://apply.ala.org/attachments/8869.

Smith, Kelly, Matthew Irvin, Jens Arneson, Kwan Yi, Todd King, and Chad Adkins. "Library Resource Usage and Student Success at Eastern Kentucky University." Assessment in Action. Accessed January 5, 2017. https://apply.ala.org/attachments/20592.

Data Analysis

Chadock, Ted, Yelena Bailey-Kirby, Courtney Danforth, Shelley Fischer, Linda Foreman, Pamela Gallion, Christopher Perkins, Carrie Preite, Caprice Roberson, and Laura Yavitz. "Attitudes Matter: Student Success beyond Information Literacy." Assessment in Action. Accessed January 5, 2017. https://apply.ala.org/attachments/20460.

Lowe, Sara, Char Booth, Sean Stone, Natalie Tagge, Alexandra Chappell, and Gale Burrow. "Librarians Matter! Impact on First-Year Information Literacy Skills at Five Colleges." Assessment in Action. Accessed January 5, 2017. https://apply.ala.org/attachments/8854.

Resnis, Eric, Carolyn Haynes, Cecilia Shore, Andrea Bakkar, Jennifer Natale, Laura Birkenhauer, Rob Casson, and Mike Bomholt. "Dedicated Technology Facilities: Impacts, Success, and Implications." Assessment in Action. Accessed January 5, 2017. https://apply.ala.org/attachments/8874.

Squibb, Sara D., Susan Mikkelsen, Laura Martin, Matt Moberly, and Anne Zanzucchi. "Assessing an Embedded Information Literacy Emphasis Introductory Writing Class." Assessment in Action. Accessed January 5, 2017. https://apply.ala.org/attachments/20502.

Design

Baillargeon, Tara, Martha Jermé, Josh Know, and Sharron Ronco. "Flipped Learning and Evidence Based Medicine Skills." Assessment in Action. Accessed January 5, 2017. https://apply.ala.org/attachments/20495.

Murphy, Sarah A., Elizabeth L. Black, Sophie Tullier, Emily Slager, and Alexis Collier. "AiA and the Second-Year Transformational Experience Program." Assessment in Action. Accessed January 5, 2017. https://apply.ala.org/attachments/8873.

Nicholson, Karen, Melanie Parlette-Stewart, Kim Garwood, and Trent Tucker. "Evaluating the Impact of Face-to-Face and Online Information Literacy and Writing Skills Instruction Using a Mixed Methods Research Design." Assessment in Action. Accessed January 5, 2017. https://apply.ala.org/attachments/8860.

Ray, Jacquelyn, Cheri Kendrick, and Craig McIntosh. "Expanding Our Reach: Pedagogical Strategies and Information Literacy Learning in an Online versus Traditional Classroom." Assessment in Action. Accessed January 5, 2017. https://apply.ala.org/attachments/26911.

Whitlock, Brandy, Nassim Ebrahimi, and Marjorie Paoletti. "Finding the Cocked Hat: Triangulating Assessment for Information Literacy as a College-wide Core Competency." Assessment in Action. Accessed January 5, 2017. https://apply.ala.org/attachments/8894.

Discussion

Bartholomew, Jennifer, Bruce Eldevik, Michael Chan, Terri Elton, Mark Granquist, Leonard Hummel, Amy Marga, and Laurel Forsgren. "Cultivating a Culture of Assessment Using Multiple Collaborative Assignments to Teach Information Literacy Skills." Assessment in Action. Accessed January 5, 2017. https://apply.ala.org/attachments/20538.

Lock, Mary Beth, Meghan Webb, Glenda Boyles, Le'Ron Byrd, John Champlin, and Ryan Shirey. "What's in It for Me? Success, Motivation, and Gaps." Assessment in Action. Accessed January 5, 2017. https://apply.ala.org/attachments/20513.

Sharpe, Stephanie, Kris Helbling, Carol Mollman, Ted Chaffin, Susan Lowther, and Robert Patterson. "Assessing Research and Writing Support for First-Year Writing." Assessment in Action. Accessed January 5, 2017. https://apply.ala.org/attachments/20520.

Future Work

Burkhardt, Jess, Debbie Malone, Lynne Kvinnesland, Deb Booros, Jim Castagna, and Marc Albanese. "TV or Not TV: Assessing Student Learning of Search as Strategic Exploration." Assessment in Action. Accessed January 5, 2017. https://apply.ala.org/attachments/27096.

Martinez, Josie U., Steven Wise, Brighid Gonzales, Candace Zepeda, Kirsten Komara, Sabrina Zertuche, and Andrew Hale. "Video Killed the One Shot Session: Embedding Online Tutorials in First Year Composition Classes and the Effects on Student Success." Assessment in Action. Accessed January 5, 2017. https://apply.ala.org/attachments/20532.

Reporting

Glass, Amy. "Library Assessment—the Next Frontier! Our Mission for this Project: How Does Library Instruction Impact Student Success within Sections of ENG 111 (Composition II)?" Assessment in Action. Accessed January 5, 2017. https://apply.ala.org/attachments/8765.

Liss, Ken, Tom Casserly, Gwen Kordonowy, Sarah Madsen Hardy, and Gillian Pierce. "Telling Students to 'Get Lost!': Research as Inquiry and Searching as Strategic Exploration." Assessment in Action. Accessed January 5, 2017. https://apply.ala.org/attachments/26789.

Morganelli, H., S. Tonner, L. Driver, S. Doscher, G. Pearson, and K. Perez. "The Influence of Faculty Collaboration on Students' Information Literacy." Assessment in Action. Accessed January 5, 2017. https://apply.ala.org/attachments/20477.

Topic/Problem

Bishop, Katie, Connie Sorensen-Birk, and Derek Boeckner. "Don't Wait for Them to Come to You: Partnering with Student Support Services." Assessment in Action. Accessed January 5, 2017. https://apply.ala.org/attachments/20491.

Lantzy, Tricia, Lea Roberg-Chao, and Melissa Simnett. "How Does It Measure Up? Assessing Student Learning in Online Versus Face-to-Face Instruction." Assessment in Action. Accessed January 5, 2017. https://apply.ala.org/attachments/26823.

Torres, Elizabeth, Timothy Martin, Farris Sanders, Nori Leong, Sheryl Sunia, and Han N. C. Wester. "Assessing Library Instruction for Military Students." Assessment in Action. Accessed January 5, 2017. https://apply.ala.org/attachments/26855.

Notes

1. Association of College and Research Libraries, *The Value of Academic Libraries: A Comprehensive Research Review and Report*, researched by Megan Oakleaf (Chicago: Association of College and Research Libraries, 2010), http://www.ala.org/acrl/sites/ala.org.acrl/files/content/issues/value/val_report.pdf; "An Executive Summary," *Chronicle of Higher Education* 62, no. 25 (March 4, 2016): B4; Laura Saunders, "Academic Libraries' Strategic Plans: Top Trends and Under-recognized Areas," *Journal of Academic Librarianship* 41, no. 3 (2015): 285–91; ACRL Research Planning and Review Committee, *Environmental Scan 2015* (Chicago: Association of College and Research Libraries, 2015), http://www.ala.org/acrl/sites/ala.org.acrl/files/content/publications/whitepapers/EnvironmentalScan15.pdf.
2. Association of College and Research Libraries, *Value of Academic Libraries*; Judith Broady-Preston and Alison Lobo, "Measuring the Quality, Value and Impact of Academic Libraries: The Role of External Standards," *Performance Measurement and Metrics* 12, no. 2 (2011): 122–35; Joseph R. Matthews, "Assessing Organizational Effectiveness: The Role of Performance Measures," *Library* 81, no. 1 (2011): 83–110; Jason M. Vance, Rachel Kirk, and Justin G. Gardner, "Measuring the Impact of Library Instruction on Freshman Success and Persistence," *Communications in Information Literacy* 6, no. 1 (2012): 49–58.
3. Moe Hosseini-Ara and Rebecca Jones, "Overcoming Our Habits and Learning to Measure Impact," *Computers in Libraries* 33, no. 5 (2013): 3–7; Jon R. Hufford, "Can the Library Contribute Value to the Campus Culture for Learning?" *Journal of Academic Librarianship* 39, no. 3 (2013): 288–96; Amanda B. Albert, "Communicating Library Value: The Missing Piece of the Assessment Puzzle," *Journal of Academic Librarianship* 40, no. 6 (2014): 634–37, doi:10.1016/j.acalib.2014.10.001.
4. McGraw Hill Education, *The Changing Role of Libraries* (New York: McGraw Hill, 2016), https://learn.mheducation.com/rs/303-FKF-702/images/Whitepaper_AccessEducation_RoleofLibraries_10-2016_v4%20%283%29.pdf.
5. Barbara Fister, "Critical Assets: Academic Libraries, A View from the Administration Building," *Library Journal* 135, no. 8 (2010): 24–27; Beverly P. Lynch, Catherine Murray-Rust, Susan E. Parker, Deborah Turner, Diane Parr Walker, Frances C. Wilkinson, and Julia Zimmerman, "Attitudes of Presidents and Provosts on the University Library," *College and Research Libraries* 68, no. 3 (2007): 213–28, http://crl.acrl.org/index.php/crl/issue/view/1011; Mark Robertson, "Perceptions of Canadian Provosts on the Institutional Role of Academic Libraries," *College and Research Libraries* 76, no. 4 (2015): 490–511, http://crl.acrl.org/index.php/crl/issue/view/1060.
6. Lorcan Dempsey, "The Road Ahead 4: Challenges and Opportunities for Academic Libraries" (presentation, The Future of Academic Libraries: A Symposium on Provision for Online and Distance Learning Students, The Open University, Milton Keynes, UK, March 17, 2016), http://www.oclc.org/content/dam/research/presentations/dempsey/dempsey-open-university-2016.pptx.
7. Ibid.
8. Christine Wolff-Eisenberg, *US Library Survey 2016* (New York: Ithaka S+R, April 3, 2017), http://www.sr.ithaka.org/publications/us-library-survey-2016.
9. Emmett Lombard, "The Role of the Academic Library in College Choice," *Journal of Academic Librarianship* 38, no. 4 (2012): 237–41, doi:10.1016/j.acalib.2012.04.001.
10. "About," 1st International Conference on Learning Analytics and Knowledge 2011, accessed January 4, 2017, https://tekri.athabascau.ca/analytics.
11. Margie Jantti and Jennifer Heath, "What Role for Libraries in Learning Analytics?" *Performance Measurement and Metrics* 17, no. 2 (2016): 203–10, doi:10.1108/PMM-04-2016-0020.
12. Clifford Lynch, "The Rise of Reading Analytics and the Emerging Calculus of Reader Privacy in the Digital World," *First Monday* 22, no. 4 (2017), http://firstmonday.org/ojs/index.php/fm/article/view/7414.
13. Brian Cox and Margie Jantti, "Discovering the Impact of Library Use and Student Performance," *EDUCAUSE Review*, July 17, 2012, http://er.educause.edu/articles/2012/7/discovering-the-impact-of-library-use-and-student-performance; Shane Nackerud, Jan Fransen, Kate Peterson, and Kristen Mastel, "Analyzing Demographics: Assessing Library Use across the Institution," *portal: Libraries and the Academy* 13, no. 2 (2013): 131–45.
14. Krista Soria, Jan Fransen, and Shane Nackerud, "Library Use and Undergraduate Student Outcomes: New Evidence for Students' Retention and Academic Success," *portal: Libraries and the Academy* 13, no. 2 (2013): 147–64; Margie Jantti and Brian Cox, "Measuring the Value of Library Resources and Student Academic Performance through Relational Datasets," *Evidence Based Library and Information Practice* 8, no. 2 (2013): 163–71.
15. Association of College and Research Libraries, *Framework for Information Literacy for Higher Education* (Chicago: Association for College and Research Libraries, 2015), http://www.ala.org/acrl/standards/ilframework.
16. Association of College and Research Libraries Research Planning and Review Committee, "2016 Top Trends in Academic Libraries: A Review of the Trends and Issues Affecting Academic Libraries in Higher Education," *College and Research Libraries* 77, no. 6 (2016): 274–81.
17. Kate Pitcher, "Library Publishing of Open Textbooks: The Open SUNY Textbooks Program," *Against the Grain* 26, no. 5 (2014): 22–24; Julia Hess, Alejandra J. Nann, and Kelly E. Riddle, "Navigating OER: The Library's Role in Bringing OER to Campus," *Serials Librarian* 70, no. 1/4 (2016): 128–34; Mandi Goodsett, Barbara Loomis, and Marsha Miles, "Leading Campus OER Initiatives through Library–Faculty Collaboration," *College and Undergraduate Libraries* 23, no. 3 (2016): 335–42.
18. Margaret Brown-Sica, "Using Academic Courses to Generate Data for Use in Evidence Based Library Planning," *Journal of*

Academic Librarianship 39, no. 3 (2013): 275–87; Bonnie L. Fong, Minglu Wang, Krista White, and Roberta Tipton, "Assessing and Serving the Workshop Needs of Graduate Students," *Journal of Academic Librarianship* 42, no. 5 (2016): 569–80; Kyrille Goldbeck Debose, Inga Haugen, and Rebecca K. Miller, "Information Literacy Instruction Programs: Supporting the College of Agriculture and Life Sciences Community at Virginia Tech," *Library Trends* 65, no. 3 (2017): 316–38; Robin E. Miller, "Plagiarism Curricula May Reduce Need for Punitive Plagiarism Education," *Evidence Based Library and Information Practice* 9, no. 1 (2014): 39–41; Coleen Meyers-Martin and Laurie Borchard, "The Finals Stretch: Exams Week Library Outreach Surveyed," *Reference Services Review* 43, no. 4 (2015): 510–32; Maureen Richards, "24/7 Library Hours at an Urban Commuter College," *Urban Library Journal* 22, no. 1 (2016): 1–23; Jean Hiebert and Shelly Theriault, "BLASTing the Zombies!" *College and Research Libraries News* 73, no. 9 (2012): 540–69; Jo Ann Reynolds and Laurel Rabschutz, "Studying for Exams Just Got More Relaxing—Animal-Assisted Activities at the University of Connecticut Library," *College and Undergraduate Libraries* 18, no. 4 (2011): 359–67; Elizabeth M. Smigielski and Neal D. Nixon, "The Library as Finals Resting Place: Expanding Service to Health Sciences Students during Final Exams," *Medical Reference Services Quarterly* 23, no. 1 (2004): 29–39.

19. "The 2017 Trends Report," *Chronicle of Higher Education*, accessed April 21, 2017, http://www.chronicle.com/specialreport/The-2017-Trends-Report/95.
20. Association of College and Research Libraries, *Standards for Libraries in Higher Education* (Chicago: Association of College and Research Libraries, 2011), http://www.ala.org/acrl/standards/standardslibraries; Gap Analysis Subcommittee, *Final Report to ACRL VAL Committee from Gap Analysis Subcommittee, Presented for ALA Annual Conference 2015* (Chicago: Association of College and Research Libraries, 2015), http://www.acrl.ala.org/value/wp-content/uploads/2016/04/VAL-Cmte-Gap-Analysis-FINAL-ALA-Annual-2015.pdf.
21. Lynn Silipigni Connaway, Vanessa Kitzie, Erin M. Hood, and William Harvey, with contributions from Allison Benedetti, Agustí Canals, Liliana Gregori, Eva Ortoll Espinet, Daniel Lozano, Melissa Man, Josep Cobarsí Morales, Sara Giuliana Ricetto, Riccardo Melgrati, Eva M. Méndez Rodríguez, Andrea Sada, Peter Sidorko, Paolo Sirito, Virginia Steel, and Esther Woo, *The Many Faces of Digital Visitors and Residents: Facets of Online Engagement* (Dublin, OH: OCLC Research, forthcoming).
22. Amanda Nichols Hess, Katie Greer, Shawn V. Lombardo, and Adriene Lim, "Books, Bytes, and Buildings: The Academic Library's Unique Role in Improving Student Success," *Journal of Library Administration* 55, no. 8 (2015): 622–38, doi:10.1080/01930826.2015.1085241; Kate S. Wolfe, "Emerging Information Literacy and Research-Method Competencies in Urban Community College Psychology Students," *Community College Enterprise* 21, no. 2 (2015): 93–99.
23. Lynn Silipigni Connaway, William Harvey, Vanessa Kitzie, and Stephanie Mikitish, "Changing Tack: A Future-Focused ACRL Research Agenda" (presentation, Association of College and Research Libraries [ACRL] Conference, Baltimore, MD, March 23, 2017), https://www.slideshare.net/oclcr/changing-tack-a-futurefocused-acrl-research-agenda-73607657; Lynn Silipigni Connaway, "Where Are We Going and What Do We Do Next? Demonstrating the Value of Academic Libraries in Times of Uncertainty" YouTube video, 22:26, from presentation, Research Libraries UK Conference, London, UK, March 9, 2017, https://www.youtube.com/watch?v=FyXNEwVV-q0; Lynn Silipigni Connaway, William Harvey, Vanessa Kitzie, and Stephanie Mikitish, "Action-Oriented Research Agenda on Library Contributions to Student Learning and Success" (presentation, ALA Midwinter Conference, VAL Update Session, Atlanta, GA, January 22, 2017), http://www.slideshare.net/oclcr/actionoriented-research-agenda-on-library-contributions-to-student-learning-and-success-72009285; Lynn Silipigni Connaway, Vanessa Kitzie, Stephanie Mikitish, and Jaime Hammond, "ACRL Presents: Update on ACRL Action-Oriented Research Agenda," YouTube video, 59:49, from virtual forum presented by ACRL, November 15, 2016, https://www.youtube.com/watch?v=PhOI-R3u_Gdo&feature=youtu.be; Lynn Silipigni Connaway and Alan Carbery, "What Do We Want to Know: Completing an Action-Oriented Research Agenda" (presentation, 2016 Library Assessment Conference [LAC], Arlington, VA, November 2, 2016), http://www.slideshare.net/LynnConnaway/what-do-we-want-to-know-completing-an-actionoriented-research-agenda.
24. Association of College and Research Libraries, *Request for Proposals: Action-Oriented Research Agenda on Library Contributions to Student Learning and Success* (Chicago: Association of College and Research Libraries, 2016), http://www.acrl.ala.org/value/wp-content/uploads/2016/04/ACRL-RFP-for-action-oriented-research-agenda.pdf.
25. Peter Hernon, Robert Dugan, and Danuta Nitecki, *Engaging in Evaluation and Assessment Research* (Santa Barbara, CA: Libraries Unlimited, 2011).
26. Jon R. Hufford, "A Review of the Literature on Assessment in Academic and Research Libraries, 2005 to August 2011," *portal: Libraries and the Academy* 13, no. 1 (2013): 5–35, doi:10.1353/pla.2013.0005.
27. Paul Coleman and Ada D. Jarred, "Regional Association Criteria and the Standards for College Libraries: The Informal Role of Quantitative Input Measures for Libraries in Accreditation," *Journal of Academic Librarianship* 20, no. 5–6 (1994): 273–84, doi:10.1016/0099-1333(94)90063-9; Madeline Kelly, "Applying the Tiers of Assessment: A Holistic and Systematic Approach to Assessing Library Collections," *Journal of Academic Librarianship* 40, no. 6 (2014): 585–91; Association of College and Research Libraries, *Standards for Libraries in Higher Education*.
28. Ben Hunter and Robert Perret, "Can Money Buy Happiness? A Statistical Analysis of Predictors for User Satisfaction," *Journal of Academic Librarianship* 37, no. 5 (2011): 402–8, doi:10.1016/j.acalib.2011.06.004; Graham Matthews and Graham Walton, "Strategic Development of University Library Space: Widening the Influence," *New Library World* 115, no. 5/6 (2014): 237–49; ARL Statistics home page, accessed January 5, 2017, https://www.arlstatistics.org/home.
29. Boris Teske, Michael DiCarlo, and Dexter Cahoy, "Libraries and Student Persistence at Southern Colleges and Universities," *Reference Services Review* 41, no. 2 (2013): 266–79, doi:10.1108/00907321311326174.
30. Nackerud et al., "Analyzing Demographics"; Valery King and Sara Christensen-Lee, "Full-Time Reference with Part-Time Librarians: Dealing with Staffing Realities, Meeting User Needs," *Reference and User Services Quarterly* 54, no. 1 (2014): 34–43,

doi:10.5860/rusq.54n1.34.

31. Stephen Bollinger, Nina Exner, and Octavious Spruill, "Trying to Measure Success: A Mid-size Academic Library Grapples with Assessing a Popular Tablet Loan Project," in *Mobile Devices: Services with Intention*, ed. Rebecca K. Miller, Heather Moorefield-Lang, and Carolyn Meier, *Library Technology Reports* 51, no. 7 (2015): 9–15.
32. Liangzhi Yu, Qiulan Hong, Song Gu, and Yazun Wang, "An Epistemological Critique of Gap Theory Based Library Assessment: The Case of SERVQUAL," *Journal of Documentation* 64, no. 4 (2008): 511–51, http://www.emeraldinsight.com/doi/abs/10.1108/00220410810884066.
33. Colleen Cook, Fred Heath, and Bruce Thompson, "Users' Hierarchical Perspectives on Library Service Quality: A 'LibQUAL+' Study," *College and Research Libraries* 62, no. 2 (2001): 147–53, http://crl.acrl.org/index.php/crl/article/view/15432; Martha Kyrillidou and Fred M. Heath, "The Starving Research Library User: Relationships between Library Institutional Characteristics and Spring 2002 LibQUAL+(™) Scores," *Journal of Library Administration* 40, no. 3/4 (2004): 1–11, doi:10.1300/J111v40n03_01; Colleen Cook and Bruce Thompson, "Psychometric Properties of Scores from the Web-Based LibQUAL+ Study of Perceptions of Library Service Quality," *Library Trends* 49, no. 4 (2001): 585–604, https://www.ideals.illinois.edu/bitstream/handle/2142/8369/librarytrendsv49i4d_opt.pdf; Bruce Thompson, Colleen Cook, and Martha Kyrillidou, "Concurrent Validity of LibQUAL+™ Scores: What Do LibQUAL+™ Scores Measure?" *Journal of Academic Librarianship* 31, no. 6 (2005): 517–22, doi:10.1016/j.acalib.2005.08.002; Youhua Wei, Bruce Thompson, and C. Colleen Cook, "Scaling Users' Perceptions of Library Service Quality Using Item Response Theory: A LibQUAL+™ Study," *portal: Libraries and the Academy* 5, no. 1 (2005): 93–104, http://www.libqual.org/documents/admin/scaling_perceptions.pdf; "General Information," LibQUAL+ website, accessed January 4, 2017, https://www.libqual.org/about/about_lq/general_info.
34. Lorraine J. Haricombe and Bonna J. Boettcher, "Using LibQUAL+(™) Data in Strategic Planning: Bowling Green State University," *Journal of Library Administration* 40, no. 3/4 (2004): 181–95, doi:10.1300/J111v40n03_14; Steve Hiller, "Another Tool in the Assessment Toolbox: Integrating LibQUAL+(™) into the University of Washington Libraries Assessment Program," *Journal of Library Administration* 40, no. 3/4 (2008): 121–37, doi:10.1300/J111v40n03_10; Amy E. Knapp, "We Asked Them What They Thought, Now What Do We Do? The Use of LibQUAL+(™) Data to Redesign Public Services at the University of Pittsburgh," *Journal of Library Administration* 40, no. 3/4 (2004): 157–71, doi:10.1300/J111v40n03_12; Stephen R. Shorb and Lori Driscoll, "LibQUAL+(™) Meets Strategic Planning at the University of Florida," *Journal of Library Administration* 40, no. 3/4 (2008): 173–80, doi:10.1300/J111v40n03_13; Judy T. Greenwood, Alex P. Watson, and Melissa Dennis, "Ten Years of LibQual: A Study of Qualitative and Quantitative Survey Results at the University of Mississippi 2001–2010," *Journal of Academic Librarianship* 37, no. 4 (2011): 312–18, http://www.sciencedirect.com/science/article/pii/S0099133311000735; John H. Heinrichs, Thomas Sharkey, and Jeen-Su Lim, "Relative Influence of the LibQUAL+™ Dimensions on Satisfaction: A Subgroup Analysis," *College and Research Libraries* 66, no. 3 (2005): 248–65, http://crl.acrl.org/index.php/crl/article/view/15728; Sherri Jones and Jessica Kayongo, "Identifying Student and Faculty Needs through LibQUAL+™: An Analysis of Qualitative Survey Comments," *College and Research Libraries* 69, no. 6 (2008): 493-509, http://crl.acrl.org/index.php/crl/article/view/15967; Yu et al., "An Epistemological Critique of Gap Theory Based Library Assessment"; Jeffrey N. Gatten, "Measuring Consortium Impact on User Perceptions: OhioLINK and LibQUAL+™," *Journal of Academic Librarianship* 30, no. 3 (2004): 222-28, doi:10.1016/j.acalib.2004.02.004; Tom Sanville, "Defending and Expanding Library Turf: The Need for Scalable Consumer Research," *Journal of Library Administration* 40, no. 3/4 (2004): 13–17, doi:10.1300/J111v40n03_02; Flo Wilson, "LibQUAL+(™) 2002 at Vanderbilt University: What Do the Results Mean and Where Do We Go from Here?" *Journal of Library Administration* 40, no. 3/4 (2008): 197–240, doi:10.1300/J111v40n03_15; Maria Anna Jankowska, Karen Hertel, and Nancy J. Young, "Improving Library Service Quality to Graduate Students: LibQual+TM Survey Results in a Practical Setting," *portal: Libraries and the Academy* 6, no. 1 (2006): 59–76, http://www.libqual.org/documents/admin/Jankowska_Hertel_Young.pdf; Bruce Thompson, Colleen Cook, and Martha Kyrillidou, "Using Localized Survey Items to Augment Standardized Benchmarking Measures: A LibQUAL+ Study," *portal: Libraries and the Academy* 6, no. 2 (2006): 219–30, doi:10.1353/pla.2006.0029; Michael J. Roszkowski, John S. Baky, and David B. Jones, "So Which Score on the LibQual+™ Tells Me If Library Users are Satisfied?" *Library and Information Science Research* 27, no. 4 (2005): 424–39, doi:10.1016/j.lisr.2005.08.002; Abhik Roy, Adwait Khare, Ben S. C. Liu, Linda M. Hawkes, and Janice Swiatek-Kelley, "An Investigation of Affect of Service Using a LibQUAL+™ Survey and an Experimental Study," *Journal of Academic Librarianship* 38, no. 3 (2012): 153–60, doi:10.1016/j.acalib.2012.03.018; Xi Shi and Sarah Levy, "A Theory-Guided Approach to Library Services Assessment," *College and Research Libraries* 66, no. 3 (2005): 266–77, http://crl.acrl.org/index.php/crl/article/view/15729.
35. Hunter and Perret, "Can Money Buy Happiness?"
36. Angie Thorpe, Ria Lukes, Diane J. Bever, and Yan He, "The Impact of the Academic Library on Student Success: Connecting the Dots," *portal: Libraries and the Academy* 16, no. 2 (2016): 373–92, https://muse.jhu.edu/article/613847/pdf; Osman Celik and Roxanne Peck, "If You Expand, They Will Come: Textbook Affordability through Expansion of Course Reserves: The Case of UCLA Library's Course Reserves via Strategic Partnership with the Campus Independent Bookstore," *Technical Services Quarterly* 33, no. 3 (2016): 268–78, doi:10.1080/07317131.2016.1169788; M. Sara Lowe, Char Booth, Sean Stone, and Natalie Tagge, "Impacting Information Literacy Learning in First-Year Seminars: A Rubric-Based Evaluation," *portal: Libraries and the Academy* 15, no. 3 (2015): 489–512, doi:10.1353/pla.2015.0030; Hess et al., "Books, Bytes, and Buildings"; Denise Pan, Ignacio J. Ferrer-Vinent, and Margret Bruehl, "Library Value in the Classroom: Assessing Student Learning Outcomes from Instruction and Collections," *Journal of Academic Librarianship* 40, no. 3/4 (2014): 332–38, doi:10.1016/j.acalib.2014.04.011.
37. Soria, Fransen, and Nackerud, "Library Use and Undergraduate Student Outcomes"; Atif Yousef Odeh, "Use of Information Resources by Undergraduate Students and Its Relationship with Academic Achievement," *Libri* 62, no. 3 (2012): 222–32.

38. Sue Samson, "Information Literacy Learning Outcomes and Student Success," *Journal of Academic Librarianship* 36, no. 3 (2010): 202–10, doi:10.1016/j.acalib.2010.03.002; Brian Lym, Hal Grossman, Lauren Yannotta, and Makram Talih, "Assessing the Assessment: How Institutions Administered, Interpreted, and Used SAILS," *Reference Services Review* 38, no. 1 (2010): 168–86, doi:10.1108/00907321011020806; Stephen "Mike" Kiel, Natalie Burclaff, and Catherine Johnson, "Learning by Doing: Developing a Baseline Information Literacy Assessment," *portal: Libraries and the Academy* 15, no. 4 (2015): 747–66, https://muse.jhu.edu/article/595064/pdf; Jackie Belanger, Ning Zou, Jenny Rushing Mills, Claire Holmes, and Megan Oakleaf, "Project RAILS: Lessons Learned about Rubric Assessments of Information Literacy Skills," *portal: Libraries and the Academy* 15, no. 4 (2015): 623–44, https://muse.jhu.edu/article/595058/pdf.
39. *Oxford English Dictionary* Online, s.v. "Learn," accessed January 4, 2017, http://www.oed.com/view/Entry/106716.
40. David L. Sills, ed. "Learning," in *International Encyclopedia of the Social Sciences*, vol. 9, 120, (New York: Macmillan, 1968), Gale Virtual Reference Library, http://go.galegroup.com/ps/i.do?p=GVRL&sw=w&u=new67449&v=2.1&it=r&id=GALE%7CCX3045000696&asid=b35129393a0470a5f1f0794445983fa9.
41. George D. Kuh, Jillian Kinzie, John H. Schuh, and Elizabeth J. Whitt, *Student Success in College: Creating Conditions that Matter* (San Francisco: John Wiley and Sons, 2011), iv.
42. Association of College and Research Libraries, "Assessment in Action Team Applications," accessed April 30, 2017, http://www.ala.org/acrl/aiaapplication; Association of College and Research Libraries, *Value of Academic Libraries*.
43. George D. Kuh, Jillian Kinzie, Jennifer A. Buckley, Brian K. Bridges, and John C. Hayek, *What Matters to Student Success: A Review of the Literature, Commissioned Report for the National Symposium on Postsecondary Student Success: Spearheading a Dialog on Student Success* (Washington, DC: National Postsecondary Education Cooperative, 2006), 5, https://nces.ed.gov/npec/pdf/kuh_team_report.pdf; Andrea Venezia, Patrick M. Callan, Joni E. Finney, Michael W. Kirst, and Michael D. Usdan, *The Governance Divide: A Report on a Four-State Study on Improving College Readiness and Success* (Washington, DC: National Center for Public Policy and Higher Education, September 2005), http://www.highereducation.org/reports/governance_divide.
44. Cindy A. Kilgo, Jessica K. Ezell Sheets, and Ernest T. Pascarella, "The Link between High-Impact Practices and Student Learning: Some Longitudinal Evidence," *Higher Education* 69, no. 4 (2015): 509–25, doi:10.1007/s10734-014-9788-z.
45. Agnieszka Bielinska-Kwapisz, "Impact of Writing Proficiency and Writing Center Participation on Academic Performance," *International Journal of Educational Management* 29, no. 4 (2015): 382–94.
46. Julia Bredtmann, Carsten J. Crede, and Sebastian Otten, "Methods for Evaluating Educational Programs: Does Writing Center Participation Affect Student Achievement?" *Evaluation and Program Planning* 36, no. 1 (2013): 115-23, doi:10.1016/j.evalprogplan.2012.09.003.
47. M. Kade Callahan and Donalda Chumney, "'Write Like College': How Remedial Writing Courses at a Community College and a Research University Position 'At-Risk' Students in the Field of Higher Education," *Teachers College Record* 111, no. 7 (2009): 1619–64.
48. E. Ní Fhloinn, O. Fitzmaurice, C. Mac an Bhaird, and C. O'Sullivan, "Student Perception of the Impact of Mathematics Support in Higher Education," *International Journal of Mathematical Education in Science and Technology* 45, no. 7 (2014): 953–67, doi:10.1080/0020739X.2014.892161.
49. Ibid.
50. Elizabeth D. Phillips, "Improving Advising Using Technology and Data Analytics," *Change: The Magazine of Higher Learning* 45, no. 1 (2013): 48–55.
51. Ibid., 48.
52. Kilgo, Sheets, and Pascarella, "The Link between High-Impact Practices and Student Learning."
53. George D. Kuh, *High-Impact Educational Practices: What They Are, Who Has Access to Them, and Why They Matter* (Washington, DC: Association of American Colleges and Universities, 2008).
54. Rosalind Latiner Raby, Gary M. Rhodes, and Albert Biscarra, "Community College Study Abroad: Implications for Student Success," *Community College Journal of Research and Practice* 38, no. 2/3 (2014): 174–83.
55. Benjamin F. Hadis, "Gauging the Impact of Study Abroad: How to Overcome the Limitations of a Single-Cell Design," *Assessment and Evaluation in Higher Education* 30, no. 1 (2005): 3–19, doi:10.1080/0260293042003243869.
56. Association of College and Research Libraries, *Request for Proposals*.
57. Lynn Silipigni Connaway, William Harvey, Vanessa Kitzie, and Stephanie Mikitish, How Far Have We Come and What Do We Do Next? An Agenda for Action-Based Research on Student Learning and Success, Excerpt of Proposal: Narrative (Dublin, OH: OCLC Research, 2016), 4, http://www.oclc.org/content/dam/research/themes/acrl-agenda.pdf.
58. Association of College and Research Libraries, *Value of Academic Libraries*.
59. Association of College and Research Libraries, *Documented Library Contributions to Student Learning and Success: Building Evidence with Team-Based Assessment in Action Campus Projects*, prepared by Karen Brown with contributions by Kara J. Malenfant (Chicago: Association of College and Research Libraries, 2016). http://www.ala.org/acrl/sites/ala.org.acrl/files/content/issues/value/contributions_y2.pdf.
60. Ibid.
61. ACRL Research Planning and Review Committee, *Environmental Scan 2015*.
62. Association of College and Research Libraries Research Planning and Review Committee, "2016 Top Trends in Academic Libraries."
63. ACRL Research Planning and Review Committee, *Environmental Scan 2015*.

64. Association of College and Research Libraries Research Planning and Review Committee, "2016 Top Trends in Academic Libraries."
65. Ibid.
66. Dagobert D. Runes, *The Dictionary of Philosophy* (New York: Philosophical Library, 2001), 346.
67. For a discussion on mixed methods, see Lynn Silipigni Connaway and Marie L. Radford, *Research Methods in Library and Information Science*, 6th ed. (Santa Barbara, CA: Libraries Unlimited, 2017), 229–33.
68. Matthew B. Miles, A. Michael Huberman, and Johnny Saldaña, *Qualitative Data Analysis: A Methods Sourcebook*, 3rd ed. (Los Angeles: Sage Publications, 2014); Earl R. Babbie, *The Practice of Social Research*, 14th ed. (Boston: Cengage Learning, 2016); Norman K. Denzin and Yvonna S. Lincoln, *Handbook of Qualitative Research* (Thousand Oaks, CA: Sage Publications, 2002); John W. Creswell, *Qualitative Inquiry and Research Design: Choosing among Five Approaches* (Thousand Oaks, CA: Sage Publications, 2007); David Kaplan, *The Sage Handbook of Quantitative Methodology for the Social Sciences* (Thousand Oaks, CA: Sage Publications, 2004); I. K. Ravichandra Rao, *Quantitative Methods in Library and Information Science* (New York: Halsted Press, 1983).
69. Association of College and Research Libraries, *Value of Academic Libraries.*
70. Ibid.
71. Association of College and Research Libraries, "Assessment in Action: Academic Libraries and Student Success," accessed January 4, 2017, http://www.ala.org/acrl/AiA.
72. Alfred E. Goldman and Susan S. McDonald, *The Group Depth Interview* (Englewood Cliffs, NJ: Prentice Hall, 1987), 7.
73. Victoria L. Young, "Focus on Focus Groups," *College and Research Libraries News* 54, no. 7 (July/August 1993): 391.
74. Connaway and Radford, *Research Methods*, 250.
75. Ibid., 253.
76. Ibid.
77. John W. Cresswell, *Research Design: Qualitative, Quantitative, and Mixed Methods Approaches*, 4th ed. (Thousand Oaks, CA: Sage Publications, 2014), 251.
78. Ibid., 240.
79. Lynch et al., "Attitudes of Presidents and Provosts"; Fister, "Critical Assets"; Robertson, "Perceptions of Canadian Provosts."
80. Leigh S. Eastbrook, *What Chief Academic Officers Want from Their Libraries: Findings from Interviews with Provosts and Chief Academic Officers* (Chicago: Association of College and Research Libraries, 2007), http://www.ala.org/acrl/sites/ala.org.acrl/files/content/publications/whitepapers/Finalreport-ACRLCAOs.pdf; Adam Murray and Ashley Ireland, "Provosts' Perceptions of Academic Library Value and Preferences for Communication: A National Study," *College and Research Libraries*, forthcoming.
81. Connaway and Radford, *Research Methods*, 241.
82. Ibid., 176.
83. Ibid., 300.
84. For a discussion of how to create codebooks, examples of how they can be used, and their effectiveness, see chapter 6 and chapter 10 in Connaway and Radford, *Research Methods.*
85. Earl Babbie, *The Practice of Social Research*, 10th ed. (Belmont, CA: Thomson/Wadsworth Publishing Company, 2003).
86. Hae-Young Kim, "Statistical Notes for Clinical Researchers: Post-Hoc Multiple Comparisons," *Restorative Dentistry and Endodontics* 40, no. 2 (2015): 172–76.
87. Runes, *Dictionary of Philosophy*, 346.
88 Creswell, John W. *Research Design: Qualitative, Quantitative, and Mixed Methods Approaches.* (Thousand Oaks, CA: Sage Publications, 2013), 3.
89. Creswell, *Qualitative Inquiry and Research Design.*
90. Association of College and Research Libraries, "Assessment in Action: Academic Libraries."
91. Association of College and Research Libraries, "Assessment in Action Team Applications."
92. Wolff-Eisenberg, *US Library Survey 2016.*
93. Ma Lei Hsieh, Susan McManimon, and Sharon Yang, "Faculty-Librarian Collaboration in Improving Information Literacy of Educational Opportunity Program Students," *Reference Services Review* 41, no. 2 (2013): 313–35; Danielle Barandiaran, Betty Rozum, and Becky Thorns, "Focusing on Student Research in the Institutional Repository," *College and Research Libraries News* 75, no. 10 (2014): 546–49; Betty Rozum, Becky Thoms, Scott Bates, and Danielle Barandiaran, "We Have Only Scratched the Surface: The Role of Student Research in Institutional Repositories," in *Creating Sustainable Community: The Proceedings of the ACRL 2015 Conference*, ed. Dawn M. Mueller, 804–12 (Portland, OR: Association of College and Research Libraries, 2015), http://www.ala.org/acrl/sites/ala.org.acrl/files/content/conferences/confsandpreconfs/2015/Rozum_Thoms_Bates_Barandiaran.pdf; Lisa Junghahn and Richard Buckingham, "Research Competition Awesomeness," *AALL Spectrum* 18, no. 3 (2013): 17–18; Clementine Lewis, "Enhancing the Role of the Library in the Research Process: A Review of the Research Review Competition," *Technical Services Quarterly* 28, no. 1 (2011): 17–30; Afra Bolefski, "Creating Partnerships with Business Student Organizations: Effectively Promoting and Providing Business Case Competition Research Sessions," *BF Bulletin* 152 (2014): 13–14.
94. Joe C. Clark, "User-Centered Events in a Performing Arts Library," *Fontes Artis Musicae* 59, no. 2 (April–June 2012): 158–67; Hubert David Womack, Susan Sharpless Smith, and Mary Beth Lock, "Large-Scale, Live-Action Gaming Events in Academic Libraries," *College and Research Libraries News* 76, no. 4 (2015): 210–14; Justin L. Otto, Qing Meade, Jeffrey Stafford, and Pa-

tricia Wahler, "Library Lights Out," *Digital Library Perspectives* 32, no. 3 (2016): 192–208; Thomas Courtier Devlyn and John DeLooper, "Hosting a Super Smash Bros. Tournament at the Hudson County Community College Library," *Library Hi Tech News* 34, no. 1 (2017): 11–16.

95. Kathryn M. Crowe, "Student Affairs Connection: Promoting the Library through Co-curricular Activities," *Collaborative Librarianship* 2, no. 3 (2010): 154–58; Ian Chant, "Academic: Univ. of Michigan Libraries Open Nap Stations," *Library Journal* 139, no. 10 (2014): 20; Elizabeth Schobernd, Toni Tucker, and Sharon Wetzel, "Closing the Gap: Use of Student Volunteers in an Academic Library," *Technical Services Quarterly* 26, no. 3 (2009): 194–98.
96. Shannon Najmabadi, "How One College Put Information Literacy into Its Curriculum," *Chronicle of Higher Education*, February 26, 2017, http://www.chronicle.com/article/How-One-College-Put/239293; Abrizah A. Samaila, Inuwa Samaila, and N. Afiqah-Izzati, "Systematic Literature Review Informing LIS Professionals on Embedding Librarianship Roles," *Journal of Academic Librarianship* 42, no. 6 (2016): 636–43; Carl R. Andrews, "An Examination of Embedded Librarian Ideas and Practices: A Critical Bibliography," *Codex* 3, no. 1 (2014): 69–87; Michelle Reale, *Becoming an Embedded Librarian: Making Connections in the Classroom* (Chicago: American Library Association, 2015); Lindsay Blake, Darra Ballance, Kathy Davies, Julie K. Gaines, Kim Mears, Peter Shipman, Maryska Connolly-Brown, and Vicki Burchfield, "Patron Perception and Utilization of an Embedded Librarian Program," *Journal of the Medical Library Association* 104, no. 3 (2016): 226–30; Pramod Sharma, Kamal Kumar, and Parveen Babbar, "Embedded Librarianship: Librarian Faculty Collaboration," *DESIDOC Journal of Library and Information Technology* 34, no. 6 (2014): 455–60; Raymond Pun, "The Embedded Librarian as an Entrepreneur in a Startup University," *Reference Services Review* 43, no. 3 (2015): 439–49.
97. Harry Glazer, "'Likes' Are Lovely, but Do They Lead to More Logins?" *College and Research Libraries News* 73, no. 1 (2012): 18–21; Timothy McClelland, "What Exactly Do You Do Here? Marketing-Related Jobs in Public and Academic Libraries," *Journal of Library Administration* 54, no. 5 (2014): 347–67; Matthew Ismail, "Marketing Academic Libraries—Marketing Is Communication with Our Users," *Against the Grain* 26, no. 1 (2014): 68–69.
98. Sonia Yaco, Caroline Brown, and Lee Konrad, "Linking Special Collections to Classrooms: A Curriculum-to-Collection Crosswalk," *American Archivist* 79, no. 2 (2016): 417–37; Matthew Cook, "Build It and They Will Come: Integrating Unique Collections and Undergraduate Research," *Collection Building* 34, no. 4 (2015): 128–33; Morgan Daniels and Elizabeth Yakel, "Uncovering Impact: The Influence of Archives on Student Learning," *Journal of Academic Librarianship* 39, no. 5 (2013): 414–22; Lindsay Anderberg, "STEM Undergraduates and Archival Instruction: A Case Study at NYU Polytechnic School of Engineering," *American Archivist* 78, no. 2 (2015): 548–66.
99. Rebecca Jackson and Kristine Stacy-Bates, "The Enduring Landscape of Online Subject Research Guides," *Reference and User Services Quarterly* 55, no. 3 (2016): 219–29; Amy Suiter and Heather Lea Moulaison, "Supporting Scholars: An Analysis of Academic Library Websites' Documentation on Metrics and Impact," *Journal of Academic Librarianship* 41, no. 6 (2015): 814–20; Lauren Wallis, "Building a Virtual Reference Shelf," *Serials Librarian* 67, no. 1 (2014): 52–60.
100. Mary Dugan, George Bergstrom, and Tomalee Doan, "Campus Career Collaboration: 'Do the Research. Land the Job,'" *College and Undergraduate Libraries* 16, no. 2/3 (2009): 122–37; Jennifer Wilson and Laurence Morris, "Promoting Library Engagement through Employability (Among Other Things)," *CILIP Update,* 205 (2016): 44–45.
101. Cox and Jantti, "Discovering the Impact of Library Use and Student Performance"; Nackerud et al., "Analyzing Demographics."
102. Joseph R. Matthews, "Assessing Library Contributions to University Outcomes: The Need for Individual Student Level Data," *Library Management* 33, no. 6/7 (2012): 389–402, doi:10.1108/01435121211266203; Shun Han Rebekah Wong and T. D. Webb, "Uncovering Meaningful Correlation between Student Academic Performance and Library Material Usage," *College and Research Libraries* 72, no. 4 (2011): 361–70, http://crl.acrl.org/index.php/crl/article/view/16168..
103. McGraw Hill Education, *Changing Role of Libraries.*
104. Shannon Najmabadi, "Information Literacy: It's Become a Priority in an Era of Fake News," *Chronicle of Higher Education,* Special Report, February 26, 2017, http://www.chronicle.com/article/Information-Literacy/239264.
105. George D. Kuh and Robert M. Gonyea, "The Role of the Academic Library in Promoting Student Engagement in Learning," *College and Research Libraries* 64, no. 4 (2003): 256–82; Mark Emmons and Frances C. Wilkinson, "The Academic Library Impact on Student Persistence," *College and Research Libraries* 72, no. 2 (2010): 128–49; Lynch et al., "Attitudes of Presidents and Provosts"; Fister, "Critical Assets."
106. Coleman and Jarred, "Regional Association Criteria and the Standards for College Libraries," 274.
107. US Department of Education, "FAQs about Accreditation," Database of Accredited Postsecondary Institutions and Programs, accessed May 31, 2017, https://ope.ed.gov/accreditation/FAQAccr.aspx.
108. Thomas D. Snyder, Cristobal de Brey, and Sally A. Dillow, *Digest of Education Statistics 2015*, 51st ed., NCES 2016-014 (Washington, DC: National Center for Education Statistics, 2016), https://nces.ed.gov/pubs2016/2016014.pdf; ACRL Research Planning and Review Committee, "Top Trends in Academic Libraries: A Review of the Trends and Issues Affecting Academic Libraries in Higher Education," *College and Research Libraries News* 75, no. 6 (2014): 294–302; Katy Mathuews, "Moving beyond Diversity to Social Justice: A Call to Action for Academic Libraries," *Progressive Librarian,* no. 44 (Spring 2016): 6–27, http://progressivelibrariansguild.org/PL/006.pdf.
109. Susan Bailey and Megan Slemons, "Halt! Who Goes There? Assessing Library Use with Turnstile Data" (lightning talk, Library Assessment Conference [LAC], Seattle, WA, August 4, 2014), http://libraryassessment.org/bm~doc/12baileylightningtalk.pdf; Gabriela Castro Gessner, Damon E. Jaggars, Jennifer Rutner, and Kornelia Tancheva, "A 2CUL Collaborative Ethnographic Assessment of Humanities Doctoral Students," *Evidence Based Library and Information Practice* 10, no. 2 (2015), https://jour-

nals.library.ualberta.ca/eblip/index.php/EBLIP/article/view/24128/18394; Cheryl A. McCarthy and Danuta A. Nitecki, "An Assessment of the Bass Library as a Learning Commons Environment," (presentation, Library Assessment Conference [LAC], Baltimore, MD: October 25, 2010), http://libraryassessment.org/bm~doc/mccarthy_cheryl.pdf; Bertha P. Chang, "Assessing the Impact of a New Library on Graduate Students' Use of Library Spaces," (lightning talk, Library Assessment Conference [LAC], Seattle, WA, August 6, 2014), http://libraryassessment.org/bm~doc/20changlightningtalk.pdf; John K. Stemmer and David M. Mahan, "Assessing the Library's Influence on Undergraduate Outcomes with Student Usage Surveys," *Evidence Based Library and Information Practice* 10, no. 2 (2015), https://journals.library.ualberta.ca/eblip/index.php/EBLIP/article/view/24157/18389.

110. Nackerud et al., "Analyzing Demographics"; James Sponsel, Sara Swanson, and Linda LeFauve, "Co-curricular Students as Stakeholders: Gauging Perceptions of an Academic Library," Assessment in Action, 2016, https://apply.ala.org/aia/docs/project/13997; Sofia Leung, Stephanie Gamble, Ellen Raimond, Anne Madden Johnson, and Amalia Monroe-Gulick, "Exploring Undergraduate Student Use of Learning Studio Space at the University of Kansas (KU)," Assessment in Action, 2016, https://apply.ala.org/aia/docs/project/13909; Anne Giffey, Ryan Lynch, Leah Adams-Curtis, Helen Hoyt, and Jeff Douglas, "The Seats Don't Lie: Study Preferences of STEM Students," Assessment in Action, 2016, https://apply.ala.org/aia/docs/project/10203; Mary Beth Lock, Meghan Webb, Glenda Boyles, Le'Ron Byrd, John Champlin, and Ryan Shirey, "What's in It for Me? Success, Motivation, and Gaps," Assessment in Action, 2016, https://apply.ala.org/aia/docs/project/10189.
111. Kymberly Keeton, J. Mark Leslie, Lois Heldenbrand, Rachel Sale, Jessie Adolph, and Haiying Qian, "Creating a Research Writing Environment with Personalized Library Instruction" (poster presentation, ALA's 2016 Annual Conference, Orlando, FL, June 23–28, 2016) Lincoln University, Library Faculty and Staff Publications and Presentations, 2016, http://bluetigercommons.lincolnu.edu/libfac_pubs/9; Terence K. Huwe, "Toward a Broader View of the User Experience," *Computers in Libraries* 36, no. 7 (2016): 15–16; Mark Bilandzic and Daniel Johnson, "Hybrid Placemaking in the Library: Designing Digital Technology to Enhance Users' On-Site Experience," *Australian Library Journal* 62, no. 4 (2013): 258–71.
112. Jon Ritterbush, "Assessing Academic Library Services to Distance Learners: A Literature Review of Perspectives from Librarians, Students, and Faculty," *Reference Librarian* 55, no. 1 (2014): 26–36, doi:10.1080/02763877.2014.853274; Hufford, "Can the Library Contribute Value."
113. Holly A. Jackson, "Collaborating for Student Success: An E-mail Survey of U.S. Libraries and Writing Centers," Wright State University Libraries, Campus Online Repository, 2016, http://corescholar.libraries.wright.edu/ul_pub/178.
114. Association of College and Research Libraries, *Standards for Libraries in Higher Education*; Gap Analysis Subcommittee, *Final Report to ACRL VAL Committee*; Albert, "Communicating Library Value"; Saunders, "Academic Libraries' Strategic Plans"; Rachel A. Fleming-May, Regina Mays, and Rachel Radom, "'I Never Had to Use the Library in High School': A Library Instruction Program for At-Risk Students," *portal: Libraries and the Academy* 15, no. 3 (2015): 433–56, doi:10.1353/pla.2015.0038.
115. Murray and Ireland, "Provosts' Perceptions of Academic Library Value."
116. Ibid.
117. Association of College and Research Libraries, *Value of Academic Libraries*; Association of College and Research Libraries, *Standards for Libraries in Higher Education*; Hufford, "Can the Library Contribute Value"; Saunders, "Academic Libraries' Strategic Plans"; Maggie Gallup Kopp, "Academic Libraries, Institutional Mission, and New Student Recruitment: A Case Study," *Reference Services Review* 41, no. 2 (2013): 192–200, doi:10.1108/00907321311326192; Amanda Bird, Kelly Rhodes McBride, and Elizabeth Cramer, "Modeling ACRL's Standards for Libraries in Higher Education," *College and Research Libraries News* 75, no. 11 (2014): 614–18,http://crln.acrl.org/index.php/crlnews/article/view/9228/10243 .
118. Shannon Najmabadi, "How Colleges Can Teach Students to Be Good Citizens," *Chronicle of Higher Education*, January 13, 2017, http://www.chronicle.com/article/How-Colleges-Can-Teach/238891.
119. "2017 Trends Report," *Chronicle of Higher Education*; Najmabadi, "How One College Put Information Literacy into Its Curriculum"; Najmabadi, "Information Literacy."
120. Najmabadi, "How One College Put Information Literacy into Its Curriculum."
121. Dempsey, "The Road Ahead 4"; Najmabadi, "How One College Put Information Literacy into Its Curriculum."
122. State Higher Education Executive Officers Association, *SHEF: FY 2015*.
123. Megan Oakleaf and Martha Kyrillidou, "Revisiting the Academic Library Value Research Agenda: An Opportunity to Shape the Future," *Journal of Academic Librarianship* 42, no. 6 (2016): 757–64, doi:10.1016/j.acalib.2016.10.005; Hufford, "Review of the Literature on Assessment in Academic and Research Libraries"; Ritterbush, "Assessing Academic Library Services to Distance Learners"; Jody Condit Fagan, "The Effectiveness of Academic Library Deans and Directors: A Literature Review," *Library Leadership and Management* 26, no. 1 (2012): 1–19; Margaret Weaver, "Student Journey Work: A Review of Academic Library Contributions to Student Transition and Success," *New Review of Academic Librarianship* 19, no. 2 (2013): 101–24, doi: 10.1080/13614533.2013.800754.
124. Murray and Ireland, "Provosts' Perceptions of Academic Library Value."
125. Connaway and Radford, *Research Methods*, 106.
126. Ibid., 229.
127. Eastbrook, *What Chief Academic Officers Want.*
128. Wil Weston, "Revisiting the Tao of Resource Sharing," *Serials Librarian* 69, no. 1 (2015): 47–56; Bob Kieft, "Curating Collective Collections—What Exactly Are We Retaining When We Retain That Book? Part One," *Against the Grain* 26, no. 5 (2014): 100–101; Joe Lenkart, Thomas H. Teper, Mara Thacker, and Steven Witt, "Measuring and Sustaining the Impact of Less Commonly Taught Language Collections in a Research Library," *College and Research Libraries* 76, no. 2 (2015): 222–33; Lindsay

C. Farinella, "Collaborative Print Serial Retention: A Multiple Case Study of Academic Library Projects in the United States" (master's thesis, University of North Carolina, Chapel Hill, 2014), https://cdr.lib.unc.edu/record/uuid:210cee2e-b057-4152-8832-2267702b3895; Bernard F. Reilly Jr., "The Future of Cooperative Collections and Repositories," *Library Management* 34, no. 4/5 (2013): 342–51; Yi Shen and Virgil Varvel, "Developing Data Management Services at the Johns Hopkins University," *Journal of Academic Librarianship* 39, no. 6 (2013): 552–57; Sue F. Phelps, Heidi E. Senior, and Karen R. Diller, "Learning from Each Other: A Report on Information Literacy Programs at Orbis Cascade Alliance Libraries," *Collaborative Librarianship* 3, no. 3 (2011): 140–53; Editors, "Data Management Skills for LIS Professionals," *CILIP Update* 12, no. 1 (2013): 7, http://edition.pagesuite-professional.co.uk//launch.aspx?eid=89ee4930-c7ce-4cbb-9d94-13142298a567; Ixchel M. Faniel, Adam Kriesberg, and Elizabeth Yakel, "Social Scientists' Satisfaction with Data Reuse," *Journal of the Association for Information Science and Technology* 67, no. 6 (2016): 1404–16; Jared Lyle, "OpenICPSR." *Bulletin of the Association for Information Science and Technology* 40, no. 5 (2014): 55–56; Martha Fallahay Loesch, "UK Data Archive," *Technical Services Quarterly* 32, no. 2 (2015): 233–34; Wallis, "Building a Virtual Reference Shelf"; Faye A. Chadwell, "Assessing the Value of Academic Library Consortia," *Journal of Library Administration* 51, no. 7/8 (2011): 645–61; Denise Pan and Yem Fong, "Return on Investment for Collaborative Collection Development: A Cost-Benefit Evaluation of Consortia Purchasing," *Collaborative Librarianship* 2, no. 4 (2011): 183–92; Elizabeth Mengel and Vivian Lewis, "Collaborative Assessment: North American Academic Libraries' Experiences Using the Balanced Scorecard to Measure Performance and Show Value," *Library Management* 33, no. 6/7 (2012): 357–64; J. Stephen Town and Martha Kyrillidou, "Developing a Values Scorecard," *Performance Measurement and Metrics* 14, no. 1 (2013): 7–16, doi:10.1108/14678041311316095.

129. Association of College and Research Libraries, *Request for Proposals*, 3.
130. Ibid.
131. Association of College and Research Libraries, "Learning Analytics: Strategies for Optimizing Student Data on Your Campus," ACRL e-Learning Webcast Series, 2016, http://www.ala.org/acrl/learninganalytics; ARL Statistics home page.
132. Connaway and Radford, *Research Methods*, 60–63.
133. Institute for Research Design in Librarianship home page, accessed May 26, 2017, http://irdlonline.org; Connaway and Radford, *Research Methods*; Barbara M. Wildemuth, *Applications of Social Research Methods to Questions in Information and Library Science,* 2nd ed. (Santa Barbara, CA: Libraries Unlimited, 2017).
134. Connaway and Radford, *Research Methods.*
135. Fister, "Critical Assets"; Lynch et al., "Attitudes of Presidents and Provosts"; Robertson, "Perceptions of Canadian Provosts."
136. Fister, "Critical Assets"; Lynch et al., "Attitudes of Presidents and Provosts"; Robertson, "Perceptions of Canadian Provosts."
137. Fister, "Critical Assets"; Lynch et al., "Attitudes of Presidents and Provosts"; Robertson, "Perceptions of Canadian Provosts."
138. Lynch et al., "Attitudes of Presidents and Provosts," 226.
139. Robertson, "Perceptions of Canadian Provosts."
140. Fister, "Critical Assets."
141. Marie R. Kennedy and Kristine R. Brancolini, "Academic Librarian Research: A Survey of Attitudes, Involvement, and Perceived Capabilities," *College and Research Libraries* 73, no. 5 (2012): 431–48.
142. Paula Kaufman and Sarah Barbara Watstein, "Library Value (Return on Investment, ROI) and the Challenge of Placing a Value on Public Services," *Reference Services Review* 36, no. 3 (2008): 226–31.
143. Trudi Bellardo Hahn and Paul T. Jaeger, "From Practice to Publication: A Path for Academic Library Professionals," *College and Research Libraries News* 74, no. 5 (2013): 240, http://crln.acrl.org/index.php/crlnews/article/view/8944/9675.
144. Ibid.
145. See Lynn Silipigni Connaway and Marie L. Radford, "Seeking Synchronicity: Evaluating Virtual Reference Services from User, Non-user, and Librarian Perspectives," funded by the Institute of Museum and Library Services (IMLS), 2005–2008, http://www.oclc.org/research/themes/user-studies/synchronicity.html.
146. Karen E. Fisher, Sandra Erdelez, and Lynne (E. F.) McKechnie, eds., *Theories of Information Behavior* (Medford, NJ: Information Today, 2005).
147. Sarah J. Tracy, *Qualitative Research Methods: Collecting Evidence, Crafting Analysis, Communicating Impact* (West Sussex, UK: Wiley-Blackwell, 2013); Connaway and Radford, *Research Methods.*
148. Wildemuth, *Applications of Social Research Methods*, 2nd ed.
149. Fister, "Critical Assets"; Lynch et al., "Attitudes of Presidents and Provosts"; Robertson, "Perceptions of Canadian Provosts."
150. Wolff-Eisenberg, *US Library Survey 2016.*
151. Lombard, "Role of the Academic Library in College Choice."
152. Ibid.
153. Tracy, *Qualitative Research Methods*, 36; see also Connaway and Radford, *Research Methods*, 50, 230.
154. Tracy, *Qualitative Research Methods*, 36; see also Connaway and Radford, *Research Methods*, 50, 230.
155. Connaway and Radford, *Research Methods.*
156. John W. Creswell and Vicki L. Plano Clark, *Designing and Conducting Mixed Methods Research*, 2nd ed. (Thousand Oaks, CA: Sage Publications, 2011).
157. Thomas R. Lindlof and Bryan C. Taylor, *Qualitative Communication Research Methods,* 3rd ed. (Thousand Oaks, CA: Sage Publications, 2011), 45.
158. Alan Bryman, "Integrating Quantitative and Qualitative Research: How Is It Done?" *Qualitative Research* 6, no. 1 (2006): 97–99; Connaway and Radford, *Research Methods*, 319.

159. See Miles, Huberman, and Saldaña, *Qualitative Data Analysis,* 31–32; Tom Wengraf, *Qualitative Research Interviewing: Semi-structured, Biographical and Narrative Methods* (Thousand Oaks, CA: Sage Publications, 2001); Edward Blair and Johnny Blair, *Applied Survey Sampling* (Los Angeles: Sage Publications, 2015).
160. Connaway and Radford, *Research Methods,* 243.
161. Ibid., 135.
162. Amalia Monroe-Gulick and Julie Petr, "Conversations with Students: Assessment Leads to Adjustment," in *Proceedings of the 2012 Library Assessment Conference: Building Effective, Sustainable, Practical Assessment,* ed. Steve Hiller, Martha Kyrillidou, Angela Pappalardo, Jim Self, and Amy Yeager, 523–32 (Washington, DC: Association of Research Libraries, 2012).
163. Wengraf, *Qualitative Research Interviewing.*
164. Association of College and Research Libraries Research Planning and Review Committee, "2016 Top Trends in Academic Libraries"; Association of College and Research Libraries, "Learning Analytics."
165. "About," 1st International Conference on Learning Analytics and Knowledge.
166. Lynch, "Rise of Reading Analytics."
167. "About," 1st International Conference on Learning Analytics and Knowledge.
168. Matthews, "Assessing Library Contributions to University Outcomes"; Ken Varnum, "Editorial Board Thoughts: Library Analytics and Patron Privacy," *Information Technology and Libraries* 34, no. 4 (2015): 2–4; Amanda Nichols Hess, Rachelle LaPorte-Fiori, and Keith Engwall, "Preserving Patron Privacy in the 21st Century Academic Library," *Journal of Academic Librarianship* 41, no. 1 (2015): 105–14; Michael Zimmer and Kenneth Blacks, "Assessing the Treatment of Patron Privacy in Library 2.0 Literature," in *Proceedings of the 2012 iConference,* 501–503 (New York: ACM, 2012).
169. Jantti and Heath, "What Role for Libraries in Learning Analytics?"
170. Connaway and Radford, *Research Methods,* 212–13.
171. Connaway and Radford, *Research Methods*; Barbara M. Wildemuth, *Application of Social Research Methods to Questions in Information and Library Science* (Westport, CT: Libraries Unlimited, 2009).
172. Kuh et al., *What Matters to Student Success.*
173. Cox and Jantti, "Discovering the Impact of Library Use and Student Performance"; Nackerud et al., "Analyzing Demographics."
174. Soria, Fransen, and Nackerud, "Library Use and Undergraduate Student Outcomes"; Jantti and Cox, "Measuring the Value of Library Resources."
175. Connaway and Radford, *Research Methods*; Wildemuth, *Applications of Social Research Methods,* 2nd ed.; Matthews, "Assessing Library Contributions to University Outcomes"; Varnum, "Editorial Board Thoughts," 2; Hess, LaPorte-Fiori, and Engwall, "Preserving Patron Privacy."
176. Adam Murray and Melissa Bowles-Terry, *Value of Academic Libraries Statement* (Chicago: Association of College and Research Libraries, 2015).
177. Soria, Fransen, and Nackerud, "Library Use and Undergraduate Student Outcomes."
178. Association for College and Research Libraries, *Framework for Information Literacy.*
179. Connaway and Radford, *Research Methods,* 381.
180. See Nancy L. Leech, Karen C. Barrett, and George A. Morgan, *IBM SPSS for Intermediate Statistics: Use and Interpretation,* 4th ed. (New York: Taylor and Francis Group, 2011).
181. Connaway and Radford, *Research Methods.*
182. Kathy Charmaz, *Constructing Grounded Theory: A Practical Guide through Qualitative Analysis,* 2nd ed. (Thousand Oaks, CA: Sage Publications, 2014); see also Wildemuth, *Applications of Social Research Methods,* 2nd ed.; Connaway and Radford, *Research Methods.*
183. Norman K. Denzin and Yvonna S. Lincoln, *The Sage Handbook of Qualitative Research,* 4th ed. (Thousand Oaks, CA: Sage Publications, 2011); Statistical Associates Publishing, "E-Book Catalog," accessed May 26, 2017, http://www.statisticalassociates.com/booklist.htm.
184. Wildemuth, *Applications of Social Research Methods,* 2nd ed.; Connaway and Radford, *Research Methods.*
185. "2017 Trends Report," *Chronicle of Higher Education.*
186. Brown-Sica, "Using Academic Courses to Generate Data."
187. Fong et al., "Assessing and Serving the Workshop Needs of Graduate Students"; Debose, Haugen, and Miller, "Information Literacy Instruction Programs"; Miller, "Plagiarism Curricula May Reduce Need for Punitive Plagiarism Education"; Meyers-Martin and Borchard, "Finals Stretch"; Richards, "24/7 Library Hours"; Hiebert and Theriault, "BLASTing the Zombies!"; Reynolds and Rabschutz, "Studying for Exams Just Got More Relaxing"; Smigielski and Nixon, "The Library as Finals Resting Place."
188. Fong et al., "Assessing and Serving the Workshop Needs of Graduate Students"; Debose, Haugen, and Miller, "Information Literacy Instruction Programs"; Miller, "Plagiarism Curricula May Reduce Need for Punitive Plagiarism Education."
189. Brown-Sica, "Using Academic Courses to Generate Data."
190. Connaway and Radford, *Research Methods.*
191. Association of College and Research Libraries, "Academic Library Building Design: Resources for Planning: Home," accessed May 26, 2017, http://acrl.libguides.com/buildingresources.
192. Association of College and Research Libraries, *Standards for Libraries in Higher Education.*
193. Association of College and Research Libraries, "Assessment in Action Team Applications."

194. Association of College and Research Libraries, *Standards for Libraries in Higher Education*; Gap Analysis Subcommittee, *Final Report to ACRL VAL Committee.*
195. Association of College and Research Libraries, "Assessment in Action Team Applications."
196. Connaway et al., *Many Faces of Digital Visitors and Residents.*
197. Hess et al., "Books, Bytes, and Buildings"; Wolfe, "Emerging Information Literacy and Research-Method Competencies."
198. Association of College and Research Libraries, "Assessment in Action: Academic Libraries."
199. Anne Epperson, James Henderson, and Evan Welch, "Designed and Furnished for Success: Fostering an 'Academically Social' Campus Space!" Assessment in Action, accessed June 1, 2017, https://apply.ala.org/attachments/8881; Elizabeth Torres, Timothy Martin, Farris Sanders, Nori Leong, Sheryl Sunia, and Han N. C. Wester, "Assessing Library Instruction for Military Students," Assessment in Action, accessed January 5, 2017, https://apply.ala.org/attachments/26855; Lock et al., "What's in It for Me?"; Heather Jagman, Lisa Davidson, Lauri Dietz, Jodi Falk, and Antonieta Fitzpatrick, "'I Felt Like Such a Freshman!' Creating Library Insiders," Assessment in Action, accessed January 5, 2017, https://apply.ala.org/attachments/8865.
200. Hess et al., "Books, Bytes, and Buildings."
201. Wolfe, "Emerging Information Literacy and Research-Method Competencies."
202. Connaway and Radford, *Research Methods.*
203. Hess et al., "Books, Bytes, and Buildings."
204. Kristi Morton, Magdalena Balazinska, Dan Grossman, and Jock Mackinlay, "Support the Data Enthusiast: Challenges for Next-Generation Data-Analysis Systems," in *Proceedings of the VLDB Endowment* 7, no. 6 (2014): 453–56; Sarah Hackney, Dinah Handel, Bianca Hezekiah, Cassie Hickman, Jessica Hochman, Amy Lau, Chris Alen Sula, Margie Ticknor, and Ruojing Zhang, "Visualizing Identities in LIS Literature" in *iConference 2016 Proceedings* (IDEALS [Illinois Digital Environment for Access to Learning and Scholarship], 2016), https://www.ideals.illinois.edu/bitstream/handle/2142/89356/Hackney519.pdf; Eric Phetteplace, "Effectively Visualizing Library Data," *Reference and User Services Quarterly 52*, no. 2 (2012): 93–97.
205. *Wikipedia*, s.v. "Brushing and linking," last updated November 23, 2015, https://en.wikipedia.org/wiki/Brushing_and_linking.
206. "Organize Your Gmail Inbox Using Labels," Gmail Help, accessed June 19, 2017, https://support.google.com/mail/answer/118708?co=GENIE.Platform%3DDesktop&hl=en.
207. Connaway and Radford, *Research Methods*, 176.
208. Hernon, Dugan, and Nitecki, *Engaging in Evaluation and Assessment Research.*
209. "About," 1st International Conference on Learning Analytics and Knowledge.
210. Kuh et al., *What Matters to Student Success*, 5.
211. Runes, *Dictionary of Philosophy*, 346.
212. Kuh et al., *What Matters to Student Success*, 5.
213. For further instruction about how NVivo can be used for coding of data, see Connaway and Radford, *Research Methods*, 290–96.
214. For a discussion on ICR, see Connaway and Radford, *Research Methods*, 315–17.
215. Ibid, 299.
216. Jason Hsu, *Multiple Comparisons: Theory and Methods* (Boca Raton, FL: CRC Press, 1996); Yosef Hochberg and Ajit C. Tamhane, *Multiple Comparison Procedures* (Hoboken, NJ: Wiley, 2009); Juliet Popper Shaffer, "Multiple Hypothesis Testing," *Annual Review of Psychology* 46, no. 1 (1995): 561–84; Editor, "Post-Hoc and Multiple Comparison Test—An Overview with SAS and R Statistical Package," *International Journal of Statistics and Medical Informatics* 1, no. 1 (2016): 1–9, https://ssrn.com/abstract=2944598.
217. Connaway and Radford, *Research Methods.*
218. Babbie, *Practice of Social Research*, 10th ed.
219. Yoav Benjamini and Yosef Hochberg, "Controlling the False Discovery Rate: A Practical and Powerful Approach to Multiple Testing," *Journal of the Royal Statistical Society, Series B (Methodological)* 57, no. 1 (1995): 289–300, http://www.stat.purdue.edu/~doerge/BIOINFORM.D/FALL06/Benjamini%20and%20Y%20FDR.pdf.
220. Association of College and Research Libraries, *Request for Proposals*, 3.
221. For recent discussions of library space and issues related to diversity and inclusivity, see: Svanhild Aabo and Ragnar Audunson, "Use of Library Space and the Library as Place," *Library & Information Science Research* 34, no. 2 (2012): 138-49; Joanna Bryant, Graham Matthews, and Graham Walton, "Academic Libraries and Social and Learning Space: A Case Study of Loughborough University Library, UK," *Journal of Librarianship and Information Science* 41, no. 1 (2009): 7-18; Seung Hyun Cha and Tae Wan Kim, "What Matters for Students' use of Physical Library Space?," *Journal of Academic Librarianship* 41, no. 3 (05, 2015): 274-79; James K. Elmborg, "Libraries as the Spaces between Us: Recognizing and Valuing the Third Space," *Reference & User Services Quarterly* 50, no. 4 (2011): 338-50; Shelia Gaines, "You Want Coffee with That? Revisiting the Library as Place," *The Christian Librarian* 59, no. 1 (2016): 79-86; Kirralie Houghton, Marcus Foth, and Evonne Miller, "The Continuing Relevance of the Library as a Third Place for Users and Non-Users of IT: The Case of Canada Bay," *Australian Library Journal* 62, no. 1 (2013): 27-39; Susan E. Montgomery and Jonathan Miller, "The Third Place: The Library as Collaborative and Community Space in a Time of Fiscal Restraint," *College & Undergraduate Libraries* 18, no. 2-3 (2011): 228-38; Margaret E. Moore, K. T. L. Vaughan, Barrie E. Hayes, and Wallace McLendon, "Developing an Interdisciplinary Collaboration Center in an Academic Health Sciences Library," *Medical Reference Services Quarterly* 24, no. 4 (2005): 99-107.